BRAIN MOVIES

HARLAN ELLISON'S BLOOD'S A ROVER

EDITED BY JASON DAVIS

Brain Movies *presents*
Harlan Ellison's® Blood's a Rover
is an Edgeworks Abbey® offering in association with Jason Davis.
Published by The Kilimanjaro Corporation.

Assistant Editor: Cynthia Davis

ISBN: 978-1-946542-07-6

First Edition

Thanks to L. Q. Jones, Bo Nash, William K. Schafer & Subterranean Press.

201902032010

Harlan left behind a list of dedications he planned to use for future books.

In accordance with his wishes, Susan dedicates this book to

George Carlin

Contents

nota bene:

The teleplays in this book were reproduced from the author's file copies. They originated on a manual typewriter, hence the idiosyncrasies that set them apart from the sanitized, word-processed pages of today. The progressive lightening of the text followed by a sudden darkening of the same, indicates the author has changed the typewriter's ribbon; it is not a printing defect.

Throughout the works presented herein, there is evidence of the author's revision: struck-out text, handwritten emendations, and typewritten text printed over passages that were cancelled with correcting tape. These artifacts have been maintained to preserve the evidence of the writer's process.

Huck and Tom: The Bizarre Liaison of Ellison and Jones

L. Q. and I have known each other for a long time, like two burs under the same saddle; and I always say of him, "He's like a cold you can't get rid of." And I'm sure he says the same sort of thing about me. We are two curmudgeons, perfectly matched. It's as if our missions in life were devised to annoy each other. We're a set of cranky bookends, and I'm very, very fond of him. I think he's a spectacular, innovative director who could well have done a good many *really* individual films, were he not as big a pain in the ass as I am. His ability to endear himself is only exceeded by his Ellisonian capacity for pissing people off. I mean, he really is indeed a consummate ache in the butt.

But as far as the film is concerned, here's how it went: I wrote—oh, I guess it was about the first six, seven minutes of the movie. But I was *tired*. I had been writing for years and years without a break, and I wasn't blocked. I was just so damned *tired* I couldn't work. So L. Q. went ahead and *he* did the script. I guess he probably *had* sent me his final script; I'm not sure I ever got around to reading it, though. He went ahead and he filmed, using my opening scene. They were out in the desert, mostly, the high desert, so I never actually went on a set. At that time, I was doing a picture at Paramount, so I was straight-ahead busy while he was deep in principal photography. It was as if we were a continent separated. But I trusted him.

When he finally got it done, when he had the preliminary final cut, he called me, anxious, in fact almost giddy, for me to see it at a screening room. There was terrific anticipation, and I went; and I *loved* it. I thought he had done a *wonderful* job. What I *didn't* love was that he had changed the last line of the story. I despised it, not only because I thought it cheapened the picture, but because it was so misogynistic! It was so anti-female, AND he had put the misogynistic words into the *dog's* mouth. The dog is the only real spokesperson for civilization and kindness and decency in this film of societal barbarism, of people reduced to little more than the behavior of beasts, and he cheapened Blood by putting that cruel, insensitive line in the dog's mouth, just for the sake of getting a mean laugh from idiot fraternity boys. But, in addition, (which you don't see in the picture today), there was a plethora of similar, all-wrong, mean lines the dog spoke—particularly when they're in the boiler room—in the conversation with Vic after the night in which Vic and the girl have had sex. And Vic, this bestial young boy, has had his first *inkling* of human feeling for another person. In other words, he's found love but he doesn't know it. That is to say, he doesn't even know it's *called* "love" and, jarringly, terribly out of phase, the dog keeps referring to her as, "That cow can't come with us," or "She's a dumb-ass," and on and on and on.

Apart from the fact that *this* wise, telepathic dog as his character has been carefully built would not use anthropomorphic animal terms for a human, it was *virulently* misogynistic. Now, the movie is misanthropic to begin with, and the story is as well; but it *ain't* misogynistic. There's nothing anti-female in the story. The things that happen to women in my story are clearly presented negatively, as being the debasement of the human spirit. And men and women are treated equally badly. Only the dog has human compassion in a very calculated reversal of man/beast behavior. Historically, it's accurate. After a debilitating war, one of the things that becomes of value as booty, loot, "spoils of war," is women, because most women get killed in such a total war. And so, there was that tricky, open to criticism, aspect of it. But it works only if the internal logic of the basic idea isn't used for egregious exploitation, if it isn't compromised by forcing misogynistic words into Blood's mouth. Ironically, if you talk to Barbies—witless, parvenu little poppets who are just discovering their first taste of feminism—and they know virtually no history at all...they only know the p. c. blather of the moment...so they cannot differentiate between *I Know What You Did Last Summer*—in which every girl in a thong gets her throat ripped out—and something that is historically correct, seriously intended, non-exploitative—they lump this film in with the prevalent teen-trash that debases and/or objectifies women into nothing nobler than Britney or Shakira or J. Lo clones. So "A Boy and His Dog," from the git-go, has that trembly potential for being politically-correctly misunderstood. It's *already* got that danger going for it. It's a tough story, in that way. Dangerous.

But L. Q. is a good old Texas boy, purebred male chauvinist, lovable but primordial; and a man of his time. Well, as I see it, he was a little late in coming to incorporate "women as equals" in his basic world-view. I do not mean that in a nasty way, nor even in a denigrating way; it's just that some people are older and slower to get to it; and during that period, it was not entirely gone. It was a commonly-held attitude. It was on it's way out, but it wasn't yet gone. A lot of sexism was everyday, it was passingly acceptable.

So the lines he put in there were prototypical of the kind of stuff that you would see regularly in movies of that day, the sort of dopey remarks you would hear from ordinary people who weren't thinking very clearly, who were not, well, *courant.* Thus, when I saw that cut of the movie, and heard my dear alter ego Blood saying things that cheapened his lovely character, I was appalled, I was not just upset, I was up-in-arms. I was *crazed* behind it, and I said, "You cannot *do* that! You just can't do it!" Now, I didn't have a lot of say in such matters at the time, because I had sold the rights to L. Q. and he had made the film as he had said he would, so I had no clout to be laying down such *obiter dicta* and, in truth, even my writing contract had been terminated, so I was actually a bystander. I didn't make a lot of money off it, but it was *his* movie, and I was 98 percent satisfied with it. The things he had changed, I thought, were very sensible. The ways he got around cinematically unworkable aspects of the original novella as published, that couldn't be filmed on his budget, were absolutely brilliant. No hyperbole: entertaining, innovative, ingenious, I think, to this day. It's a very, very well-turned-out movie, filmically solid, and an excellent piece of true science fiction. I still like it a lot, and—obviously—it's stood the test of time, which is always Posterity's yardstick.

But there was that one canker on the rose, that one worm in the apple, and I knew that as time passed, and contexts would fade in the memory of young filmgoers (as they so tragically have) the p. c. dangers of those lines would come back to bite us in the ass, and I said, "This cannot stand! This cannot be, L. Q." I pleaded: "Please! You've got to throw the picture back up on the editing table, you're gonna have to over-dub. You're going to have to dub in new lines." And he looked at me, and he started to *laugh*! And I said, "What part of that is so hilarious?" And he said, "Listen, Numb Nuts!" (That's the way he talks. That's what he calls me: "Numb Nuts.") He said, "Listen, Numb Nuts! I haven't got a goddamned penny! I haven't got a cent! Where the hell do you think I'm gonna get the money to do more editing?!" I said, "Well, how much would it take to edit all that stuff out?" "Hell, I don't know! It would take about five thousand dollars!" And I said, "Well, I'll *get* it for you." And he said, "Where the hell are you gonna get it? You ain't got a pot to piss in!" And I looked at him and I said, "I'll get it! I. Will. Get. It!" Making money is a thing I can do...so I went to the convention (the 1974 World Science Fiction Convention in Washington, D. C.), and I pressured the committee to book me on the primetime Saturday evening in which I could premiere *A Boy and His Dog.*

Well, it was a bravura nightmare of technological ineptitude. They didn't have the right projector, they didn't have the right speed, they didn't have the right this, the right that. Their sound system went dead. It took three hours or four hours to run the film, and every time it would break, or every time it would go black, or every time the sound would go out, they would stop it; the audience would groan, boo hiss, clap...and they would start it over again! And every time—five, ten, who knows how many times—I had to bounce up on the stage and do my dog-and-pony show to keep the thing going! And no one left! The auditorium was *jammed*, from the start, and *no one* left! It was one of the most difficult platform stunts I've ever pulled! Sometimes I'll wake, in the dead of night, in a cold sweat, and remember what it was like! I don't know how many there were at that D. C. convention, but it must've been four, five, six thousand of them at least, and however many could get into that auditorium squeezed and jammed and pushed in as the long hours dragged painfully on.

People were sitting on the floors. People were sitting in the aisles. People were sitting on each other's laps in the seats. They brought in chairs and put them down along the side aisles. The fire marshal came in and was appalled. People were sitting on the edge of the stage so they were looking up Don Johnson's nostrils. I held them there like Martin Luther King, Jr. exhorting the congregation, like Hitler inciting the mob to set the Reichstag fire, like Robin Williams on massive infusions of Jamaican Blue Mountain coffee, Demerol, and horse trank cut with pure molasses! I talked as fast as I could, and what I said to them was, "There are lines in this movie that have to go! Please help me get these lines out of the movie. Will you contribute a dollar? Will you give me two dollars? *Any*thing!" And some fans went through that vast, restless (incredibly patient) audience with supermarket paper bags, and the constituency just went crazy! It was like a feeding frenzy. I did my stump-revivalist routine, and preached, "Will ya give us some money?! Can I have an *Amen*? Can I see a sea of green, please!?" I shamelessly did "The Sea of Green," the standard televangelist routine, and there were three huge paper bags filled with money when we were done. From top to bottom. Some people gave $10, and some people gave $20. Mostly, people just gave a dollar, but, whatever it was, I came back to L. A., and I went to L. Q.'s office, and he said, "Hi, Numb Nuts, how ya doin'?" And *I* said, "I'll *show* ya how I'm doin'!" and I turned the bags over on his desk, and a mountain of money fell in front of him.

Zorro muddlefuggin' strikes again! Aaaaa-*men*!

L. Q. took out all of the lines that I objected to, with the exception of that damned miserable last line, because he had been "testing" the picture at colleges and universities, and you know what pin-headed pseudo-macho college boys are like. *They* thought it was a great line, and they *roared* with laughter! He liked that, so he kept it in, even though I tore my hair, rent my garments, threatened to burn his home to the ground, threatened to shatter all his Gene Autry and Tex Ritter 78s. And it's embarrassed me ever since. I have to explain all of the lugubrious foregoing history to people, you know; particularly because they show it frequently in college film or science fiction classes now; and, in fact, get *this*: On my website, there's some teacher who always assigns this picture and then says, "Go to the website, and talk to the people at Ellison Webderland (www.harlanellison.com) and find out the background," and there'll always be some young woman, some college sophomore, and she'll say. "I think Ellison is a terrible person. I don't think he likes women at all, because blah blah blah," and everyone jumps on her case and pounds the verbal crap out of her, explaining that A) the movie is not the story, B) I didn't write the movie, I wrote the story, C) it was not intended to be misogynistic, and D) nowhichway is that idiotic, cruel last line my doing.

And, thanks again, L. Q.!

The salient essential I think any aficionado of this movie needs to know is that "A Boy and His Dog" is only one part of a very much *larger* novel which is titled BLOOD'S A ROVER. The largest part of it—the novel, which is close to 100,000 words—is what follows the section published as a short story under the title "Run, Spot, Run" in the January 1981 issue of *Amazing Stories*. It was included in the graphic novel, *Vic and Blood*, that I did with the definitive "Boy and His Dog" artist, the great Richard Corben. (Copies available through the Harlan Ellison Recording Collection. See the notice at the conclusion of this splendid essay for information. This has been a "Keep The Author Out of the Poorhouse" message.) So the full novel has yet to be published. I've got the manuscript sitting here on my desk. I wrote it as a two-hour movie for NBC. I'll finish it one of these days before I croak.

We were commissioned by NBC when Deanne Barkley was the head of production at NBC. She only *loved A Boy and His Dog*, and L. Q. and I went in, and we talked about doing the sequel to it. That was cool. But poor old senile L. Q. hasn't got his memories particularly straight about the way the story unfolds. After all, it *was* I who wrote it! My idea was, at the end of "Run, Spot, Run," Vic is, ostensibly, dead. There's no telepathic communication between the boy and Blood. The link is severed. Blood has seen Vic being swallowed up by a giant spider, so finally he goes wandering off down what used to be a freeway. *Blood's a Rover* opens on a "solo" named Spike, who's a girl, and the opening line is, "Spike was 'on the rag.'" She's having her period and she's got terrible menses and cramps, and she's in a fire fight with a rover-pak that's trying to kill her. She's in hiding somewhere on the Pacific coast, something like Monterey, and she's down behind a rock and the first thing that happens is a voice says to her, "When I count to six, get up and fire at the eleven o'clock position and you'll hit a guy. One, two, three, four, five..." And when the voice says, "Six," she pops up and, sure enough, there's a guy taking aim, and she blows his head off. She has no idea that it was Blood, of course, who has wandered across the country, staying alive, ekeing out an existence, making do as best he could...and looking for someone new to hook up with. And now he's established a telepathic communication—which is rare for him—with this girl, this tough solo, Spike. The story picks up from there and becomes a love triangle among Vic, Spike, and Blood. And it's a wonderful, wonderful story. (He said, with uncommon humility.) (It's tragic how even a mediocre intellect like L. Q.'s turns to tapioca as the years bear down on him. We can only sigh with compassion. Right, Numb Nuts?)

Well, Deanne Barkley sparked to the material in our "pitch session," and she commissioned a script for a two-hour tv movie; and I wrote it; and they paid me a lot of money; and NBC approved it; and the production company that was going to do it loved it; and the deal was made. Then L. Q. insisted—quite properly, in my opinion—"I want to direct." Well, you know networks: the cowardly suits waffle and consult and wool-gather and re-cast every goddamned thing to get in whoever they think is the "Flavor of the Week," and they would not approve L. Q. as the director of the film, even though he'd been the guiding intelligence that had made a movie good enough for the morons to want a sequel in the *first* place! They came to me, to try and split us (because I owned the rights to the underlying material), and I said, "If L. Q. goes...I go. We're a package. We're a postage-due package, but we're linked at the hip." So, sadly, reluctantly, they blew off the project; and all of it reverted to me. So I just said, "All right, I'll just hang onto the script and I'll just convert it into prose when the time comes." Well, the time will be coming soon. I'll be retiring. I'm 68 now and I'll be retiring in another ten years or so, and I'll finish the whole novel, as I said, before I go to hear the choir invisible. On the other claw, maybe I'll complete the book *after* I croak, just to be a pain in the ass.

But Byron Preiss and iBooks, next June, will be reissuing the adventures of Vic and Blood, the graphic novel with the Richard Corben artwork, plus all three of the stories in their text form. It'll be the first time that the text stories and the comics have been presented together, and we think it's going to sell very well. It'll be an Edgeworks Abbey offering, in conjunction with iBooks.

BLOOD'S A ROVER, the name of the novel, is from a quote by A. E. Housman, who wrote A SHROPSHIRE LAD, and it's a line (from "Reveille") that goes, "Clay is still, but blood's a rover, / Breath's a ware that will not keep. / Up Boy! When the journey's over / There'll be time enough to sleep." My friend, the most excellent writer, the late Chad Oliver, had a story in *Analog* long ago, back in the '50s, called "Blood's a Rover," and I've even got a statement from Chad, long before he died, that he didn't mind my using it as the title for my book. Blood, being the dog's name, a pun on "Rover," also a nickname for dogs, (I have no idea if Chad got Housman's okay, since he was long dead at the time...but who knows...)

I look forward to writing that book. I've been wanting to finish it for a long time. I *love* writing the Vic and Blood stuff. I just grin like a fool, sitting there and being the voice of the dog. That's my voice. And, in fact, when L. Q. talks about them doing different people who would've been the voice of the dog, one of them was me. I tested for it, and he said the problem was I sounded too much like Jimmy Cagney. The irony of it all was that Jimmy Cagney then wanted to do it himself! But I don't think anybody could've done it better than Tim McIntire, who was the son of John McIntire, the *Wagon Train* master and, years later, when I was having dinner at Roddy McDowall's house with my wife, Susan, and a whole room full of stellar people—writers and brain surgeons and directors and actors—Jeannette Nolan was seated next to me. We talked about Tim, who had passed away some years earlier.

Jeannette Nolan, a spectacular actress, was, of course, Tim McIntire's mother, and we had a long, long talk about it, and she was still broken up about what a self-destructive guy Tim had been, because he was a fantastic talent. If you've ever seen him in *American Hot Wax*, I do mean, he's remarkable. Or in *Brubaker*: he played the head guard, co-starring with Robert Redford. Tim had it in him to be one of the really important actors, on the quality level of a Forest Whitaker, and that's about as high praise as I can say, because that's who I wrote "Mefisto in Onyx" for. Dammit, I never got to *meet* McIntire, but I did talk to him on the phone; and he loved having done Blood.

The dog, of course, was spectacular. But everybody was spectacular in the movie, and it's a very adventurous piece of extrapolative film making. L. Q. understood, for instance, the subtleties of portraying an inbred, totalitarian-yet-rural society, cut off from the rest of the world. When he put the clown-white on people's faces, which was a brilliant, inexpensive way of showing an idiosyncratic societal fad, some critics scratched their dumb heads and went "Duh?" and they asked, "Why is that?" And I said, "What do you mean, 'Why is that?' Why do women change their hair-styles and hemlines every year? Why do guys shave their head and put tattoos all over themselves?" Cultures develop their own faddish make-up systems. You're cool if you wear this, and you're not if you wear that. And L. Q. understood that cultural idiosyncrasy. Our society is just as forced-conformity. If you go to a business meeting, you've got to wear a sober, sincere tie. It's a reflection of our society, and it was a reflection more of the '50s–'60s society at the time, which was *very* conformist until the middle '60s, when things started busting loose.

Working with L. Q. has been an interesting part of my life. We yell and argue at each other like Tweedle Dum and Tweedle Dumber, but I hold him in very high esteem; he's a good guy: and if there's ever a re-make of this film, or if there's ever a sequel made, L. Q. will be absolutely involved. I will not make a deal that L. Q. will not be involved in. I don't give a shit what the other people want to do. I don't care if they want Shyamalan or Ken Burns, or Twohy or Darabont (who are the best), to direct it, it'll still have L. Q. involved there, somehow. The director is probably not going to be my call, but I would never go back to war with that story without L. Q. being involved. We are linked at the hip, heaven help me; and the film is as much his as the story is mine. Further, deponent sayeth not.

A Boy and His Dog

When producers L. Q. Jones and Alvy Moore optioned "A Boy and His Dog," it was assumed Harlan Ellison would adapt his own novella for the screen. This assumption continued, as Jones fulfilled various acting commitments, but Ellison couldn't finish the screenplay. After yet another delivery date with no script, Jones issued an ultimatum: either Ellison finish the screenplay, or Jones would add *writer* to his credits. Ellison, creatively spent after nearly two decades of non-stop writing, conceded defeat and handed off the fourteen pages he'd finished to Jones, who completed the work and—despite his intentions—added *director* to his credits when the original fell out.

Ellison's pages are published here for the first time, reproduced from a poor-quality photocopy, the only extant version in his files.

The unfinished screenplay is followed by Ellison's notes on which dialogue should be re-dubbed, as explained in the preceding essay.

FADE IN:

1 SERIES OF BLACK AND WHITE STILL PHOTOGRAPHS

(Using various methods of photographic engraving: tonal separation, line resolution, contour, mezzoprint, spiral, cross line, tone line and full reverse print.)

Shots of bombed-out cities.

They should tighten down from full aerial shots through closer angles to a group of close shots on buildings blasted off like beheaded corpses, wastelands, cities lying in ruin, scarred and scorched earth, final and ultimate urban desolation. The after-effects of a war.

NARRATION OVER as still photos flash.

VIC'S VOICE O.S.

World War Three lasted from June 25th, 1950 when the Republic of Korea was invaded by 60,000 North Korean troops spearheaded by over 100 Russian-built tanks...to January 1st, 1983 when the Vatican armistice was signed between the Eastern and Western blocs. World War Three, hot and cold, lasted 33 years. Then it was over.

(beat)

World War Four lasted five days, until the last of the missiles left their silos on both sides and there wasn't much of anything left to fight over.

(beat)

Five days.

(beat)

Then what was left belonged to anybody who wanted it. But it was a different world. Sixteen years ago, in the year of our lord 2024, I got born and it was my turn. You know how I know all about it? Blood told me.

My dog

The photos run their sequence till we HOLD on the final shot, a bombed-out slum area. PHOTO RESOLVES INTO ACTUAL LIVE SHOT. CAMERA PANS RIGHT to pick up a lizard scuttling through the debris.

2 CLOSEUP PAN WITH LIZARD - DAY

An electric blue and green lizard, obviously unlike any creature alive today. An atomic mutation, through which we establish the strangeness of the new world in one quick image. It slithers along through rubble. In counterpoint we HEAR a WOMAN'S VOICE OVER speaking with bedroom passion.

WOMAN'S VOICE OVER
(huskily)
Lover...lover...come on, lover...

CAMERA WITH lizard as the VOICE OVER CONTINUES in a highly sexual tone, the voice of a woman having heavy intercourse. Abruptly, a booted foot comes into the frame and crushes the lizard undeffoot as the woman says:

WOMAN'S VOICE OVER:
Lover...oh, Jesus, Lover...don't kill me, Lover...don't kill me...

There is a shot. Then another. Then three or four more, not close together, spaced apart as though someone is taking his time doing an unspeakable act.

As SHOTS SOUND OVER the CAMERA TILTS UP from the boot to show VIC and BLOOD crouching amid the rubble of bombed-out buildings. Vic is a sixteen-year-old boy who looks older. He's rangy, and though he has neither beard nor character lines in his face, he looks deadly competent. The look we see in Matthew Brady photographs of teen-aged soldiers in the Civil War, the look of the jungle predator, the look of the scavenger, the adult-before-his-time look we see on the faces of ghetto kids who've had to live by their wits. That's the way Vic looks. He's sixteen, going on fifty. He's got two bandoliers of shells crossed over his shoulders, he's got a .45 holstered in a shoulder rig, he's got a knife sheathed at his side and the hilt of a throwing-knife protruding from his boot. He has his 30.06 hunting rifle (probably a Husquvarna) aimed at the shack across the way from the rubble in which he crouches. Having crushed the lizard, he is again watching the shack. Beside him is Blood, his dog. Blood also watches the shack.

(CONTINUED:)

2 CONTINUED:

CAMERA HOLDS several beats on the faces of Vic and Blood then PANS LEFT across the rubble in the direction they are staring. The shack. The door opens. Half a dozen ROVERS come out of the shack, one of them pulling his pants up and buckling his belt. There are two dogs with them, mean-looking guard dogs. The rovers are in their early teens (none older than 18) and they laugh and chuckle as they walk away. All are armed in a manner similar to Vic. CAMERA HOLDS on them as they walk away and disappear amidst the rubble. CAMERA PANS BACK TO VIC AND BLOOD.

VIC (FILTER OVER)
We'll go take a look.

BLOOD (FILTER OVER)
(bored)
So we'll go take a look.

Vic gives the dog a hard look. They rise to go.

NOTE: this is the first time we hear Blood talk. Yes, that's right, the dog talks. Telepathically. Not the way a TV talking horse talks, nor with animated mouth. Vic and Blood are linked mentally, and when they converse, they do it in filter over. Sometimes Vic speaks vocally, but when Vic and Blood are engaged in a heavy conversation Vic can either talk aloud or in his head. Blood's tones are usually very wise, very bored, very much above it all. He's intelligent, and he has a sense of his own worth that makes much of what he hears and sees not even worth commenting on. He is a joker in that he has a gallows sense of humor, and he is a realist, even as Vic is a realist. They are out here alone together, hustling as best they can, and there is no fantasy in their manner or their view of the world.

3 WITH VIC AND BLOOD

as they approach the shack, carefully. There may be more rovers in there. Vic crouches and looks through a break in the wood panelling of the door. The windows are boarded-up. He looks at Blood.

VIC (FILTER OVER)
I can't see a thing in there.
Smell it, willya?

(CONTINUED:)

3 CONTINUED:

The dog looks back at him and blinks. Blood is a weird looking animal. He is big, but kind of floppy. He can be very dangerous when he has to be, but his appearance is a cross between a dinosaur and a Walt Disney cutie.

BLOOD (FILTER OVER)
I thought you were doing the scouting.

VIC (FILTER OVER)
(snaps)
Dammit, Blood, stop giving me a hard time. Smell it!

The dog heaves a sigh and his eyes close. In a second he looks back at Vic.

BLOOD (FILTER OVER)
It's clean. Just the chick.

Vic rises and pushes open the door with the barrel of the rifle. It is dim inside as they enter.

4 INT. SHACK - DAY

Piled up with refuse. On a plank table a naked woman lies, her legs dangling over. Because of the angle of the shot, we cannot see all of the body, but there is blood running down the arm that dangles over the side. She is obviously dead. Keep it dim and the angle right and we will have the feeling of brutality without having to show it.

VIC (ALOUD)
Ain't that a shame.

BLOOD (FILTER OVER)
Better luck next time.

VIC (ALOUD)
Now that's what I call a waste. They din't haveta kill her. She could of been used two, three more times.

BLOOD (ALOUD)
War is hell, Vic.

Vic looks sharply at Blood and CAMERA COMES IN on Blood's face till it fills the frame and FREEZES:

MAINTITLES OVER

5 CLOSEUP ON BLOOD

as the face resolves into a tonal separation of the dog's features and we expand the image until it becomes a series of dots and blotches THROUGH WHICH CAMERA MOVES IN until one of the dots becomes a photo of a bombed-out street. CAMERA IN ON PHOTO.

6 BOMB CRATER STREET

as the photo resolves into LIVE SHOT. The street is pocked with steaming bomb-craters that give off an eerie disease-green glow from radiation. The buildings are in various degrees of falling-down. On the street corner, standing beside the melted and twisted shape of a lamp post, are Vic and Blood. CAMERA IN ON THEM as telepathic VOICE OVERS progress.

NOTE: from this point on in the script, when telepathic communication is indicated, FILTER OVER will be written simply as F.O. for convenience. If F.O. does not appear it will indicate the speech is spoken ALOUD

VIC F.O.
Come on, you worthless dingo.

BLOOD F.O.
You're funny when you get horny.

VIC F.O.
Funny enough to kick you upside your ass. I said find! I ain't kidding!

BLOOD F.O.
For shame, Albert. After all I've taught you. Not ain't kidding... I'm not kidding.

Vic raises the rifle as if he will club the dog.

VIC F.O.
Find, you son of a bitch...and stop calling me Albert. My name is Vic and you know it damned well!

BLOOD F.O.
(hurt)
You'd club a poor defenseless animal? You're not a good person, Albert.

(CONTINUED:)

6 CONTINUED:

The dog pauses a moment, as though taunting Vic, then he flops over on his back, lies rigid, and we HEAR the sound of TELEPATHIC SEEKING as Blood sniffs for women. (This should be a SPECIAL SOUND used only for this purpose. Suggest electronic sound devised for this use.)

After a moment, the dog stands up, licks his chops and sits down, staring at Vic.

BLOOD F.O.
I detect nothing...sir. I have cast and I have sniffed...sir. And I get a negative reading.
(beat)
Sir.

Vic sits down on the shattered curve. He pulls out a cleaning rag with gun oil on it, and begins polishing the .45 as Blood sits beside him.

VIC
Why do you always call me Albert when you know it'll annoy me?

BLOOD F.O.
You wouldn't understand.

VIC
Why wouldn't I understand?

BLOOD F.O.
Because, essentially, Vic, you're stupid.

VIC
Don't talk to me like that. I can read, I can do figures, I even know history.

BLOOD F.O.
Only because I taught you. If it weren't for me, Vic, you'd be like any other solo.

VIC
You're a dog. What the hell d'you know!?!

(CONTINUED:)

6 CONTINUED: - 2

Blood licks his paw in a truly disinterested way.

BLOOD F.O.
I know you need me to find girls.
And I know you wouldn't last ten
minutes in this city without me.

VIC
Yeah, sure. Like hell.

BLOOD F.O.
And you know it, too.

They sit there in silence for a short while. Finally:

BLOOD F.O.
I call you Albert, after Albert
Payson Terhune. He wrote dog
stories, about eighty years ago.

VIC
That's dumb.

BLOOD F.O.
I thought you'd think so.

VIC
It annoys me.

BLOOD F.O.
That's why I do it.

VIC F.O.
Why are you always so crummy to
me, Blood? I thought we was
friends?

BLOOD F.O.
Were. Not _was_: were.
(beat)
We _are_ friends, Vic. But sometimes
I _find_ it difficult to contain my
hostilities toward you. I'm
dependant on you, even as you are
on me...and I resent it sometimes.

VIC
(after a beat)
Whaddaya wanta to do tonight?

7 ON BLOOD

he tries to look unconcerned. Licks a paw, yawns.

BLOOD F.O.
Doesn't matter to me. Whatever
you'd like to do, Al...Vic.

CAMERA ANGLE EXPANDS as Vic stands up and stretches, looking down at Blood with a nasty smile on his face.

VIC
We could always take in a movie.

BLOOD F.O.
(tries to be
offhand)
We could do that.

VIC
IF you'd rather not...

BLOOD F.O.
(quickly)
No, no, that'd be fine, Vic.
(beat)
We could even get some popcorn.

VIC
(with an evil
undertone)
Would you like that?

BLOOD F.O.
You bastard!

Vic walks away, laughing. Blood watches him for a moment then gets up and follows. CAMERA HOLDS ON THEM STARTING THROUGH RUBBLE as we

LAP DISSOLVE TO:

8 thru 12 SERIES OF TRAVELING SHOTS - ARRIFLEX

ANGLES ON THEM as they pick their way through rubble and down bombed-out streets, giving us a thorough looks at the devastation of the city. VOICES OVER as they travel through:

(CONTINUED:)

8 CONTINUED:
thru
12

VIC F.O.
I hear Our Gang got in some old Cagney films.

BLOOD F.O.
Did you ever see "Public Enemy?"

VIC F.O.
Uh-uh. Good?

BLOOD F.O.
Sensational.
(beat)
Is that turf safe, Vic?

VIC F.O.
As far as I know. It was last time. They've really got it locked up. Neutral ground.

BLOOD F.O.
You know why they call themselves Our Gang, don't you?

VIC F.O.
No.

BLOOD F.O.
It was the name of a series of short comedies made in the 1930's. About a gang of kids.

VIC F.O.
Well, shit, dog. Our Gang ain't... isn't no comedy bunch. I heard how they cleaned out a rumble at the old Loew's Utopia Theater when a roverpak tried to steal some Rory Calhoun movies they'd found.

13 THEATER STREET - TOWARD EVENING

The sun is going down. Red and bloated the way a sunset looks through ugly smog. There is a lone building, obviously a theater, standing amid rubble. Blood and Vic are walking toward it. Blood stops and quivers.

BLOOD F.O.
We've got trouble.

14 ON VIC

as he unships the rifle. He stops and squats, making a smaller target. There is no cover.

VIC F.O.
What do you sniff?

BLOOD F.O.
Three of them, with dogs. Behind that car.

Vic looks down the street. A junked car is lying on its side. Suddenly VOICES come from that direction.

OUR GANGER #1
Stand and deliver, mother!

OUR GANGER #2
We gotcha pinned. Move and we open ya.

VIC
Who are you?

OUR GANGER #1
You tell us who you are?

VIC
I'm a solo. Me and my dog are goin' to the movie.

OUR GANGER #2
You ain't a scout?

VIC
I told ya, ya wimp! I'm a solo.

Vic stands and holds the rifle out away from his body but doesn't drop it. Then three ragged kids, aged approximately fifteen to eighteen, thin and not at all like hoods, come out from behind the car. One of them has an old Thompson submachine gun. The others have rifles. They walk slowly toward Vic, well apart from one another. Two large, vicious dogs accompany them.

15 WITH THE GANGERS

LOW SHOT from them to Vic. As they come up to him. They stop and appraise him.

OUR GANGER #2
What'd you bring to pay?

(CONTINUED:)

15 CONTINUED:

Blood comes over to Vic and sits beside him. Vic gives a start as though hearing something and, though he doesn't take his eyes off the kids, he gives Blood a quick eye-shift.

BLOOD F.O.
Two of them are bluffing. The tommy gun is empty and the barrel of the .22 is plugged. The other rover's got two rounds in his rifle.

OUR GANGER #2
What'd that dog say to you?

VIC
He said we don't have to pay any goddam guards in the street. We deliver at the box office, like always.

OUR GANGER #2
You got a smart mouth, boy.

He raises the rifle. Vic tenses.

OUR GANGER #1
Angelo. Cool it.
(beat; to Vic)
Okay, you can pass. But Spanky'll walk with you.

He nods to the third Ganger, who has not spoken. The one with the loaded rifle. Vic moves out. As Blood passes the other two dogs, they growl at one another.

VIC F.O.
C'mon!

Blood comes along. ~~SPANKY~~ SPANKY, a fat kid with acne, follows behind, rifle at port arms.

BLOOD F.O.
Just letting those egg-suckers know I'm no roverpak mutt.

CAMERA WITH the trio as they cross to the theater where a hand-lettered sign reads BIG TRIPLE FEATURE TONIGHT! Two guards lounge in front of the bomb-ravaged theater. Spanky turns them over with a look and walks back to his fellows.

16 LOBBY OF THEATER - EVENING

as Vic and Blood come past the two guards, who turn to watch him enter. He comes to a coat-check room at the side of the lobby where two more guards stand with the flaps of their sidearm holsters open. Another Our Gang kid is inside the cloak room. There are weapons hung on pegs behind him: rifles, pistols, knives. There is a leaking water pipe running across the ceiling of the coat room.

CHECKER
Buy yer tickets first.

Vic digs down in his old army jacket pocket and brings up a tin of sardines.

CHECKER
(calls back over his shoulder to someone we can't see in booth)
Sardines.

BOOTH VOICE
Okay, we can use 'em.

The Checker takes the tin of sardines.

CHECKER
That's good for a start. Now the mutt.

VIC
He's no mutt.

CHECKER
You wanna see the movies or doncha?

Vic digs down again, comes up with a can without a label. He puts it on the counter.

CHECKER
What the hell's that?

VIC
Peaches.

CHECKER
How the hell do I know that?

(CONTINUED:)

16 CONTINUED:

VIC
'Cause I <u>said</u> so, pissbrain, that's how.

The checker glares at him, but takes the can. He speaks to the voice inside again.

CHECKER
Peaches. For a dog.

BOOTH VOICE
Okay. Pass 'em.

CHECKER
Shower down your weapons, pistolero.

Vic hands him the rifle and the .45 and the Checker hangs them.

VIC
Hey, move 'em over. That pipe's leakin'.

The checker ignores him. Vic leans across and grabs him by the front of his T-shirt.

VIC
Hey you mammygrabbin' toad, you move my stuff over the other side! It goes to rust fast an' it picks up any spots, man, I'll break your bones!

The checker starts to yell for help from the two guards who already have their pistols drawn, but one of them nods and the VOICE from the Booth jumps in.

BOOTH VOICE
Alfalfa! Move his heat. We don't need no trouble tonight.

The Checker slumps back as Vic lets him loose and moves the rifle, farther down the line where it's dry. He pegs the .45 beneath it.

Vic stares at him for a long moment and the Checker looks worried. Then Vic and Blood turn, they stare a moment at the guards, who holster their pistols as Vic stares them down. Then Vic and Blood move toward the swinging doors into the theater proper.

17 THE LOBBY

WITH THEM as they pass a popcorn stand tended by two guards with bren guns.

BLOOD F.O.
I want popcorn.

VIC
Forget it.

BLOOD F.O.
You <u>said</u> we'd get popcorn.

VIC
<u>You</u> said. I didn't say shit, man.

BLOOD F.O.
Come on, Albert, buy me popcorn.

VIC
I'm tapped out. You can live without popcorn.

BLOOD F.O.
You're just being a creep!

VIC F.O.
Remember that the next time you call me Albert.

He goes into the theater by the swinging door, leaving Blood sitting in front of the popcorn stand. Blood looks up wistfully at the brown paper sacks of wilted popcorn, till one of the bren gun guards snarls at him.

BLOOD F.O.
I hope the next time you play with yourself you go blind!

Then, tail high, jauntily, haughty, he walks to the swinging doors and nudges one open with his nose.

18 CAMERA WITH BLOOD

as he enters the darkenes theater. It is filled with rovers, solos and their dogs, all in seats. The film is an old RKO gangster film with much shooting. Blood stops in the aisle. He can't find Vic. He barks. VOICES come from the dark, ad lib: "Shut the hell up!" "Shut that damn mutt up!" Blood barks again.

(CONTINUED:)

REVISED DIALOGUE FOR
"A BOY AND HIS DOG"

OLD DIALOGUE	NEW DIALOGUE
BLOOD: Shut up, cow!	BLOOD: Shut up, Circe!
BLOOD: And I'm right about this simpering cow.	BLOOD: And I'm right about this female. [Optional add, if possible:] She's a wrongo if I ever smelled one!
BLOOD: Give them the cow.	BLOOD: Let the Seven Dwarfs have Snow White and we can get out of here with all our parts.
VIC: What the hell's lumbering you? BLOOD: Last night. And your cow. We should have vacated this place and left her for the Pak; that would've been the intelligent thing to do. VIC: I wanted her. BLOOD: Yeah, I know you "wanted" her; about a half a hundred times. But why're we still hanging around? VIC: I want her some more. BLOOD: Well, listen, my friend, I want to get rid of this pain in my side and I want to get away from here; those screamers could come back any time, you know. VIC: Oh, what the hell are you worried about that for? We can handle all that. (BEAT) It don't mean she can't go with us. BLOOD: Go with us!?! You're out of your mind if you think I'm going to team up with a ridiculous, lusting [Word unclear: pile or vial] of female stupidity and clumsiness! VIC: You know, you're starting to sound like a goddam poodle!	VIC: What the hell's lumbering you? BLOOD: Your headlong plunge into stupidity. Last night was inexcusable. Leaving her for the Pak, that would've been the survival thing to do. VIC: I wanted her. [Identical dialogue from here to] It don't mean she can't go with us. BLOOD: Go with us!?! I must be going crazy; I didn't hear that! I didn't! This is a nightmare. It's all we can do just to keep us fed! What the hell good is she? Did you see her with that gun last night? She damn near unloaded on me! Go with us??? That damned thing shaves its legs and armpits! VIC: You know, you're starting to sound like a goddam poodle! BLOOD: You're starting to sound like a jackass!

Revised Dialogue for
"A BOY AND HIS DOG"
(continued)

In the Fellini scene, with Blood and Vic in cutaway shot as one of Fellini's slaves plays the guitar off-camera, Blood says, "I wish he'd tune that thing."

Substitute line:

"When I'm elected God I'm going to make it a felony to strangle guitars like that."

In the love scene in the boiler, when Quilla June and Vic have an extended period of staring at each other with doe-eyed lust, an intercut of Blood staring at them ruefully could be accompanied by this new,

Substitute line:

"Terrific. Soulful glances. Heavy breathing. Quaint mating habits of the brain-damaged natives."

Blood's a Rover

First Draft Teleplay
14 May 77

BLOOD'S A ROVER

by Harlan Ellison

Pilot Teleplay

based on

the award-winning novella
and film

A BOY AND HIS DOG

created by
HARLAN ELLISON

BLOOD'S A ROVER

by Harlan Ellison

ACT ONE

FADE IN:

1 EXT. BLASTED WASTELAND - DAY - EXTREME LONG SHOT

This is a land that has been pounded by calamity. Barren, stark, high-contrast gold and black. Desert that was very likely a city once...we can see obviously man-made shards of Brancusi-like metal thrusting up spindly arms and angles from the hard-packed ground. The rear end of a buried car juts its silhouette into the dawn sky. A red, molten ball of sun rises over the horizon. And topping a rise, coming toward us, two figures in sharp black relief against the low sky. One seems to be a human, the other a dog. LARGE IN F.G. we see the barrel of a rifle aimed toward them.

BLOOD IN VOICE OVER
(sprightly)
First thing in the morning, don't you hate it when someone lectures you?
(beat)
So do I.
(beat, elfishly)
Here's today's lecture.

(CONTINUED:)

1 CONTINUED:

As the boy and the dog continue on a straight line into the muzzle of that rifle, aimed at them with only the slightest wavering to advise us it is well-manned and ready to shoot.

BLOOD V.O.
World War III lasted from 25 June 1950 when the Republic of Korea was invaded by 60,000 screaming North Korean troops spearheaded by something in excess of 100 Russian-built tanks...through a long 'cold war'...and several small 'hot ones' ...to 1 January 1983 when the Vatican Entente Cordiale was signed between the Eastern and Western blocs.
(beat)
Paying attention? This is called 'history.'

As the boy and the dog reach mid-B.G. the CAMERA PULLS BACK SLIGHTLY to show us three extremely raggedy young boys (12 years old, fifteen and sixteen years old, clearly tough juveniles) lying out on their bellies, rifles aimed at the pair moving toward us. They wear bandoliers of bullets crossed on their chests, patched combat fatigues, one of them has on a dented crash helmet such as the kind stock car drivers wear, tied to his head with a bandana; another has a WWII-style "pot" helmet and a pair of ancient aviator goggles a la Lucky Lindy; one has his feet wrapped in rags, burlap, cardboard, tied together with friction tape.

The boy and the dog ramble toward us, the boy pausing from moment to moment to kick at the dirt, as if hunting for something buried in the ground. Blood continues speaking.

BLOOD V.O.
World War III--hot and cold--lasted thirty-three years.
(beat)
World War IV lasted five days, until the few remaining missiles that had jammed in their release phase had left their silos beneath the Painted Desert and the Urals and the Gobi Altay; but by then there wasn't anything much left to fight over. Five days, and 'civilization' as humans knew it was gone. Blotto. Finito. Isn't that sad?

As the preceding V.O. dialogue has progressed, the boy and the dog have come into the MID-SHOT and we can see now that they are VIC and his dog BLOOD. Vic walks on, but Blood suddenly stops, drops to his belly and casts about.

2 CLOSE SHOT ON VIC

he is fourteen years old, but a very tough and hardened kid for that age. He is fourteen, going on forty. He wears a forage cap, has a rucksack on his back, a thong sack slung from one shoulder, a .45 holstered on his hip, a bolo knife in an oiled sheath just showing over his right shoulder, twin crossed bandoliers of bullets for the 30.06 hunting rifle with the telescopic sight he carries at port arms, a can opener on a thong around his neck, heavy hiking boots, and a ragtag wardrobe that is topped off by a Howdy Doody T-shirt revealed under his open battle jacket. We TRUCK WITH VIC IN CU for a few steps till he realizes Blood isn't with him, then HOLD as he turns and SHOOT PAST and DOWN to Blood lying behind him half a dozen paces on the desert.

VIC
Now what's the matter?

The VOICE OF BLOOD IN FILTER OVER--our way of indicating the dog is telepathic, communicating mind-to-mind with Vic--is heard, as the dog looks warily this way and that.

BLOOD (FILTER)
We have trouble.

VIC
Don't start _that_ again! You had a whole can of little sausages just about three hours ago.

BLOOD (FILTER)
Not a _whole_ can, an _entire_ can; and I'm not talking about food.

VIC
Then what?

BLOOD (FILTER)
I smell three rovers with freshly-oiled weapons.

VIC
Damn!

BLOOD (FILTER)
No doubt. But it doesn't change a thing.

(CONTINUED:)

2 CONTINUED:

Vic now looks around warily. The dog keeps low to the ground.

VIC
Can you pick up a location on them?

At that moment, the three ROVERS open fire. Vic falls on his face right beside Blood.

BLOOD (FILTER)
Yeah. Right over there.

VIC
(ruefully)
Thanks a lot.

Now begins firing back and forth between the rovers and Vic.

3 LONG SHOT - THE DESERT

as we HOLD the two groups with considerable space between them, firing at each other, and Blood's voice OVER goes on with the history, and the firefight can be HEARD IN B.G. (By this time, having heard the erudite voice spinning the history, and having heard the same voice in filter as coming from the dog, the viewer is primed to accept the dog is telepathic. This will be strengthened very shortly.)

BLOOD V.O.
Then what was left of the world belonged to anybody who wanted it. Anybody with a taste for radiation and rubble. But it was a very different world. The 'good folks,' the nice, fat middle-class folks, sank their caisson cities, their sterile Downunders deep in the earth. And they locked out all the rabble. The cities were abandoned to the survivors, vicious roverpaks of parentless young boys and girls...and their telepathic dogs. Noble, loyal, intelligent dogs. Such as myself. You can call me what my pet boy, Vic, calls me...

HARD CUT TO:

4 CU ON VIC - PAST HIM TO BLOOD

as the dog starts to scuttle away on his belly. Vic's scream dovetails exactly with the last beat of the preceding speech.

VIC
(paniced)
Blood! Blood! Don't leave me!

BLOOD (FILTER)
Noble, loyal and intelligent, Massa' Vic, that's me. Just keep busy till I get back...

and he scuttles away across the desert and over a low dune as Vic, in horror, watches him go; and we FREEZE-FRAME that look of horror as we FLASH

MAINTITLES OVER

CUT TO:

5 SERIES OF VIGNETTE SHOTS
thru
10 as MAINTITLES run, we see the following:

A. Vic firing at the rovers.

B. Rovers firing at Vic.

C. Blood poking his head over the dune as Vic sees him.

D. Vic crawling flat along ground toward Blood.

E. Vic looking around on the other side of the dune for a vanished Blood, crawling a little further and then, in a shadow of the dune, suddenly slipping head first into an otherwise invisible hole, and disappearing. The desert is empty again.

F. The rovers suddenly realizing there's no answering fire, looking confused, raising up to look around...seeing nothing...looking at each other bewilderedly.

END MAINTITLES

CUT TO:

11 INT. GROCERY STORE - UNDERGROUND - ON CEILING

as Vic comes falling through in a shower of dirt and broken ceiling parts. He FALLS INTO CAMERA and CAMERA WITH as he crashes to the filthy floor amid shattered bottles and broken crates. He lies there on his back, his legs up in the air for a moment, till Blood comes into SHOT and licks his face.

12 CLOSE ON VIC & BLOOD

BLOOD (FILTER)
What an entrance! What grace, what form, what a klutz!

Vic is still upside-down.

VIC
How would you like the butt of my rifle up your nose?

BLOOD (FILTER)
(mock affronted)
This is a way to talk to man's best friend? Why, Albert...!

VIC
Stop calling me Albert! You only do it 'cause it annoys me.

BLOOD (FILTER)
Very perceptive analysis. Perhaps you would be a tot less cranky if you roused yourself from all that broken glass, faithful master.

Vic realizes he's in pain, winces, and rights himself. Now he sits in the gloom, staring around. Blood sits beside him, cozy and friendly as you please.

VIC
Where the hell are we?

BLOOD (FILTER)
(sternly)
I've spoken to you about your foul mouth on numerous occasions, Vic. Coarse language is the sign of a sterile imagination.

VIC
I'm sorry, I'm sorry! Where the... uh...where the dickens are we?

BLOOD (FILTER)
(thoughtful)
Dickens is so archaic. Try bleep.

VIC
(furious)
Will you please...!

(CONTINUED:)

12 CONTINUED:

Blood, sensing a cuffing, decides not to rag him any further.

BLOOD (FILTER)
We are in the buried remains of what was once an abundantly-stocked food shoppe. Not to put too fine a point on it, a grocery.

VIC
(amazed)
You found food? But I thought when dogs got telepathy they lost the ability to hunt for food?

BLOOD (FILTER)
Quite true. But we acquired the ability to hunt people, which is why dogs were used as skirmishers in World War III. I offer as living proof of that fact, the gentleman over yonder...

He nods his head toward a dim corner and Vic looks as CAMERA MOVES TO INCLUDE the corner. There is a dead man lying there.

BLOOD (FILTER) CONT'D.
...well, perhaps living isn't the precise term.

VIC
He must not have bought it too long ago, or you'd never have smelled him.

BLOOD (FILTER)
I'd say he went to that big supermarket in the sky just about the time I fell in on him. Landing on him probably didn't help his case much.

VIC
(warily)
What killed him?

BLOOD (FILTER)
(laconically, licking himself)
Probably that big rattlesnake.

Vic's eyes widen, and he looks more closely as CAMERA COMES IN on the leg of the dead man, and a huge snake that comes slithering out to coil itself and rattle terrifyingly.

13 FULL SHOT

as Vic leaps up, going "yoick!" He grabs his rifle, jumps sidewise as the snake strikes, and bats the thing like Johnny Bench batting a ground-rule double.

14 CLOSER SHOT

as Vic clubs the thing (out of camera). He stops, breathes heavily. Looks at Blood, who is panting happily.

VIC
Y'know, you've got a real
morbid sense of humor.

BLOOD (FILTER)
It comes from hanging about with
low, bestial types.
(beat)
Care to stock the larder, Albert?
Er...Vic?

Vic continues to look at him with annoyance, then slowly looks around the grocery.

15 FULL SHOT - FROM VIC'S POV

It is gloomily lit from above by shafts of light dropping through the ruined ceiling. It is what is left of a small grocery store. FULL 360° VIEW, and then Vic moves INTO SHOT, picking among the cans and bottles for what is left intact.

VIC
Beans...Campbell's tomato soup...
pitted California black olives...
beets...a bar of soap...

BLOOD (FILTER)
Forget the beets. Yucchhh!

VIC
You didn't say that about two
weeks ago when we didn't have anything
else.

BLOOD (FILTER)
Deprivation can make even the noblest
creature debase himself slightly.
Forget the beets.

(CONTINUED:)

15 CONTINUED:

VIC
(ruminating)
Not much here. Enough to tide us over a few days...but not what I really need.

BLOOD (FILTER)
Yes, isn't it tragic they never learned to can or bottle females.

VIC
I don't mean a woman...I mean ammunition.

He flips a hand across the bandoliers, which are now virtually empty. They were full when we first saw him.

BLOOD (FILTER)
Tsk-tsk, you've been profligate with your shots again, Vic.

VIC
You shouldn't have left me alone up there so long.

BLOOD (FILTER)
And unless I'm losing my amazing abilities, we won't be alone down <u>here</u> much longer.

VIC
They're sniffing around up there?

BLOOD (FILTER)
They're not too bright, but they're certainly persistent. Perhaps it was something you said.

Then Vic spies something sticking out from under a pile of rubble. He goes over, pulls it out, and lifts up a bottle of cheap wine.

VIC
Oh boy! Just a time to get cornered by three clowns who want to kill me.

(CONTINUED:)

15 CONTINUED: - 2

BLOOD (FILTER)
Try to remember the plural, Albert. That's _us_ they wanto to kill.
(beat)
What's that you have there?

VIC
Sweet Betsy Pike fruit wine. 92 proof. Six unbroken bottles.

BLOOD (FILTER)
You pick some dandy times to consider oblivion.

VIC
Not for me, dodo. We can use three of these for barter with the roverpak that makes ammunition.

BLOOD (FILTER)
_If_ we can get out of this hole alive.

At that moment, dirt begins falling into the hole, and a face appears, blotting out the sunlight.

Vic raises his rifle. He is about to shoot.

BLOOD (FILTER)
Hold it. I've got what is certainly a brilliant idea. Unscrew that bottle of wine and pour a little here on this rock.

VIC
Are you nuts? This stuff is valuable!

BLOOD (FILTER)
Is it dearer to thee than thy life, oh mouth-that-walks-like-a-man?

Vic looks at him, then does as he was bid.

BLOOD (FILTER) CONT'D.
Now...unwrap that bar of soap...

Vic stares at him as we

DISSOLVE THRU TO:

16 INT. UNDERGROUND GROCERY - ANOTHER ANGLE

FAVORING CEILING and the hole in the dirt and rubble, as it is kicked in and jammed in by rifle butts. The slope of fallen-in dirt that permitted Blood exit and entrance is added-to by the dirt falling on it. Blood and Vic are nowhere to be seen, but the piles of boxes and rubble may well be concealing them. We HOLD on the ceiling as a face appears. It is ROVER #1, the one who held the rifle in Scene 1. The face withdraws quickly. Then comes back for a longer look, the rifle protruding into the hole. When there is no shooting, the face withdraws and after a moment Rover #1 swings his legs in and drops, sliding down the dirt mound. He is followed by Rover #2. A third face appears in the hole, framed by sunlight, but Rover #3 is clearly being left up there to cover their back and to hold a tactical position down on the room below.

17 WITH THE ROVERS

as they bound to their feet, rifles swinging in all directions. No one there. They look around warily: maybe this wasn't where that solo and his dog went. Suddenly there is a terrible MOAN from the darkness.

They swing around and around. But the face in the hole up there is blocking their light. Rover #1 waves Rover #3 out of the hole and sunlight pours down. Now we see Vic, lying beside the dead man, almost cuddling him. It is a sight at once frightening and (because we know Vic isn't wounded) funny. Vic moans again. Horribly.

They throw down on him, ready to shoot him, and Vic raises a trembling finger, pointing behind them. His face is grotesquely twisted.

VIC
(groaning)
Look out...m-mad d-dog...

They swing around, holding rifles on Vic nonetheless.

18 REVERSE ANGLE - ROVER'S POV - WHAT THEY SEE

Blood, with soap all over his face, fangs bared, crouched there suddenly growling maniacally.

19 MED-CLOSE SHOT - FAVORING ROVERS

as stark terror flushes their faces.

20 ON VIC

VIC
R-run for your life! He killed my partner and I'm a goner for sure...oooooohh...!

21 SAME AS 19

on the Rovers' faces, as CAMERA PULLS BACK to include Blood, who starts barking ferociously, and then begins running around, knocking over empty cartons, like a nut.

ROVER #2
(hysterically)
Shoot him! Shoot him!

ROVER #1
In here? You idiot, a ricochet could kill <u>me</u>!

He starts scrambling for the hole and it galvanizes the second rover, who almost knocks #1 down in his attempt to scramble up the dirt mound. #1 kicks him and down goes #2...as #1 practically flies up the mound and out the hole. Rover #2 is stuck there on his back, and Blood puts on a terrific performance, drooling and fanging and jumping at him. Vic continues to moan.

Rover #2 gains his feet and bolts up the mound, and struggles through the hole, kicking out at Blood who is nipping at his boots.

Vic struggles out of the corpse's embrace, as Blood rushes up the slope of the dirt mound and jumps through the hole in the ceiling. Vic dashes after him.

22 EXT. DESERT - FAVORING HOLE IN GROUND

as Vic comes up through the aperture. There goes Blood after the three rovers, who are screaming and running for their lives. Vic gains the surface and stands up. His thong sack clanks: the bottles of wine. His rucksack bulges prominently with food. He watches Blood for a moment until the dog screeches to a halt and watches the three rovers disappearing in the distance. Then the dog lopes back to Vic.

BLOOD (FILTER)
A demonstration of how my noble ancestors made the saber-tooth tremble.

(CONTINUED:)

22 CONTINUED:

VIC
You look stupid with that soap on your jaw.

BLOOD (FILTER)
And you looked just swell cuddling that corpse.

VIC
I could have picked them off when they came down through the hole.

BLOOD (FILTER)
And wasted some of the few bullets we had left. Intelligence is always a better weapon than violence.

VIC
(wearily)
Here comes another lecture on ethic and morality.

BLOOD (FILTER)
(seriously)
A lecture on survival, friend. It is a nasty, brutish and usually fatal life we live, and if you know nothing else about me after two years together, you'd better know that I am interested in survival. First, last and always.

VIC
Okay, okay. Gimme some slack.
(beat)
Let's go get some ammunition.

They start to walk away from CAMERA.

BLOOD (FILTER)
That's what I adore about you, Albert. You learn so quickly.

And they walk away as we

LAP-DISSOLVE TO:

23 EXT. CRATER CITY - EVENING - EXTREME LONG SHOT - MATTE

If the desert seemed to be what remained of a city, hammered into oblivion, then what we see of that city, this vista we now hold in LONG PANORAMA SHOT, is even more heartbreaking. Rubble everywhere. The snaggle-toothed remains of what were high rises. Pits filled with water where basements once hid in darkness. Craters everywhere, filling the street so one has to weave and pick one's way through. Ivy growing up twisted lampposts. A scene of desolation and ruin.

LAP-DISSOLVE HOLDS Vic and Blood from preceding scene, walking away from us as the image fades and LONG SHOT fades in of them walking toward us (so they both co-exist for a double moment) through the craters and rubble of the city. While we HOLD THIS SHOT we HEAR the VOICE OF BLOOD OVER.

BLOOD V.O.

During the last years of World War III, geneticists working with the basic building blocks of life, the gene material known as DNA, began expanding rapidly on Kornberg's experiments. Recombining DNA for the war effort resulted in the skirmisher dogs, of whom I'm a direct lineal descendant. Ahbhu, my great-great-great grandfather was only the first dog injected with the amplified spinal fluid of dolphins. He acquired the limited telepathic ability to communicate mind-to-mind with a few commandos. His war record was impressive.

(beat)

Using X-rays and drugs, the gene change mutation bred true.

Vic and Blood move into mid-F.G. of FULL SHOT, DOMINATING FRAME. They go carefully, listening, swinging the rifle around, crouching, going from shadow pool to pool, Blood always sniffing. Once, a face appears at a window on the second floor of a building they pass, and Vic throws down on him...and the face vanishes. Another momentary incident presents itself as they pass a huge, old steamer trunk. As they pass, the lid is raised from within. Two tiny children, perhaps no older than ten or eleven, filthy, have made their home in the big trunk. Hands, faces and gun barrels protrude; but the boy and the dog are clearly not looking for trouble, and they are allowed to pass the trunk without difficulty. As they PASS CAMERA we HOLD TRUNK IN F.G. and CAMERA SLOW PANS WITH Vic and Blood shooting down street in opposite direction.

(CONTINUED:)

23 CONTINUED:

Blood's V.O. CONTINUES through these passage scenes.

BLOOD V.O.
Not all dogs are telepathic. Not all people, either. Certain dogs can talk to certain men or women.
(beat)
In the roverpaks, the ones who can work dog get the best food, the best sex, the warmest bed out of the rain.
(beat)
But there are always a few dogs and humans who can't cut it in a roverpak. They're called solos.
(beat)
That's Vic and me. It's not a cushy life, but we stay alive. And isn't that what it's all about? We keep living to say no to death.

DISSOLVE TO:

24 EXT. CRATER CITY - NIGHT - AT THE WHARF

The black ribbon of the River stretches out there, with more rubble on the other side of the shore, indicating another city that has died. But the wharf has been maintained in good order. Possibly by the roverpak that lives on the huge garbage scow out there in the middle of the water. We see all this as CAMERA PULLS BACK from a hand-painted, crude sign that shows a gun and a scow and a skull-&-crossbones and the numbers 82. The sign is at the entrance to the wharf. Vic and Blood come sauntering into the frame.

BLOOD V.O.
What remains of civilization is a kind of "turf" mentality. Each roverpak provides a service. Our Gang have found old films and run the movies in exchange for food. Ted's Bunch keep the three wells clean so there is always water.
(beat)
And the roverpak that calls itself the 82nd Airborne take food in exchange for ammunition.
(beat)
They ~~[illegible]~~ have their lathes and reloading presses and die sets out on a scow in the middle of the river where they ~~[illegible]~~ can't be attacked.

(CONTINUED:)

16.

24 CONTINUED:

The boy and the dog walk out onto the wharf, toward the end where a lantern and a big old ship's bell hang from an iron post. It is a moonlit night. We can see the scow out there clearly against the black water. A lantern flickers at the stern. Blood's V.O. CONCLUDES:

BLOOD V.O.
It's a good and smart thing, being out there on the water, where they're safe. In our world, bullets are the second most valuable thing you can own.
(beat)
Modesty and good taste prevent my naming the most valuable.

Vic grabs the rope hanging from the bell and rings the big brass clapper. The sound rushes off across the river.

They wait a beat, then another lantern appears out there on the scow. Vic cups his hands and yells.

VIC
(yells)
Hey, Skipper! Walter!

A VOICE (probably amplified by a megaphone of the Rudy Vallee variety) calls back. It is a mean voice.

SNAKE
(faintly, over water)
Yeah, who is it? Whaddaya want?

VIC
(yells)
Tell Skipper and Walter it's Vic and Blood.

SNAKE
(faintly, over water)
What kinda loads you need?

VIC
(yells)
Thirty-ought-six dum-dums and forty-five automatics.

SNAKE
(faintly, over water)
Whaddaya got for barter?

(CONTINUED:)

24 CONTINUED: - 2

VIC
(yelling)
Three bottles of wine! Good stuff!

There is a longer beat, several seconds, as they (and we) wait. Then:

SNAKE
(faintly, over water)
Stay where we can see you, in the light! We'll send the skiff!

25 WITH VIC AND BLOOD

as Vic drops down, feet dangling over the edge of the quay. Blood circles him, then comes to sit beside him. Both look out across the water, where we see activity around the scow.

BLOOD (FILTER)
Just so it shouldn't be a waste of time while we're waiting, name me the Presidents of the United States after Franklin D. Roosevelt.

VIC
(distracted)
Don't want to.

BLOOD (FILTER)
What's the matter, brain in repose?

VIC
(suddenly very sad)
Get off me.

BLOOD (FILTER)
(jollying him)
Come on, take a crack at it. I'll get you started: Truman, Eisenhower...

Vic is ignoring him, kicking at the water, clearly unhappy. Blood pauses, then in a much tighter, stricter, more schoolmasterly voice, pushes him again--

BLOOD CONT'D. (FILTER)
(annoyedly)
Truman...Eisenhower...

(CONTINUED:)

18.

25 CONTINUED:

Out there on the water we HEAR the SPLASH of the skiff being dropped overside. More movement. But here, on the wharf, Vic suddenly snaps his head around and glares at Blood, and answers him in vicious tones:

VIC
(angrily)
Damn you, Blood! Truman, Eisenhower, Kennedy, Johnson, Nixon, Carter, Brown, Kennedy, Kennedy, Kennedy! I told you I didn't want no lesson now!

BLOOD (FILTER)
(easily)
Any lesson, watch your grammar; and you forgot Ford.

VIC
(yells)
Oh, f—buzz off! Lemme alone!

And he gets up, and walks away along the quay as Blood watches. He stops at a piling and sits on it. Blood waits a moment, then pads after him.

BLOOD (FILTER)
(gently)
Hey, what's the trouble, kiddo?

Vic is silent a few beats, then speaks sadly.

VIC
Nuts. I don't know. Just feeling very crummy. That dead guy in the grocery, no women for almost a month, all this running and jumping just to stay ahead of Fellini and his roverpak, or some crazy solo with one slug too many...all this history and junk you keep telling me till my head hurts. Every day's just like every other day, just hustling for food.

BLOOD V.O.
My pet boy was suffering from battle fatigue.

(CONTINUED:)

25 CONTINUED: - 2

Blood jumps up on the next piling, and looks at Vic.

BLOOD (FILTER)
(gently)
I think I've picked up a flea behind my right ear. Would you mind doing me a scratch?

Vic reluctantly moseys over, idly begins to scratch Blood behind the right ear. They continue to stare out at the skiff coming toward the pier.

BLOOD (FILTER)
Listen, Vic: this is only temporary. One day very soon, something's going to start happening in this country. Someone's going to settle down and start a farm, start planting food right in the ground--I know you think that's impossible, but it used to happen all the time, <u>right in the ground so you could eat any time you wanted</u>. And they'll put up a stout wall to keep out big roverpaks like the one Fellini runs, and after a while someone else will join them, and then there'll be two, and then three, and after a while it'll be a real settlement.

VIC
Bull. More of that mythology you're always trying to tell me.

BLOOD (FILTER)
It will happen! It may already <u>be</u> happening somewhere. The war's been over for forty years. Humans have a tribe instinct; if we could just get away from this area, look around, you'd see I'm right. You keep hearing rumors all the time from the minstrels that pass through...don't you?

VIC
It's all ramadoola. Bull.

BLOOD (FILTER)
Maybe not.

(CONTINUED:)

25 CONTINUED: - 3

VIC
(angrily)
That's your idea of Heaven, ain't it? "Over the hill."

BLOOD (FILTER)
Isn't it. "Over the hill" is as good a name for Heaven as any other.

The skiff pulls in at the dock, with three rovers in it. Vic shoves off from the piling and walks toward the wharf end again.

VIC (FILTER)
Yeah, well, "over the hill" my butt, dog. We ain't never gonna see it!

BLOOD V.O.
I didn't correct his grammar. One day soon I'd maneuver him into going out looking for "over the hill" and he'd find out. But: I'd certainly get even for his calling me "dog." How'd he like it if I called him "boy"?

26 SHOT PAST ROVERS IN SKIFF TO DOCK

as Vic strolls toward them, Blood padding alongside. There are three members of the 82nd Airborne in the little boat, with a lantern hanging from the stern on a pole, like a Venetian gondola. All three rovers carry pump shotguns, leveled at Vic and Blood.

SNAKE
Hold it.

Vic stops.

SNAKE CONT'D.
Drop the rifle, hands way out onna side, get down on yer face and spread.

Vic just stares at him.

BLOOD V.O.
Oh boy.

(CONTINUED:)

26 CONTINUED:

The three pump guns lock down on Vic.

SNAKE
I said: spread!

VIC
(coldly)
Who're you?

SNAKE
Snake. I said drop and spread!

Vic moves several slow steps forward. He makes no move to comply.

VIC
Well, well. Snake, huh?
(beat)
Listen, stupid: you're here, so that means Skipper and Walter know me and sent you over, and that means I'm okay, so stop playing Jimmy Cagney and move your butt so we can get in.

In response, all three pump guns emit the sound of their hammers being pulled back. The beat goes on...

BLOOD V.O.
God save me from idiots who have to do their machismo number.
(beat)
My wonderful self is about to be killed very dead.

HOLD THE SHOT beat beat beat as we:

FADE TO BLACK

and

FADE OUT.

END ACT ONE

ACT TWO

FADE IN:

27 EXT. RIVER - MEDIUM SHOT - WITH SKIFF - NIGHT

as it is rowed back across from the wharf to the scow, lying dead in the water directly ahead. Two of the rovers, one of whom is SNAKE, stand up in the boat. Vic and Blood are seated amidships. As we near the scow, we HEAR BLOOD'S VOICE OVER:

BLOOD V.O.
Like most machismo encounters of male humans, it was considerable sound and fury, signifying muscle-flexing and not much else.

They reach the scow and a ladder is lowered. Vic grabs Blood under the belly and climbs up one-handed.

SNAKE
(from below)
Can't that eggsucker get up on board by hisself?

There is nasty, ridiculing laughter from the three rovers.

BLOOD (FILTER)
I've decided that Snake person has a somewhat less than sparkling manner.

VIC (FILTER)
Ignore him. We need the bullets.

BLOOD (FILTER)
Calling a noble canine an "eggsucker" is about as actionable an insult as I care to imagine.

VIC (FILTER)
You can explain what it means to me later. Right now, cool it.

CAMERA RISES TO HOLD VIC as he goes over the taffrail. He is met by two members of the 82nd Airborne with bren guns. Snake and his partners come up behind him.

28 EXT. DECK OF SCOW - NIGHT - WITH VIC

Snake gestures with the pump gun as Vic drops Blood. The gesture is toward a superstructure erected on the mid-deck. It is a house of spare bare boards, oil drums, something that looks like the remains of a quonset hut. It is a gimcrack residence the Seven Dwarfs might inhabit. Vic and Blood start for it in the shadowy dimness. The five 82nd Airborne rovers follow, guns leveled.

BLOOD (FILTER)
How do they live with this smell?

VIC (FILTER)
Keep your mouth shut. They're very sensitive.

BLOOD (FILTER)
They can't hear me, only you. And I'm sorry I maligned their delicate natures. Pee-yoo!

They approach the entrance to the superstructure, and the door flies open. A short, swarthy, very jolly-looking boy of about fifteen stands there. It is SKIPPER.

SKIPPER
(volubly)
Vic! Hey, c'mon in!

VIC
(dourly)
Hiya, Skipper. Good to see you again. How's chances of your getting this clown with the pump gun to back off?

SKIPPER
Snake! Damn it, this solo's a friend of mine.

SNAKE
He gimme trouble. Him an' that little eggsucker.

BLOOD (FILTER)
That's <u>twice</u>! Aren't you going to say something to defend my good name?

VIC
(to Snake)
Hey, pinhead: don't call my dog no eggsucker.

Skipper sees trouble, and grabs Vic, brings him inside. Blood rushes through quickly. Snake and two others follow.

29 INT. SCOW - FULL SHOT

A larger room than it seemed from outside. Found materials furnish the place. Bunk beds in which very young boys are sleeping, a fireplace made from bricks and a length of stove-pipe. A chicken turning on a spit in the middle of the room. It is smokey. Everything is dim and faint, as if shot by Altman for a film of primitive existence. A long, lean kid with a patch over one eye, wearing a fedora with a feather in it, sits in a rickety rocking chair. He is WALTER, Skipper's partner.

VIC
Hello, Walter. How they jumpin'?

WALTER
(grunting)
Okay. Same dog?

VIC
Same dog. Over two years.

SKIPPER
Sit down.

He kicks one of the littest kids off a crate. Vic sits down.

WALTER
Let's see the barter.

BLOOD (FILTER)
Big on hospitality, aren't they?

Vic fishes around, pulls out the three bottles of Sweet Betsy Pike fruit wine, hands them to Skipper, who hands one to Walter, who examines it.

WALTER
This's been opened.

VIC
Needed a couple of drops to save my life this afternoon. Just a few drops.

SKIPPER
Looks good to me, Walter.

WALTER
Jus' fine. Got a boot, Vic?

Vic nods, shrugs out of his rucksack and fishes around in it till he comes up with a western-style boot, cut off halfway up the side. He hands it to Skipper.

30 WITH SKIPPER

as he hefts the boot, and shakes it. It clatters from things inside.

SKIPPER
How much brass you got in here?

VIC
About thirty .45 casings, and maybe forty of the 30.06 shells.

SKIPPER
We'll give you fifteen for the pistol and twenty for the rifle.

Vic stands up, takes the bottle from Skipper.

VIC
When was the last time you had booze?

WALTER
Twenty-five and twenty-five.

Vic takes the second bottle, shoves it back in the thong bag. Blood is already at the door.

VIC
Tell 'em not to hoist up that skiff.

Skipper, laughing, takes the second bottle back.

SKIPPER
Okay, okay. Full reload.

He hands the boot full of brass to a little boy of about ten, PIDGE, and slaps Vic on the bicep. Vic shies away, he doesn't like being touched, not even by a "friend."

SKIPPER CONT'D.
(to Pidge)
Pidge, take this to the shop. Tell Coop to reload 'em all.

The little kid goes out a door into a corridor that must lead back to the stern, to the shop. Vic hands Skipper the third bottle.

WALTER
That'll take a while. Sit and tell us what it's like on the land.

(CONTINUED:)

30 CONTINUED:

Vic nods, sits down again. Blood comes over to him. The boy reaches into the sack and brings out two more bottles.

VIC
Here. I'll contribute to the party.

There is general all-around whooping from the eager, hungry kids in the room, all of whom have been watching that wine like hungry animals. Tin cups are suddenly in every hand, and as the bottles are uncapped and passed around, Blood settles down unhappily on his stomach, head between paws.

BLOOD V.O.
Why do I know I'm going to hate this?

The party gets underway as we:

DISSOLVE TO:

31 INT. SCOW - ANOTHER ANGLE - LATER

It is an unpleasant scene. These children are unused to even the mildest wine. Most of the kids are sick, lying about clutching their heads and stomachs. Every once in a while one of them rushes for the door to whooops over the side. Vic is lying up against a bulkhead, more than a little green.

BLOOD CONT'D. V.O.
There are few things in this life as nasty-looking as a human filled with alcohol. They call it hung-over, and if one need any proof that we members of the canine species are smarter than humans, one need only point out that a dog with any self-respect will not touch the filthy stuff.
(beat)
Headaches, stomach aches, blurred vision, vomiting and a great many dumb remarks. These are the manifest benefits of getting, as my pet boy puts it, ripped. Very anti-survival.

Vic rises up. He looks at Blood. He doesn't look good.

32 TWO-SHOT - VIC & BLOOD

He extends a tin cup to the dog.

VIC
(slurred)
Hey, Blood...have a drink.

Blood lifts his nose and turns his head away. Affronted.

SKIPPER
(drunkenly)
Whassa madder, he don' wanna drink with us? Too good to drink with us? Dog ain't s'spossed to drink with us? Somethin' wrong he don' wanna drink with us?

BLOOD (FILTER)
That was a stupid move. Saying it out loud so they could hear it. Tell them I don't drink or use dope, and that I have sworn a vow of sexual abstinence. Tell them at least one of us has to stay pure, so we can hope to survive. Tell them, if you can form the words.

SNAKE
(drunkenly)
Whassa matter with the li'l eggsucker?

BLOOD (FILTER)
That's three.
(beat)
I'm going for a walk. I can bear this vile display no longer.

He gets up and strolls through the door into the corridor leading to the shop. Behind him there is laughter of ridicule.

33 WITH BLOOD

as he wanders down the corridor composed of old crates nailed together. From ahead of him we HEAR the SOUND of sizing die machines and reloading presses.

BLOOD V.O.
If one's "master" cannot, or will not protect one's honor, then perhaps a noble and talented sniffer ought to find a new relationship.

34 INT. SHOP - ON DOORWAY - LOW ANGLE

as Blood comes in through the opening. The shop is set up with ancient machines: a Lyman reloading press, primer seater, powder scale, Saeco sizing die, C-H Tool & Die Corp. bullet swaging die set, canneluring tools, lathes, etc. Piles of shavings litter the floor. Half a dozen 82nd Airborne rovers are working reloading Vic's ammunition. Blood pads about, looking at this and that, amid the noise, till a big, muscular kid of perhaps eighteen, COOP, looks down, sees the dog, and throws a piece of metal at him.

COOP
G'wan, get outta here, you damned eggsucker!

Blood shies from the throw and rushes back down the corridor.

BLOOD V.O.
That's it! I've had it! The next miserable human who calls me a foul name is going to go to his grave with my teeth in his throat!

35 SAME AS 31

as Blood comes back into the "main saloon" of the scow. If everyone was smashed before, they look like death warmed over now. There is nothing appealing about this. Anyone who might ever contemplate drinking, seeing this scene, should be repelled. Vic is lecturing on "life on the land."

VIC
(pontifically)
So things're getting tighter out there. Most of the fast easy food you can dig up is gone. Fellini has the biggest roverpak, and he's scared off most of the solos. He hates me...I keep gettin' to the buried food before he does...an' sometimes I just swipe it from him once they've dug it up.

BLOOD (FILTER)
The Lone Ranger rides again.

He settles down by the bulkhead.

VIC
Fellini's got that big slave wagon, and all them kids pull it.

(CONTINUED:)

35 CONTINUED:

Blood is near Snake, he suddenly realizes...as Snake kicks out to shove the dog further from him. Blood reluctantly scoots over a few feet. They appraise one another.

VIC CONT'D.
He's really organized. About two dozen top guns hanging around all the time. Won't be long now.

SKIPPER
What won't be long now?

VIC
Till he takes over the city.

They all seem startled. Everyone is listening-up hard. Like one of those commercials for the stockbroker in which all movement and sound stop as everyone leans in to catch the eavesdrop. It should be made clear by their perplexed expressions that they have no sense of history; that the past is one minute gone and that because they have no sense of imagination they cannot conceivc of the future.

WALTER
I don't unnerstan'.

VIC
(warms to topic)
Stands to reason. Fellini can't let any solos run loose because they might find some store of ammo or food, and he needs all he can get to feed his people. And it's those troops that keep some solo like me from getting close enough to put a bullet in his fat head.
(beat)
He can't feed 'em, he loses 'em; and he loses 'em...he's just another fat old man.

SKIPPER
Yeah, but what's that got to do with us? We ain't solos. We're organized. We know where the mine is to get the powder for the loads. Nobody can get to us here...an' they need us to do the reload of their brass.

VIC
(laughing)
Dream on, Skipper. Fellini doesn't need you. He could torture the mine location out of you; so he doesn't think he needs you. Same thing.

36 ON BLOOD

as he raises up his head and looks at Vic.

BLOOD (FILTER)
Careful, Vic. I've told you a million times that stupid people resent smart people.

37 ANOTHER ANGLE - FEATURING VIC & SKIPPER

But Vic is too sloppy drunk to be paying attention. He doesn't respond to Blood's warning, but keeps talking.

SKIPPER
Yeah, but the <u>other</u> roverpaks need us. We don't need Fellini's business to stay alive.

VIC
(braggartly)
For how long, man? As soon as Fellini cleans out or scares off the solos in the area, all the independants, then he'll start taking over the roverpaks one by one.

WALTER
(warily)
How do you know all this? Some minstrel lay it on you?

VIC
(puffing up)
Hell, no. I just figured it out. As George Santayana said in <u>The Life of Reason</u>, 'Those who cannot remember the past are condemned to repeat it.' That's a book; I've read books; it's called history; I've studied history. I <u>know</u> that's what'll happen.

BLOOD (FILTER)
That tears it. Now they'll <u>know</u> we're different. We've got trouble.

There is nervous agitation in the room as rovers slowly reach for their weapons as they watch Skipper and Walter move back away from Vic as if he were a pariah, a leper. There is a deathly hush in the place, just the hissing and crackling of the open fires. Snake gets to his feet, the pump gun suddenly very much in evidence.

38 ANGLE PAST SNAKE TO VIC ON FLOOR

He is tensed, the gun not quite pointing at Vic, but ready.

SNAKE
(mean)
Where'd you get all that garbage?

Vic suddenly realizes he's in trouble. He licks his lips. He looks around in silence, looking for an alibi, an out, an excuse.

VIC
(trapped)
Uh...uh...
(then suddenly)
I got it all from Blood!

The dog's head snaps up sharply in amazement.

BLOOD (FILTER)
Why, you...you...<u>fink</u>!

Snake turns to look down at the dog. His face is the meanest thing anybody has ever seen. Ever.

SNAKE
(viciously)
I wouldn't take all that stupid crap from no stupid <u>eggsucker</u>!

Blood cannot control himself. His fangs bare. He tenses.

BLOOD V.O.
<u>That's it</u>! <u>Nobody</u> talks that way to <u>the noblest</u> creature on Earth! An avenging angel, a death-dealing instrument of destruction, a lone heroic beast defending his honor against the Philistines, a juggernaut of power and pain...launching himself on a mission of vengeance...

All this as he leaps and springs IN SLOW MOTION. The V.O. is swift, fast, running together as if he is thinking it, but his movement, caught in SLOW MOTION, shows him arching up and out, as Snake ducks, Blood sails past through the air...and hits the wall. He falls down, stunned, as we HEAR in VOICE OVER, slowly, stupefiedly...

BLOOD CONT'D. V.O.
How fleeting is grandeur.

39 WITH SNAKE - TO BLOOD - DOWN ANGLE

as the rover throws down on the dog, thumbs back the hammers on the over-and-under pump gun, and begins to sight.

SMASH-CUT TO:

40 thru 51 SERIES OF INTERCUTS - INSTANTANEOUS

BLOOD LOOKING HALF-CONSCIOUS BUT TERRIFIED.

VIC SUDDENLY LOSING HIS DRUNKEN MANNER.

SNAKE'S MEAN LITTLE EYES NARROWING.

VIC OPENING HIS MOUTH TO YELL.

SNAKE'S FINGER TIGHTENING ON THE TRIGGERS.

VIC SLAPPING HIS HAND ACROSS HIS .45's HOLSTER, UNSNAPPING THE FLAP, GROPING FOR THE GUN.

BLOOD SEEING DEATH.

SNAKE'S FINGERS PULLING TRIGGERS BACK.

VIC WHIPPING UP THE AUTOMATIC.

A BLUR OF LIGHT THAT IS VIC'S GUN FIRING.

EXTREME CLOSEUP OF THE PUMP GUN FLYING THROUGH THE AIR TO LAND IN ONE OF THE OPEN FIRES, SCATTERING CINDERS & SPARKS.

52 FULL SHOT WITH VIC

as he bounds to his feet, the .45 in one hand, the rifle in the other. We see a dim shape lying against the wall. BUT WE HAVE NOT SEEN SNAKE BEING KILLED OR HIS BODY CLEARLY! All around the room rovers are grabbing for weapons. But Walter sits in his chair and doesn't move. Skipper leaps to his feet. Vic grabs him around the throat with the arm that ends in the hand holding the .45 and we can see the weapon is pressed against Skipper. Vic slings the rifle. He is wearing his rucksack already.

VIC
Freeze, you turkeys!

He manhandles Skipper over to the fallen Blood, forces Skipper to his knees as he, Vic, gets to his knees, and then, awkwardly, he manages to lift the dog over his shoulder, and with Blood woozily assisting, he forces the dog head-down into the rucksack. Blood's back end sticks out, tail drooping.

53 ANGLE ON VIC - PERSPECTIVE ON ROOM

as we see the mass of 82nd Airborne rovers swaying toward Vic and their captured leader. It is almost a unified movement, a gestalt. They want to do something, but Vic has Skipper pinioned. They edge forward as Vic moves back toward the door; he unslings the rifle again, awkwardly, the weight of Blood on his back giving him trouble balancing. He now uses the rifle to clear rovers out from around him as he goes for the door. He backs against it, then turns Skipper slightly.

VIC
(to Skipper)
Open it.

SKIPPER
(chokingly)
You'll never get another slug reloaded, man!

VIC
Just open it, Skipper. I've got no beef with you.

WALTER
(from chair)
Why don't we talk this out, Vic.

VIC
I don't care if you _think_ I'm stupid; just don't _talk_ to me like I'm stupid.
(beat, to Skipper)
Open it!

Skipper reaches around, opens the door onto the deck. Vic edges out, pulling Skipper with him as the rovers move in to fill the empty spaces. Walter does not leave his chair.

54 ON DECK - NIGHT - WITH VIC & SKIPPER

as Vic pulls Skipper toward the skiff, hoist up on lanyards. As they reach it, Vic gets behind him and looks back at the door to the superstructure. A head pops out, and Vic snaps off a warning shot to get the rover do dodge back inside.

55 PAST VIC & SKIPPER

as the shot tears wood out of the wall.

VIC
Stay off the deck!
(beat, to Skipper)
Drop the skiff. Do it, man!

(CONTINUED:)

55 CONTINUED:

Skipper starts letting the skiff down. It hangs over the side, a little below the taffrail.

VIC
Hold onto that rope and get in.

SKIPPER
We'll come after you, Vic.

VIC
Not unless you can walk on water.
Get in!

Skipper crawls over taffrail, holding onto lanyard, and gets in the skiff. Vic, keeping the .45 on him, crawls over and gets in. Blood moves sluggishly.

56 OVERHEAD SHOT - INTO SKIFF

VIC
Okay. Lower us.

Skipper does it. They hit the water.

VIC CONT'D.
Start rowing.

SKIPPER
You gonna kill me, Vic?

VIC
You should of thought'a that when you let that Snake creep throw down on my dog. Row!

He starts rowing away from the scow, into the darkness, as the 82nd Airborne rushes out on deck, rifles and bren guns aimed at them.

VIC CONT'D.
(to rovers on deck)
He bleeds, too! Don't try anything!

The OVERHEAD SHOT assumes a FLATTER ANGLE as the skiff goes away from us, toward the darkness. One of the rovers grabs the lantern and holds it up, but all that can be seen is the skiff disappearing in the night until there is the SOUND of a big SPLASH, and then thrashing in the water, and Skipper swims out of the darkness toward the scow.

SKIPPER
Throw me a line, you stupid buncha--

FLIP-FRAME TO:

57 thru 62 SERIES OF ARRIFLEX SHOTS - TRAVELING WITH VIC

as he climbs up on the wharf with Blood still upside-down sticking out of the knapsack on his back. He starts running. TRUCKING and PANNING SHOTS with VIC as he runs and runs, trying to get as far away from the wharf and the scow, and the implied threat of the 82nd Airborne coming after him as he can. WITH HIM as he dashes down a main street littered with rubble, as he jumps what is left of a shattered wall, as he dodges into an open doorway, as he emerges from the rear of a blasted building. And every once in a while, on a street, we should SEE a crater that emits an ominous green glow. This need not be explained for now. WITH HIM in his flight till he is HELD IN MED-LONG SHOT at the far end of an alley, running TOWARD CAMERA. He rushes INTO MED-CLOSE SHOT at the end of the alley nearest us, and collapses. He falls down and shucks out of the rucksack, dumping the now-revived Blood out on the filthy pavement amid cans and sheathed knives and clothes and other oddments of survival. He falls back against the wall of the alley, and just breathes hard.

Blood circles woozily for a few beats, getting his legs under him. He sits down in front of Vic, who is sitting against the wall with his aching head in his hands. He says nothing for a while. Then Vic looks up at him.

BLOOD (FILTER)
(embarassed, but cheery)
How's it going, kiddo?

VIC
(angrily)
Stupid damned short-tempered imbecilic moron dog! Nearly got us killed! Spoiled my night! Lost us the only armorer in the territory! We're nearly outta ammo and _you_ gotta get insulted, stupid looney lousy ..._eggsucker_!

Blood looks the other way, lifting his nose. Above it. Vic, having vented his spleen, drops his head back into his hands. Blood watches him for a few beats, then speaks very softly.

BLOOD (FILTER)
I was getting tired of this town, anyway.

Vic gives him a quick look of disbelief and anger.

(CONTINUED:)

62 CONTINUED:

VIC
Are you nuts? We're down to five or six slugs. You got us dead!

BLOOD (FILTER)
Take it easy.

VIC
Easy!? You just got us marked lousy with the 82nd Airborne...and every other roverpak in the territory needs them...and that means we're open targets for everybody! Easy?!

BLOOD (FILTER)
We could look on the bright side: take this as a good chance to go look for 'over the hill.'

Vic spits in his direction. Blood dodges.

BLOOD (FILTER)
(getting angry, too)
Look, kiddo, it wasn't all my fault! I admit to losing my temper, but if you hadn't gotten bagged and started showing off your education...

VIC
(warning)
Watch it, dog...

BLOOD (FILTER)
...or if you'd stopped Snake when he started insulting me, I wouldn't have run amuck. It's your responsibility, too.

Vic stands up. He's had it.

VIC
That's it.

Then Vic walks straight out of the alley. And he's gone. Leaving rucksack, contents, dog, everything. Blood just sits there, staring.

BLOOD (FILTER)
I don't believe this.

63 ON BLOOD

as he nudges the goods back into the rucksack and then drags it to the mouth of the alley. He drops the strap from his mouth and looks around the wall carefully.

BLOOD V.O.
Oh no.

ANGLE ELEVATES to HOLD the street. Vic is stumbling, still half-drunk, down the middle of the street. In plain sight. And he's heading directly toward one of those glowing green craters.

BLOOD V.O.
Have you ever seen a screamer? I have. Radiation poisoning victims. They glow the prettiest green. Touch one and you die. Slowly. Screaming. That's why they call them screamers.

He starts running down the street toward Vic way ahead of him.

BLOOD (FILTER)
Vic! Vic, look out, you drunken idiot! Screamer crater right in front of you!

VIC (FILTER)
(drunken)
Damned lousy stupid dog!

BLOOD (FILTER)
(frantic)
Look out, look out, Vic! Dodge, stop, don't go any further!

64 DOLLY SHOT - IN FAST WITH BLOOD

as he runs full out. Now we ZOOM IN on the crater and see a hand clawing at the edge of the crumbling pavement in the street. It is scabrous and glowing faintly green. Blood is still yelling as we PULL BACK FAST as Vic goes away from us, BACK TO BLOOD who is running as fast as his little legs will carry him. He is almost upon Vic, as Vic nears the edge of the crater. Blood leaps, hits Vic in the back, knocking him sidewise, but the force of the jump carries Blood over the edge, right over the bulk of something indistinguishable, but clad in rags, and quite hideous to see, even though we can't tell what it is.

65 INT. CRATER - ARRIFLEX - WITH BLOOD

as he hits the bottom, doesn't stop for breath, goes scrabbling up the other side and out and down the street, full tilt. Behind him we HEAR the SOUND of FEET RUNNING.

38.

66 TRACKING SHOT - STREET

as BLOOD RUSHES PAST going a mile a minute. HOLD CAMERA as Vic comes rushing behind him.

67 EXT. STREET CORNER - MEDIUM SHOT

as Blood runs into the FRAME, looks behind him, sees Vic, and collapses in the gutter. He falls on his back, legs in the air, and we HEAR HIM panting ferociously.

Vic runs INTO FRAME and flops down on the curb.

They lie that way for a few beats. Then Blood gets to his feet. He stares at him.

BLOOD (FILTER)
That was stupid of you.

VIC (FILTER)
Get away from me.

BLOOD (FILTER)
I saved your miserable life, you sixteen year old ingrate!

Vic picks up a rock.

VIC
I said: get away from me!

BLOOD (FILTER)
Wouldn't you be just as happy with <u>some</u> sense?

Vic throws the rock at him. Blood dodges and it misses.

VIC
We're finished...two years with you is enough! If I'm gonna die, I'll do it alone! Get out of here!

Blood walks off a pace or two. He stares.

BLOOD (FILTER)
(matter-of-factly)
Your knapsack and goods are back in that alley.
(beat)
Take care of yourself, kiddo.

And he walks away, into the darkness, leaving Vic staring after him. COME IN CLOSE ON VIC'S EXPRESSION as we

FADE TO BLACK

and

FADE OUT.

<u>END ACT TWO</u>

ACT THREE

FADE IN:

68 EXT. ROCKY SEACOAST - HIGH MEDIUM SHOT - MORNING

as CAMERA COMES DOWN on a single person, behind a big boulder, holding a .22 fitted with a scope. It is a young woman, SPIKE. Behind her on the ground is a small pile of cans and several bandoliers of bullets. She is dressed in camouflage suit and her dirty long hair is bound up in a knot at the back of her head. She wears dark-tinted sunglasses. We HEAR a SHOT and a ricochet spangs off the top of the rock behind which she hides. CAMERA DOWN TO CLOSE on Spike.

She pops up, bangs off a shot and ducks back.

Another shot comes at her. She starts to pop up and get off another shot, when we (and she) HEAR A VOICE.

BLOOD (FILTER)
I wouldn't do that if I were you.

She drops back, spins around, swings the rifle.

69 PAST SPIKE - HER POV

just the cliff and the sea and that's it. No one. She does a full 360° appraisal, and then goes back to her original position, looking worried.

BLOOD (FILTER)
Now if you count to seven slowly, and then track left to 10:00, you might get one.
(beat)
Go ahead, try it. Now count to five.

We see her counting slowly, then up on one knee, and snapping off a shot. From the distance, where more rocks are piled, we HEAR a howl of pain.

(CONTINUED:)

69 CONTINUED:

SPIKE
(aloud)
Who's there? Who are you?

BLOOD (FILTER)
Your fairy godfather; come to save you.

A couple of shots spang off the rock.

SPIKE
I can't see you.

BLOOD (FILTER)
I'm here, don't worry about it. You can trust me. What's your name?

SPIKE
Spike. Who're you?

BLOOD (FILTER)
You can call me Blood.
(beat)
They're trying to flank you, by the way. One coming around from the left, the other over that rise on the right.

Spike looks around frantically. Trapped.

BLOOD (FILTER)
Try the cliff.

Spike gathers up her stuff, shoves it into a rucksack, slings the bandoliers, and crawls on her stomach to the cliff.

70 ANGLE DOWN CLIFF

she slithers over the side. There is a small ledge there. She gets down onto it.

BLOOD (FILTER)
Keep going to your left. I'll meet you at the cave about a quarter of a mile up the beach.

Then silence. Spike crouches on the ledge.

SPIKE
Hey! Hey, where are you?

(CONTINUED:)

70 CONTINUED:

No answer. She keeps going as CAMERA TRACKS HER LEFT. Down the little ledge, to a path, down the path, and then off into the distance as we:

DISSOLVE TO:

71 INT. CAVE - DAY

right near the sea. Spike comes trudging across the sand, and sitting on his haunches in the middle of the mouth of the cave is Blood, panting prettily. Spike comes up to the cave, not too close, rifle ready, waiting for Blood's master to show himself...but there's only the dog.

BLOOD (FILTER)
What've you got to eat?

She stares at him in wonder.

BLOOD (FILTER)
I'll take anything but beets. I haven't had a square meal in three days. What I mean to say is, lady, can you spare a meal for a terrific sniffer like me?

She comes to him, squats down, still cautious.

SPIKE
You saved me up there?

BLOOD (FILTER)
Modesty forbids my answering that question.
(beat)
Hunger forces the truth from me. It was I.

SPIKE
But I can hear you. Inside my head.

BLOOD (FILTER)
It's called telepathy. Very rare these days. You're clearly an exceptional person: I can talk to you.

SPIKE
I've heard about skirmisher dogs, and I even saw one working with a roverpak once. But--

71 CONTINUED:

BLOOD (FILTER)
Listen, kiddo: I'd love to discuss the state of the world with you, but I'm <u>really</u> hungry.

SPIKE
(cautious)
Is that why you helped me up there? So I'd feed you?

BLOOD (FILTER)
I've always mistrusted humanitarians.

SPIKE
(totally confused)
Huh?

BLOOD (FILTER)
Forget it. The answer is yes, I lent you a paw up there in hopes you'd spring for a meal. Anything wrong with that?

SPIKE
No one ever helped me before.

BLOOD (FILTER)
(a little sadly)
Yes, I can imagine. Well, a new day is dawning. There'll be a lot of that going around.

Spike shucks out of the rucksack, starts digging around for food. She continues talking to Blood.

SPIKE
You talk funny. But you're a smart pup.
(beat)
How does this talking-in-the-mind work?

BLOOD (FILTER)
(checking the cans)
Do you know what you've got there?

(CONTINUED:)

71 CONTINUED: - 2

SPIKE
Not much. I'm fat on ammo, but real thin on food.

BLOOD (FILTER)
No, I mean do you know what's in those cans?

She looks bewildered.

SPIKE
Food.

BLOOD (FILTER)
Do you know what kind of food?

SPIKE
How the hell can I know till I open them?!

BLOOD (FILTER)
(quietly)
Read what's left of the labels.

She looks even more bewildered. She turns the cans in her hand, assaying the decaying labels. It is obvious: she cannot read. Blood comes to her, looks over her arm.

BLOOD CONT'D. (FILTER)
That one is corned beef hash. This one is crushed pineapple. That one has no label, so I don't know what it is.

She stares at him in amazement. A dawning interest in him grows as we study her face, seeing the cunning of the wily predator.

SPIKE
You work with a roverpak?

BLOOD (FILTER)
No. I'm solo.

SPIKE
Where's your master?

BLOOD (FILTER)
(haughtily)
I'm my own dog. No one owns me. I go where I choose.

(CONTINUED:)

71 CONTINUED: - 3

SPIKE
Don't try running that one past me,
dog. Nobody makes it by herself
out here.

BLOOD (FILTER)
You seemed to have done it. How old
are you?

SPIKE
(bothered)
I don't know. Older than twenty,
I know that much.

She shows him the butt of her rifle. It has notches cut in it.

SPIKE CONT'D.
I tried to keep track. Every time the
snow comes, I cut another notch. But
I missed a few at the beginning.

BLOOD (FILTER)
(sadly)
I've never known a female solo this
close. It must be extremely difficult
for you.

SPIKE
(tightly)
I get by.

BLOOD (FILTER)
Why don't you join a roverpak of
females?

SPIKE
I don't like being with people.

BLOOD (FILTER)
Why don't you open those cans, I'll go
find some firewood and we can eat.
(beat)
Then we can talk some more.

He starts to trot away. She calls out to him.

SPIKE
You didn't run it past me, dog. I still
want to know what happened to your boy.

She watches him as Blood trots off down the beach looking for driftwood, as we:

DISSOLVE TO:

72 INT. CAVE - DAY

It is dim and shadowy in the cave, eerie with the flickering shapes cast on the water-worn walls by the small driftwood fire. Spike and Blood are eating.

BLOOD (FILTER)
It's been a long time since I had corned beef hash. It's delicious.
(beat, wistfully)
I had it once with a fried chicken egg on it.

SPIKE
Where did you find a chicken?

BLOOD (FILTER)
There was a roverpak that called itself The Black Gang. They raised them, used them for barter. Vic traded off three cans of--

SPIKE
Vic?

Blood is silent. He keeps eating.

SPIKE CONT'D.
Who was Vic?

No answer. Spike puts down her food, moves toward the dog, moves to touch him. Blood bares his fangs. She stops but doesn't pull back.

SPIKE CONT'D
Okay, no touching yet.
(beat)
Listen, Blood: I get the message you cut out on ~~something or other with~~ whoever was running your show...and you're looking for a new tie-up.

BLOOD (FILTER)
I'm not sure entering into a working relationship with a solo female is a good idea. You're a little scarred: looks as though you've had some bad fights. I look for the kind of solos who <u>inflict</u> scars like that.

(CONTINUED:)

72 CONTINUED:

Spike's face gets hard. She looks at him, but she's seeing a great many days and nights stretched out behind her.

SPIKE
If I had a mother and father, they had me and dropped me before I got old enough to know them on sight.
(beat)
I belonged to a roverpak for a while, till some creep saw I was getting big enough for his kind of fun, and I cut his throat and took his .22 and got out at night. I've been on my own a long time, no roverpak, no dog, no nothing but me. I'm good at it.
(beat)
Yeah, I've got scars. But the ones that gave 'em to me are dead, and I've never been raped.

Blood sits and stares at her for a long moment, then speaks very thoughtfully.

BLOOD (FILTER)
Vic and I were mates for two years. We split up. He's gone. I'm available. Maybe you'll do.

She smiles. He edges closer.

BLOOD CONT'D. (FILTER)
There's maybe a flea behind my right ear. Care to scratch him for me?

She smiles more widely, reaches out and tentatively touches him. He moves closer. She scratches as we:

DISSOLVE TO:

73 GRASSLAND AREA - EVENING - FEATURING FARMHOUSE

as CAMERA COMES DOWN on Spike and Blood crouching behind bushes. It is an old farmhouse, and they're about 100 yards in front. There is a sudden SHOT from the house, and as they watch the CAMERA ZOOMS IN to HOLD in MEDIUM CLOSEUP an old, wrinkled, grizzled man with an ancient rifle.

OLD MAN
(screams)
No food! No food! Get outta here!

He is wild, almost a crazed hermit. CAMERA PULLS BACK to Spike and Blood. They flatten as another SHOT comes.

74 EXT. CLOSEUP - SPIKE

There is a tension there, a tough streak that shows she has no patience for all this. CAMERA ANGLE WIDENS to include BLOOD.

BLOOD (FILTER)
I don't like what you're thinking.

SPIKE
Then stop reading my mind.

BLOOD (FILTER)
It's just stupid what you want to do.

SPIKE
(nods her head to their left)
You see that hole?

Blood looks left as CAMERA SWINGS WITH HIM to show us a huge, smoking hole in the earth and the blasted stump of a small tree.

75 ON SPIKE - TO BLOOD

SPIKE
Well, I don't know what made that hole when he fired at us, but whatever it is...

BLOOD (FILTER)
It's a laser rifle. Developed in the Third War.
(beat, musing)
Didn't think there were any left aboveground.

SPIKE
Yeah, well, it was that crazy old man's bad luck to come down on us...if he'd just let us take a little food...

BLOOD (FILTER)
As you say. He's crazy. And so are we if we try to take that laser out of there. Let it go.

SPIKE
I'm hungry. Sit and watch if you like.

Blood starts to say something, but she's up and off, looping out and away to the far right, off the line of sight of the farmhouse. The old man keeps screaming.

76 ARRIFLEX - WITH SPIKE

as she runs. CAMERA STAYS WITH HER but we can HEAR the VOICE OF BLOOD OVER.

BLOOD (FILTER)
Spike! For crine-out-loud! He may be old and crazy, but he's got to be good to've stayed alive this long!

No answer. (She doesn't know yet that she can speak to Blood without speaking.) She rushes through the underbrush, doubles back on the house, finds an ivy-overgrown trellis to one side, hits it softly at a dead run, dropping her rifle. She now has a hunting knife between her teeth. Up she goes.

77 WITH BLOOD - SHOT LONG TO HOUSE

as Blood in F.G. sees Spike on the shattered roof. She pries up a board and drops out of sight. There are half a dozen beats of silence as Blood starts out, a shot sends him back to cover.

BLOOD (FILTER)
Spike! Spike! What's happening?

There is a SCREAM from the house. More silence. Blood watches as we

FREEZE-FRAME and

GO TO TONE LINE (see sample below) and HOLD BLOOD as we:

DISSOLVE TO:

78 GRASSLAND AREA - UNDER BIG TREE - NIGHT

in TONE LINE EFFECT & FREEZE-FRAME that resolves itself into normal view and color. Spike and Blood under the tree, in front of them several empty cans, and the remains of some kind of meat on a spit. CAMERA COMES IN SLOWLY.

SPIKE V.O.
You're not eating.

BLOOD (FILTER) V.O.
I'm remembering. A girl named Quilla June Holmes.

(CONTINUED:)

tone line:

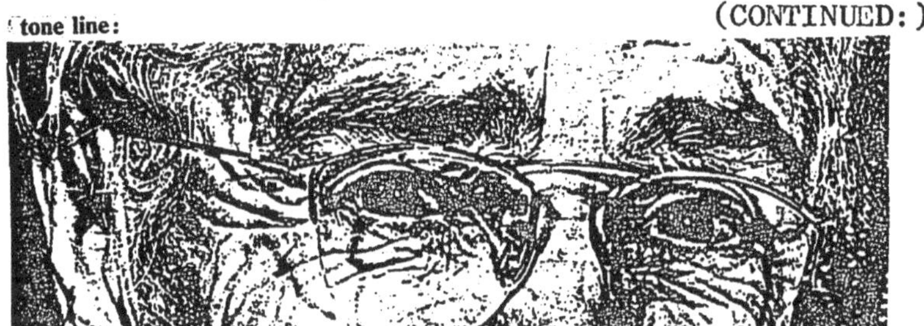

78 CONTINUED:

Spike isn't particularly concerned. She's just making conversation. She continues gnawing on a drumstick...or whatever. CAMERA IN.

SPIKE V.O.
Yeah? What happened to her?

BLOOD (FILTER) V.O.
She died.

SPIKE V.O.
Don't it always end up like that.

CAMERA COMES IN to MEDIUM CLOSE SHOT so we dispense with V.O. and can see Spike talking aloud.

BLOOD (FILTER)
(after beats)
That wasn't smart at all.

SPIKE
I got the thing didn't I?

BLOOD (FILTER)
It wasn't worth that kind of risk. It was anti-survival.

SPIKE
What's that mean?

BLOOD (FILTER)
(testily)
It means, dumb person, that we are adrift in a world of violence that wants to kill us, and anything we can do to <u>avoid</u> violence is pro-survival...meaning it is good for us...and anything that looks like trouble is anti-survival...which means <u>bad</u> for us.

SPIKE
That makes sense. Any peaches left in that can?

BLOOD (FILTER)
(loud and angry)
Now <u>listen</u> <u>to</u> <u>me</u>! If you want me to stay <u>with</u> <u>you</u>, <u>you</u>'re going to have to stop playing hotshot. No more commando games, no more unnecessary slaughter, no more--

(CONTINUED:)

78 CONTINUED: - 2

She has stopped feeding her face. The firelight on her makes her look half-animal. This is a woman who has grown tough and sharp in a bad situation, and she's never been talked to like this before.

SPIKE
Listen, dog...

BLOOD (FILTER)
And don't call me dog, "little girl!"
(½ beat)
If we're together then that means we work together! No more unilateral decisions...
(beat)
No more doing what you want to do without my agreement.

She stares at him. There is a long silence between them. The dog faces her down. She looks away.

SPIKE
(softly)
Okay...Blood.

They sit that way for several beats, then Blood says:

BLOOD (FILTER)
Okay. Now slowly pick up your rifle and get ready for somebody coming in at six o'clock, straight across the fire.

She lets her eyes widen, but other than that she makes no loss of time as she pulls the rifle to her and levels it. Then we HEAR the SOUND of FEET on the dry grass. A shape materializes, indistinct behind the fire and in the darkness. She aims.

BLOOD (FILTER) CONT'D.
Don't shoot him. He's a minstrel.

She lowers the rifle. Then calls out across the fire.

SPIKE
(asking for password)
Stop right there and take off your armband and hold it up where I can see it. The dog's a killer.

78 CONTINUED: - 3

The shape removes an armband and holds it aloft.

SPIKE
Too dark, I can't see it. Keep coming till I say don't.

The shape moves toward them. Now, as the firelight hits it, we see it is a bright yellow armband with a big black circle in the middle of it. The shape keeps coming until a young boy of perhaps eleven or twelve, with a slung .22 rifle on his back, and a battered and chewed-up Stetson, presents himself.

SPIKE CONT'D.
Hold up.
(beat, to dog)
Blood?

BLOOD (FILTER)
He's okay. He's a minstrel.

SPIKE
Could've killed the minstrel and took his armband.

BLOOD (FILTER)
Don't be silly. Nobody's that stupid.
(beat)
And talk with your head, not with your mouth.

SPIKE
(confused)
What?

BLOOD (FILTER)
Mind-to-mind. You can do it.
(beat)
Not now. Later. I'll teach you how. Let him sit down.

She is still staring half at Blood, half at the kid. She has obviously never realized she can communicate telepathically in the other direction. She pulls her eyes off the dog and gestures with the rifle for the kid to sit. He comes in and sits a proper distance away.

POKE
M'name's Poke. I've got a lot of good stuff to talk about, if you feed me.

79 SHOT (AS DESCRIBED)

Spike looking across fire at Poke, with the fire between them and Blood seen through the flames as they burn lower. Horizontally-placed in a line straight across, like two people pow-wowing.

SPIKE
Food's scarce. What've you got to tell?

POKE
(very canny)
First I eat a little, then I tell a little, then I eat some more an' then I tell some more.

SPIKE
First you tell...*then* you eat.

BLOOD (FILTER)
Oh, for pity sake, give him a piece of meat to get him started. Don't be so cheap; we can't finish it all anyhow.

Spike sighs, pulls out her hunting knife with the big mean blade, cuts off a small piece of meat from the chunk still on the spit, and tosses it across to the little boy. He goes at it ravenously.

POKE
Ouch, wow...*hot*!

He devours it in a few chomps.

SPIKE
Okay, minstrel, now what's all that good stuff you know?

POKE
(almost mystically)
I seen a far place near here, and it's nothin' but *food*. Food all over the place. Food in cans and food in jars and food in boxes. *Big* boxes. Biggest boxes you ever seen. More food than a dozen roverpaks could eat in ten years.

SPIKE
(ridiculing)
Yeah, sure; and milk runs in the river and the jack rabbits roll over so's you can cut their throats.

(CONTINUED:)

79 CONTINUED:

CAMERA BEGINS CIRCLING so we can see them from all angles in one slow revolution. MOVEMENT OF CAMERA very stately.

POKE
(defensively)
It's true. I'm a minstrel. I don't lie about what I tell. It's a lost land, a magic place, guarded by hundreds of metal soldiers and dead cars.

SPIKE
I don't believe in "lost lands."

BLOOD (FILTER)
That's what everyone said about Atlantis, until the missiles shook everything up during the Third War...and the lost continent rose.

Poke has not heard Blood's remark, so his words come almost atop Blood's.

POKE
Well, you'd better believe it, because every roverpak in the area has started gathering there.

Spike's head comes up sharply.

BLOOD (FILTER)
(very specific now)
Okay, I'll ask you the questions to ask him.

Spike nods imperceptibly, indicating she's smart enough to know the dog should run the show at this point.

BLOOD (FILTER) CONT'D.
Ask him how many days he's been traveling since he saw the "lost land." And from which direction, which roverpak turf he passed through.

POKE
(not having heard Blood)
And that far, lost place, it has a name even. They call it Eastgate Mall.

HOLD THEM for a beat as Spike leans forward to talk and

DISSOLVE THRU TO:

80 LONG SHOT ACROSS GRASSLAND AREA - DAWN

FEATURING POKE lying asleep beside the embers of the fire. It should be very very apparent that he is only sleeping, not dead or wounded. He is in F.G. LARGE as we SEE Spike and Blood hiking off toward the rising sun, red and bloody on the horizon. We HEAR their VOICES OVER in FILTER.

SPIKE V.O. (FILTER)
So that's how you talk mind-to-mind.

BLOOD V.O. (FILTER)
You're a quick learner, Spike.

SPIKE V.O. (FILTER)
You teach good, Blood.

BLOOD V.O. (FILTER)
I teach well, not good. "Well" is an adverb, "good" is an adjective. An adverb can only be used to modify a verb, or another adjective.

SPIKE V.O. (FILTER)
What's "modify" mean?

BLOOD V.O. (FILTER)
(chuckling)
We'll have a great deal to talk about on our way to the lost land, Spike, old chum.

SPIKE V.O. (FILTER)
You really think that minstrel was reporting what he saw, not just trying to beat us out of some food?

BLOOD V.O. (FILTER)
I think he was describing what used to be known as a shopping center; and the food could be there. Yes, I think it's real. And do you know why I think that?

SPIKE V.O. (FILTER)
No, why?

BLOOD V.O. (FILTER)
Because he saw Fellini and his slave wagon and all his riflemen there. And Fellini is real.

They walk into the sun as the SLOW DISSOLVE THRU

DISSOLVES TO:

81 FULL SCENE SHOT - PANORAMA - LATE NIGHT

WHAT WE SEE: we are on the ridge of an immense bowl; what might have been a suburban tract community decades before. The ridge is covered with trees and shrubbery, very dense. In the F.G. Spike and Blood are lying out staring down into the bowl.

There is an immense desertlike area at the bottom of the bowl. Here and there are the remains of structures, just poking up out of the ground. But right in the middle, looking as if it's three acres in size, is the top of what must have been a gigantic warehouse. Along its facing wall, right near the roof-line, we can make out the upper-half of block lettering, faded and sand-blasted, but still visible in the full moonlight and the light of campfires that ring the building. The words are barely discernible. (Blood will tell us what they say momentarily.)

The campfires that ring the building are far enough apart and far enough back that there is a large no-man's-land surrounding the building. We see people moving around near the various fires.

SPIKE
Is this what he called Eastgate Mall?

BLOOD (FILTER)
This is it. And I'm simply delighted to see we're not the first ones to arrive at the party.

SPIKE
How many roverpaks are there down there?

BLOOD (FILTER)
I make out seventeen, and maybe as many solos. Over there on the right, see the big wagon? That's Fellini and his bunch. About twenty-five of them...he must have hired on five or six more rifles.

SPIKE
That looks like The Nukes on the left, at about eight o'clock.

BLOOD (FILTER)
And The Jolly Stompers, and The Hole in the Wall Gang, and the Cagneys, and that female roverpak, The Flamingos.

(CONTINUED:)

56.

81 CONTINUED:

SPIKE
What kind of strength have they got?

BLOOD (FILTER)
Nukes, eleven; Stompers, sixteen --as best I can smell them--they're all rolled up together; Cagneys are running nineteen...

At that moment, a shape breaks from one of the campfires and we can make out the person broken-field running toward the buried warehouse through no-man's-land. It is all dark and distant, but suddenly there is a fussilade of machine gun shots (indicated in the darkness by tracers that light up the area) all coming from other campfires and from around the rim of the bowl, converging on that spot where the man is running. It lasts about ten seconds, all the fire pouring down on that one spot in streamers of light like the spokes of a wheel.

BLOOD (FILTER) CONT'D.
Make that eighteen.

SPIKE
Wheeew! Ain't nobody gonna get in that place for a while. It's a stand-off.
(beat)
No one group is big enough to try and take it with all them roverpaks and solos keeping them away.
(beat)
How do they know there's food in there?

BLOOD (FILTER)
Because of what it says on that buried building.

SPIKE
I can't make it out from here. Can't read, anyhow. What's it say?

BLOOD (FILTER)
Great Western Produce Market Storage.

At that moment we HEAR footsteps through the brush behind them as Blood leaps up and Spike flops over, holding the deadly laser rifle. She is about to fire, when a young man steps through the brush and looks down at them. It is Vic.

82 CLOSE ON VIC

VIC
Hello, Blood. Who's your friend?

HOLD for beat after beat after beat as we INTERCUT:

BACK & FORTH
BETWEEN:

83
thru
86 SERIES OF CLOSEUP INTERCUTS

Blood's face, looking startled.

Spike's face, looking mean and confused.

Vic's face looking bemused and wary.

Blood, as he buries his face in his paws and we

FADE TO BLACK

and

FADE OUT.

END ACT THREE

ACT FOUR

FADE IN:

87 EXT. RIM OF THE BOWL - MOONLIT NIGHT - LATER

EXTREME CLOSEUP on the almost Buck-Rogers-like muzzle of Spike's laser rifle. CAMERA PULLS BACK QUICKLY to show the young woman sighting through the scope atop the mean, futuristic weapon. Her face is even dirtier than we've seen it earlier, and more tense, colder, menacing. CAMERA BACK to WIDEN ANGLE of SHOT so we see Blood still lying there, staring across the fire. BACK FURTHER to show Vic standing there with his rifle aimed at Spike.

SPIKE (FILTER)
Blood! This the guy you left behind?

VIC (FILTER)
(bemused)
Oh, so you can talk to him, too.

SPIKE (FILTER)
Blood!

VIC (FILTER)
Good work, Blood. Can she shoot?

SPIKE
You move, you're gonna find out how good I can shoot, creep.

VIC (FILTER)
Blood...what the hell's that thing she's got there? Tell her to put it down before I blow her away.

SPIKE (FILTER)
Blood! Tell him to stop talking to you!

VIC
Blood! What's goin' on here, buddy?

(CONTINUED:)

87 CONTINUED:

Blood gets up and slowly walks around in an aimless circle as though he's thinking. CAMERA WITH HIM and IN on his contemplative dog-face. Then he stops and looks at Vic.

BLOOD (FILTER)
Put down the rifle, Vic. You were almost out of ammunition a month ago when we split up. You can't have more than a shot or two left, if that. Chances are good that thing isn't loaded, so put it down.

SPIKE
Thanks, Blood.

Blood turns to her.

BLOOD (FILTER)
If you fire that laser gun, not only will it wipe out every tree in the vicinity, but it'll draw every solo and rover on the rim. So put it down, Spike.

VIC
Thanks, Blood.
(beat)
Okay, broad, you heard him.

SPIKE
Yeah, I heard him, clown. But he don't know me that well. Put yours down or I burn your head off!

VIC
He's only guessing that I didn't come up fat with ammo...so put yours down!

BLOOD (FILTER)
(to himself)
Why me? Why do I have this endless aggravation? I'm a good person. I'm kind and decent, clean and thoughtful. Why me?

VIC
(angrily)
Who is this dippy chick?

(CONTINUED:)

87 CONTINUED: - 2

SPIKE
(furious)
I'm the "dippy chick" that's gonna slaughter you if you don't drop that thing by the time I count to three...one...two...

Suddenly CAMERA ZOOMS IN on Blood as he bares his fangs and growls deep and menacing. He looks crazed.

CAMERA BACK to include a startled Spike and Vic.

BLOOD (FILTER)
Drop them! Both of you! Now!

They are so startled that, watching each other very carefully, they lay down their weapons.

Everything suddenly settles down. And as it does, Vic jumps across the fire, spewing ashes in every direction, and goes for Spike. But she hops out of the way very quickly, and as Vic turns she hauls back and belts him as hard as she can with a roundhouse that lifts him off his feet and sends him sprawling on his back. In a second she's on top of him, knife poised to strike.

BLOOD (FILTER)
Spike! Stop it, let him alone!

She pauses, the command of the dog overriding her fever. Vic lies there, absolutely amazed at what has just gone down, including himself.

BLOOD (FILTER) CONT'D.
I mean it, Spike. Let him alone!

She slowly pulls the knife back. Then, in a very casual gesture, she slaps him twice across the cheeks, back and forth, but very gently, as an act of superiority, of disdain. To prove he's vanquished.

Then she gets off him. Vic lies there for a moment.

BLOOD (FILTER) CONT'D.
Get up, Vic.

He gets up, and stands there naked. Spike still has the knife unsheathed.

88 ON VIC - CLOSEUP

He is so chagrined, and so unseated at what has happened, he looks almost ludicrous. It is a new way for us to see Vic. And makes him more human.

VIC
(innocently)
That was awful!

SPIKE
You ever touch me again, punk,
I'll kick off your kneecaps.

VIC
But...but you're a chick! You
been handed around...you must
have...

BLOOD (FILTER)
She's a virgin. Leave her alone.

Vic regains some of his previous superior attitude.

VIC
I've had enough of this. Come on,
let's get out of here; leave this
lousy broad by herself.

SPIKE
You're the one's leaving, pukey.
Blood and me are partners.

VIC
Blood and I...
(then he stops,
horrified)
Blood and you?!?
(beat, to Blood)
Blood, what is this? I've been
looking for you for a month...

BLOOD (FILTER)
I found a new partner, Albert, old
chum.

SPIKE
Albert? I thought his name was
Vic?

(CONTINUED:)

88 CONTINUED:

VIC
(jumps on it)
See? See? We're still partners!
You called me "Albert."
(beat, to Spike)
He calls me Albert, because it's a joke; it's an iron thing from this guy who wrote dog books before the Third War...tell her, Blood.

BLOOD (FILTER)
(wearily)
An ironic thing, not an iron thing. And his name was Albert Payson Terhune. And it's all done with us, Vic. We lost faith with one another.

VIC
No, Blood, it'll still be a good deal, you'll see...

SPIKE
(angrily)
You're gettin' on my nerves, kid. I think I better just smear you now and be done with it...

VIC
(narrowly)
You just try it. You may've got me once with a sneak attack, but I'm ready for you now. Just come on!

Blood gets up and starts to trot away. Both of them look at him.

SPIKE | VIC
(simultaneously)
Hey, where you goin'? | Hey, c'mere! We got to settle this now!

Blood keeps going, doesn't turn around. SHOOT PAST THEM to his shaggy behind, bopping off toward the underbrush.

BLOOD (FILTER)
I have to relieve myself. Try not to make me an orphan till I get back.

And he's gone, leaving them alone, facing each other.

89 thru 91 FULL SCENE WITH INTERCUTS

Darkness but heavily moonlit among the trees on the rim. They stare at each other surlily. Vic tries to be very nonchalant. He turns away from her pointedly. She just stands with arms folded across her breasts, watching him.

SPIKE
(finally, mean)
He's all done with you.

VIC
You know, at first I didn't like you a lot. Now I really want to dance on your face.

SPIKE
Talk big, little fella. The dog's still with me.

VIC
I'll see you dead first!

SPIKE
Ready when you are.

VIC
Why don't you go hire on with some roverpak that needs an ugly chick to use for barter. Huh, why don'cha?

SPIKE
No wonder you need the dog so much. Only way *you* can kill somebody is to bigmouth him to death.

Vic takes a step toward her...his only response to anger is frustration and instant mayhem. Spike puts her hand on the sheathed knife. Vic looks around, can't find any exit from his frustration, kicks the ashes of the fire. CAMERA PANS PAST HIM and MOVES IN SLOWLY to show us Blood, sitting in the bushes, watching Vic and Spike.

92 WITH SPIKE - VIC IN B.G.

as she goes to her pack and takes out a dirty old chamois cloth. She squats down and reaches for the laser rifle. Vic tenses. She snickers and doesn't even look up.

SPIKE
Take it easy, hero. I won't waste you till Blood says it's okay.
(beat)
Damned animal's got a stupid soft streak in him.

(CONTINUED:)

92 CONTINUED:

VIC
(defensive)
Where the hell do you come off talking to me like that? Blood and I, we've been together two years. We're partners.

SPIKE
(cleaning rifle)
Were partners.

VIC
You'll see.

She doesn't answer him, just keeps polishing the weird futuristic weapon. Vic watches.

VIC CONT'D.
(surly, but making conversation)
What is that dumb-lookin' thing?

SPIKE
You talkin' to me?

VIC
No, I'm talking to fat old Fellini down there.
(still no reply)
Well, what is it?

SPIKE
Blood calls it a laser rifle.

Vic is suddenly fascinated, like a child.

VIC
Oh yeah!!! Wow, I've heard about those. Can I see it?

She looks at him like he's sprung a leak. His enthusiasm vanishes instantly as he realizes what he's asked.

VIC CONT'D.
Mm. No, I guess not.
(then sour grapes)
Don't make any difference. Stupid thing's no good for close work. Too much power, way I hear it.

(CONTINUED:)

92 CONTINUED: - 2

SPIKE
Keep runnin' your face, kid, and you'll find out how much power it's got.

At that moment, Blood comes out of the bushes where he's been sitting, watching them. Clearly, he has been giving them a chance to get to know each other, to let their natural antipathy sink to a lower level.

93 WITH BLOOD - UPSHOT TO VIC & SPIKE

BLOOD (FILTER)
(brightly)
Well, how are Mommy and Daddy getting along?

SPIKE
(without looking up)
Ready to let me burn this creep?

BLOOD (FILTER)
Not just yet, Spike.
(beat)
I want to talk to you two.

VIC
No time to talk. We've got to get some ammo. Let's go.

BLOOD (FILTER)
Sit down, Vic. I want to talk to both of you.

Vic stands there defiantly for a moment till Blood looks at him pointedly. Vic squats, then sits cross-legged.

BLOOD (FILTER)
Things are changing. Neither of you has ever had to work with someone else. Just Vic and me, and you all alone, Spike. But it can't go on like that.

VIC (FILTER)
Aw, c'mon, Blood; it's worked fine except for a couple of little arguments.

BLOOD (FILTER)
No, I mean all over the country, Vic. Things have to change. In a little while there'll be no room for solos or roverpaks.

94 ANGLE PAST BLOOD TO VIC - SPIKE IN B.G.

VIC (FILTER)
You mean Fellini's going to take over *everything*?

BLOOD (FILTER)
No, I mean people are going to start rebuilding.

SPIKE
(she begins aloud)
Rebuilding what?
(then, realizing she is being left out, she switches to telepathy)

SPIKE CONT'D. (FILTER)
Rebuilding what?

BLOOD (FILTER)
Rebuilding the world, Spike. Homes and factories and roads and farms and no more guns and no more digging in garbage cans for food.

VIC (FILTER)
(toward heaven)
Here we go again, folks: "over the hill," where the deer and the antelope play, and everybody grows food in the ground.

SPIKE (FILTER)
Shut up, dummy. Let the dog talk.

VIC (FILTER)
"The dog", as you call him, Lady Pinhead, has a name. He's also full of sh--

Blood's head snaps around. Vic catches himself.

BLOOD (FILTER)
Full of it or not, Vic, the three of us have a far better chance of making it, of surviving, of perhaps being one of the first units to start living like civilized, rational creatures, if--

(CONTINUED:)

94 CONTINUED:

Vic cuts him off, a wave of the hand, a dismissing gesture.

VIC
(aloud)
If what? If what damned what!?!

SPIKE
Don't even say it, Blood. No way. Forget it. I'm out of it.

Blood gets up, walks toward the bushes again. He stops, looks back at Vic.

BLOOD
Vic, come on; I want to talk to you. Spike: just wait.

He goes off into the bushes. Vic looks at Spike. She gives him a dirty look, then cursing beneath his breath, gets up and walks INTO CAMERA.

CUT TO:

95 CLEARING IN BUSHES - PAST BLOOD IN F.G.

to Vic brushing his way through the foliage. He comes into the clearing, stands with legs apart, fists on hips, waiting.

BLOOD (FILTER)
You and I have to get something important said between us.

VIC
After I knock off that Spike female.

BLOOD (FILTER)
You and I were through, Vic. Quits. I couldn't tolerate your terminal stupidity. Dumbness that awesome made me very nervous.

VIC
And she's so bloody smart? I think she's trigger happy. She would've fired that laser rifle, and brought all them rovers up here.

BLOOD (FILTER)
She's vicious, but she's smart. And you can be smart, too. But as a unit the three of us are smartest of all.

(CONTINUED:)

95 CONTINUED:

VIC
(mad as hell)
You want me to join up with that dippy chick!

BLOOD (FILTER)
I want us to join up with you.

VIC
So that's the way it is. Some rotten eggsuckin' traitor you are! Two years and you just jump right over to some other solo like that! And a female to boot!

BLOOD (FILTER)
If you could get beyond your slope-browed, prognathous-jawed Cro-Magnon sexist thinking, you might be able to stay alive till next week.

VIC (FILTER)
(yelling)
I don't know what you're sayin'! I don't know what all that means!

BLOOD (FILTER)
It means--

VIC (FILTER)
I don't give a flyin'...I don't give a darn what it means. I made it on my own before I met you, I made it on my own when we split up, I can make it on my own without you.
(beat)
An' I sure as hell can make it without her!

He turns around and stomps back through the bushes as Blood looks wearily after him.

BLOOD (FILTER)
You're not long for this life, old friend.

He patters off through the bushes, following Vic as we:

CUT TO:

96 SAME AS SHOT 87

as Vic comes out through the bushes, moving very fast. Spike is still sitting there laboriously polishing the laser rifle; she starts to get up as Vic comes straight across the little clearing without hesitation. Blood emerges from the bushes a moment behind Vic, but the boy is already on Spike. He kicks the rifle away from her and grabs her scope-mounted .22 rifle. He throws down on her.

BLOOD (FILTER)
Vic, what are you--

VIC
Both of you, just stay where you are or you're gonna be sorry.

SPIKE
You sneaky creep! Gimme my rifle!

Vic moves toward the edge of the rim, keeping low.

VIC
You were right, Blood. I was out of slugs. But this ought to do for now.

BLOOD (FILTER)
What are you going to do? Don't be crazy. Sit down and let's talk this out!

VIC
All the talkin's done. There's food and all the ammo down there I'll ever need. You won't come with, Blood...? Fine. I'll do it myself.

BLOOD (FILTER)
You aren't going to try cracking that warehouse alone? It's completely surrounded. They'll wipe you out before you even get to it.

VIC
That's _my_ worry.

And he turns quickly and vanishes over the side, into the darkness. Spike scrambles for the laser rifle and starts to aim after him, into the darkness.

(CONTINUED:)

70.

96 CONTINUED:

Blood dashes across the clearing and bumps her hard enough to throw her off-balance. She spins on the dog, furious.

BLOOD (FILTER)
We've got to stop him!

SPIKE
Damned right! He's got my rifle.

BLOOD (FILTER)
No, not kill him...stop him! We've got to save him, Spike.

SPIKE
Are you nuts? He stole my rifle!

BLOOD (FILTER)
(frantic)
Spike, we need him!

SPIKE
Like hell!

BLOOD (FILTER)
Spike, please help me save him! He's my friend.

She looks down at him.

SPIKE
I thought so.

BLOOD (FILTER)
(softly)
Won't you be my friend, too?

They look at each other for a long moment. Then she nods.

SPIKE
Now I understand why he's so angry you're with me. You're a helluva dog, Blood.

He wags his tail, pants happily, and starts off over the edge of the rim.

BLOOD (FILTER)
Come on. Follow me...I'll track a clear passage down there.

CUT TO:

97 ARRIFLEX - WITH VIC

as he rushes down the hill into the bowl. He is so angry, so frustrated, that he has thrown all caution to the winds. We can HEAR HIM mumbling curses and phrases of jumbled, disjointed words, talking to himself, wholly unlike his attitudes in the past when he was the perfect solo. CAMERA WITH HIM in all its jerky, action-indicating movement. He rushes down through the darkness, toward the campfires in the bowl. We GO WITH HIM in a long, following shot that shows how large the bowl actually is.

HARD CUT TO:

98 UP-SHOT ON THE SLOPE - TWO ROVERS IN F.G. - NIGHT

We see the backs of their heads as they are eating from tin cans, and HOLD IT FOR A BEAT as suddenly a whirlwind rushes down off the hill and is on top of them before they know what's happening. It is Vic!

99 thru 105 SAME AS 98 WITH INTERCUTS - ARRIFLEX

TILT-ANGLES and SMASH INTERCUTS to indicate wild movement but sufficient to mask the specifics of this encounter.

Vic is on them, whirling the rifle to club one, suddenly spinning to use it as a quarterstaff against the rifle of the other rover.

Three more ROVERS come out of the darkness and jump into the fray. Vic is hurled to the ground, two rovers aim their handguns at him while two others hold him down.

A blur of fur leaps out of the darkness. Blood is on them, and arms, legs, bodies, furry balls, go every which way. A mad tangle, a jumble, nothing distinct, but much action.

Then Spike is there, leveling the laser rifle and we get an even more fragmented view of the action as the CAMERA TILTS and WHIP-PANS and GOES OUT OF FOCUS so we do not see her fire the weapon at anyone specifically, but see a burst of gold and blue and red liquid light (SPECIAL EFFECT OPTICAL) and we HEAR a SCREAM and then there are rovers running away and Spike and Blood are there with Vic on the ground. Spike grabs up her .22 and slings it.

106 2-SHOT - SPIKE AND BLOOD - MEDIUM ANGLE ON THEM

Blood dances around, sniffing at Vic. Spike is looking around furtively. They are in no-man's-land and in danger.

BLOOD (FILTER)
He's okay. Out cold. Must have been coshed with a rifle. Get him up...let's get out of here!

SPIKE (FILTER)
(viciously)
I'll get him out of here, all right!

She grabs him by a leg and with uncommon strength begins to drag him back up the slope into the darkness, Vic's head bumping on the turf. CAMERA HOLDS on the group as they vanish into the darkness and we

DISSOLVE TO:

107 RIM OF BOWL LOCALE (SAME AS 87 & 96)

as Spike comes up over the lip, dragging Vic behind her. She drags him summarily to the center of the clear space in the foliage and drops the leg. Then, disgusted with him--and slightly, by implication with Blood--she goes to the far side of the clearing and squats, cradling the laser rifle. Blood comes over the lip and begins licking Vic's face. Vic starts to come back to consciousness. He shakes his head, tries to sit up, falls back, moans, then tries it again.

VIC
Ohhh...

BLOOD (FILTER)
(furious)
That was stupid. Bone, stick, stone stupid!

VIC
I--I know. Ohhhh...

He looks around, sees Spike, just watching.

VIC (CONT'D.)
(to Blood)
Did she...?

BLOOD (FILTER)
She saved your miserable hide. You owe her a big one.

(CONTINUED:)

107 CONTINUED:

Vic drags himself to his feet and wobblingly goes over to her. He stands above her for a moment, then squats so he is on her level. He extends his hand.

VIC
I was wrong. You're a tough broad and like Blood says, I owe you. You can join up with me and...

But he doesn't get it finished. Without warning, Spike swings a roundhouse and clips him full on the jaw. Vic goes over backward and is out unconscious again.

CAMERA PANS to Blood and ZOOMS in to CLOSEUP.

BLOOD V.O.
The more I see of human beings, the more attractive cockroaches look to me.

HOLD on Blood for several beats then

FADE TO BLACK

and

FADE OUT.

END ACT FOUR

ACT FIVE

FADE IN:

108 A WOODED AREA - NIGHT - MEDIUM SHOT ON LEAN-TO

Spike has erected a structure so they can have a fire and not be seen. CAMERA COMES IN SLOWLY on the lean-to as we HEAR Blood and Spike in FILTER V.O.

SPIKE (FILTER) V.O.
And what happens when he starts to act like every other guy I've ever seen?

BLOOD (FILTER) V.O.
He won't.

SPIKE (FILTER) V.O.
How do I stop it? Chain his hands together? This creep looks to me like no better than any of the others.

BLOOD (FILTER) V.O.
He is. He's smarter, quicker...

SPIKE (FILTER) V.O.
I haven't seen any sign of it.

BLOOD (FILTER) V.O.
He is, Spike. Because I taught him. The way I'm going to teach you.

SPIKE (FILTER) V.O.
I don't know how you talked me into this. But God help you if it don't work out, Blood.

BLOOD (FILTER) V.O.
Doesn't work out, not don't work out. And it'll be okay; I promise you.

CAMERA has now COME IN FULLY on the lean-to and we

CUT TO:

109 INT. LEAN-TO

Vic has been staked out in a spread-eagled position, on his back, his arms and legs tied with ropes and fastened to posts driven into the ground. Spike and Blood sit eating.

SPIKE (FILTER)
Here he comes. It's your game now.

Vic is waking up. He tries to move and, like Gulliver, finds he cannot. He raises his head, looks around blearily. He sees Spike first, realizes what has happened, and drops his head back. When he speaks, it is wearily.

VIC
Can I have some water?

BLOOD (FILTER)
Please, may I have some water.

Spike is startled by this. Obviously, Blood knows how deep runs Vic's streak of belligerance and individuality, and even though he's down and tied, Blood is determined that Vic will pull off no more nonsense. Vic sighs.

VIC
Some water...please.

Spike fills a canteen cup from a canteen, comes over to him and kneels down. CAMERA IN on them as he looks up at her with something between fear and trepidation. She takes a tiny bit of pity on him when he cannot raise up enough to sip from the cup, lifts his head, and tilts the cup so he can drink. Then she lowers him gently, and stares at him for a moment. It might be the moment in which she sees him for the first time as a human being, and not as another potential killer and rapist. She stays that way another beat, then gets up and retreats to the far side of the lean-to. Blood moves in and sits down.

BLOOD (FILTER)
(methodically)
She can fight.

VIC
(nods reluctantly)
She can fight.

BLOOD (FILTER)
You're not as smart as you think you are.

VIC
(sighing)
Sometimes I'm stupid.

(CONTINUED:)

109 CONTINUED:

BLOOD (FILTER)
We have a better chance of finding "over the hill," not to mention simply staying alive, if we join forces.

Vic is silent.

BLOOD (FILTER) CONT'D.
We have a better chance of--

VIC
Okay, okay. I hate it, but as usual you're right.

BLOOD (FILTER)
You will not touch her.

VIC
That's for sure!

BLOOD (FILTER)
Now we will remove your constraints, and you will get up and have something to eat, and then we will figure out a way to get into that warehouse.

Vic closes his eyes. He hates this a lot. He isn't used to being ordered around, not this way at least. Finally, he exhales his breath indicating he accepts Blood's terms, purses his lips and nods. Blood looks at Spike. She gets up and unknots the ropes. Vic sits up and rubs his wrists. She lets him untie his feet. He gets up and goes to the opened cans of food. He lifts one and looks at it.

VIC
(to Spike)
Were these mine or yours?

BLOOD (FILTER)
(before Spike can answer)
Ours.

VIC
(bitterly)
Right. Sure. Correct. Ours.

He sits down and begins digging out food with his fingers. No one speaks for a few moments. We can HEAR the NIGHT beyond the lean-to: crickets, birds, bullfrogs.

110 ON BLOOD

BLOOD (FILTER)
All right. Pragmatically, the situation is this...correct me if I miss anything:
(beat)
Vic is out of ammunition, and we don't have any 30.06 loads, or .45's. Only .22's and the laser rifle.
(beat)
We have a little food left, putting both our supplies together; but that'll be running out very soon.

VIC
There's plenty of everything down there in that warehouse.

SPIKE
How do you know that for sure?

Vic looks at her with annoyance. He answers reluctantly.

VIC
I've been around here for a week, trying to figure a way in. I, uh, got some data from a solo I met.

SPIKE
(chilly)
Yeah? How do we know he was tellin' the truth?

VIC
I asked him a couple of times.

There is a hidden meaning that escapes no one.

BLOOD (FILTER)
What else?

VIC
Well, they started arriving about a month or two ago. Fellini heard about it from some minstrel and got here fast. Found a small roverpak trying to break in through the roof and killed them all. But before he could get in, other started showing up.

BLOOD (FILTER)
And it's been a standoff ever since.

(CONTINUED:)

110 CONTINUED:

ANGLE HAS WIDENED to include the three of them, but still features Blood, who is running the show now.

VIC
There've been tries, but every solo in the territory's out there, not to mention just about every roverpak that ain't got a turf they've got to sit on.

BLOOD (FILTER)
Not ain't. And I suppose ever roverpak down there has a barter deal going with the ones that stayed behind?

Vic nods. He finishes eating, going through every can for what leftovers he can find. He turns them upside-down and shakes them; he's unhappy they had their fill before he came to.

SPIKE
Then that does it. No way in. So what good does our joing up together do? We're only three.

BLOOD (FILTER)
Hmmm.

VIC
What's that mean, hmmm?

BLOOD (FILTER)
It means that Spike has possibly given me a plan.

He falls on his back, legs in the air, and a soft humming SOUND can be HEARD. Spike looks alarmed.

VIC
Don't worry. He's thinking.

SPIKE
Does he always do that?

VIC
Only when it's a strain, a big think.
(beat)
Disgusting, ain't it.

SPIKE
Not ain't. Isn't it.

He gives her a class one dirty look.

111 HIGH SHOT - LOOKING DOWN FEATURING BLOOD

he lies there for several beats, humming, then rights himself and starts toward the exit to the lean-to.

VIC (FILTER)
Where you goin'?

BLOOD (FILTER)
When was the last time you had some cow's milk?

VIC (FILTER)
(perplexed)
Maybe a year ago. What's that got to do with anything?

BLOOD (FILTER)
Well, I was going to answer you with an enigmatic quote from Louis Pasteur, but then you'd have only asked me who Louis Pasteur was, and I'd have had to tell you he was the man who discovered that bacteria produced certain diseases --one of which was in milk, and then I would have said that Pasteur once made the remark, "Chance favors the prepared mind," and--as I am now doing--I would have sauntered away into the night, leaving you confused enough that you wouldn't slaughter each other till I got back.

And he saunters out of the lean-to, into the night. HOLD on Vic and Spike: she looking totally confused, he looking much put-upon.

VIC
Don't worry, it never gets any easier to take.

DISSOLVE TO:

112 EXT. ROVERPAK CAMP - SHOOTING PAST DOBERMAN

a couple of tents, a bunch of feet sticking out of the tents, some snoring. A fire being tended by a sleeping rover sentry and a wide-awake, extremely mean-looking Doberman...who suddenly perks up his head and stares into the darkness beyond the fire. A VOICE comes out of the darkness.

BLOOD (FILTER)
Good evening. Nice night, isn't it?

(CONTINUED:)

80.

112 CONTINUED:

The Doberman stares into the darkness, and now we can see --faintly--a pair of bright little eyes. The Doberman answers in a voice faintly tinged with a Bavarian accent. (NOTE: it is imperative that there be nothing "funny" about this voice. The Bavarian heritage should be there, but as easily accepted as Blood's Americanized voice.)

WOLF (FILTER)
How did you creep up on me?

BLOOD (FILTER)
Listen, Bruno--

WOLF (FILTER)
My name is Wolf, not Bruno.

BLOOD (FILTER)
Short for Wolfgang, perhaps?

WOLF (FILTER)
I am of exceeding good stock.

BLOOD (FILTER)
(impatiently)
No doubt. Listen, kiddo, how goes it around here? Enough food? The tempers of your rovers getting short? They kicking you a little too much?

WOLF (FILTER)
(haughtily)
I serve. I do not ask questions, I do not question decisions.

BLOOD (FILTER)
That's terrific. Really a bit of the old terrific. A friend to man.

WOLF (FILTER)
Das ist how I vas trained.

BLOOD (FILTER)
Yeah, right. But wouldn't you like to get a full belly, and then move out, get back to your turf?

WOLF (FILTER)
Who, it is, you are?

(CONTINUED:)

112 CONTINUED: - 2

Blood creeps in a little closer. The Doberman does not move. Should he jump, he would no doubt give Blood one hell of a fight. It is this restrained power that informs Wolf's attitude.

BLOOD (FILTER)
I'm just a wayfaring stranger, doing his best to be a Force for Good in his Own Time.

WOLF (FILTER)
I do not understand vhat it is you say. I vill signal my master and raise the alarm.

BLOOD (FILTER)
Not too smart.

WOLF (FILTER)
Vas is loss???

BLOOD (FILTER)
Wouldn't you much rather look like a champ? Bring your master and the rest of the roverpak a way of having all that food in there?

WOLF (FILTER)
You know such a ting?

BLOOD (FILTER)
What do I look like, just another pretty face? Of course I know a way.

Wolf sits up and listens attentively.

WOLF (FILTER)
I vill attend vhat you say.

BLOOD (FILTER)
Swell, becauseI've got a bunch of other mutts to see tonight, and frankly, I could do with some sleep.
(beat)
Okay. First you go to your master and you say...

DISSOLVE TO:

113 INT. LEAN-TO - EARLY MORNING

FROM MOUTH OF LEAN-TO looking in on Spike and Vic, each wrapped in soggy blanket or sleeping bag, both snoring loudly. But as Blood comes into SHOT IN F.G. they both start awake, Spike with the laser rifle in her mitts, and Vic with Spike's .22 leveled. They relax as they see it is the dog.

BLOOD (FILTER)
(wearily, sarcastic)
Oh no, don't arise on _my_ behalf.

He flops down wearily.

SPIKE
Where were _you_ all night?

BLOOD (FILTER)
Talking to the League of Nations. Did you ever try carrying on an intelligent conversation with an Akita? Between the Japanese accent and all that "honorable ancestor" nonsense, it's a wonder my brains haven't turned to puree of bat-dropping.

VIC
Come on, Blood, what's _happening_?

BLOOD (FILTER)
Softly, Albert, softly. I have a _vicious_ headache right behind my left eye. I'm tired and hungry.

VIC
You're _always_ hungry.

BLOOD (FILTER)
That was high on my list of utterly classless remarks.

He settles down and seems to be going to sleep.

SPIKE
Blood...!?!

BLOOD (FILTER)
(somnolently)
I will sleep now. If anyone comes around to see me, wake me.

(CONTINUED:)

113 CONTINUED:

And he goes to sleep. Vic and Spike stare at each other as we

IRIS IN ON BLOOD

TO

BLACK and

IRIS OUT to:

114 EXT. WOODED AREA SEEN AS NIGHT IN SHOT 108 - DAY

as three rover dogs trot up to a perimeter circle around the lean-to. A huge German Shepherd, an Akita, and Wolfgang the Doberman. They sit and watch the lean-to.

WOLF (FILTER)
(shouts)
Herr Blood! Kommen see aussen!

They wait. After a moment, Blood emerges with Vic and Spike behind him. Speaking, he trots over to them and they form a small group as Spike and Vic watch from the lean-to. CAMERA ANGLE NARROWS to the group.

BLOOD (FILTER)
Hi, fellows. What's new?

AKITA (FILTER)
(Oriental accent)
Blessings of the day to you, good messenger.

BLOOD (FILTER)
(wearily)
Please! Will you! Give me a break. Wolf, you speak for the delegation.

WOLF (FILTER)
I am honored.
(beat)
Our assembled roverpaks have agreed to your master's suggestion. We meet on the open plain at high noon.
(beat)
One representative and dog; no weapons.

BLOOD (FILTER)
Right. See you down there.

The dogs rise, turn, and leave. Blood returns to Vic and Spike.

115 THREE-SHOT - FAVORING VIC

as Blood comes up to them and sits. He looks up.

VIC
What the hell was <u>that</u>?

BLOOD (FILTER)
Peace party.

SPIKE
Blood, you'd better tell us what's happening.

BLOOD (FILTER)
Well, it's not good to let humans think we dogs are smarter than they think we are--present company exempted, of course--so I went down last night and suggested a parley.

VIC
A what?

BLOOD (FILTER)
Parley. Conference. Communal and group discussion. A sodality meeting.
(beat)
Drop the rifle, get your canteen and a couple of cans of food, and let's go.

SPIKE
Why him? I'm as much a leader of this group as he is.

VIC
No way, broad.

SPIKE
(to Blood)
Tell <u>it</u> to shut <u>it</u>'s face, before I bust <u>it</u> in the mouth.

VIC
Listen, woman, I don't have to take any of that--

SPIKE
(to Blood)
Tell <u>it</u> I'm going, and <u>it</u> can just sit here quietly.

(CONTINUED:)

115 CONTINUED:

BLOOD (FILTER)
(to Vic)
She says to tell you she's going and you--

VIC
(screaming)
I hear her, I hear her!

BLOOD (FILTER)
Except, he's right this time, Spike. Think about it.

She stops, reins in her anger, and thinks. After several beats she nods.

SPIKE
You're right, Blood. They wouldn't respect a woman and we wouldn't have as strong a voice.

BLOOD (FILTER)
(warmly)
You know, I like you more and more every day, kiddo.

Vic snorts. He stamps his foot impatiently.

BLOOD (FILTER) CONT'D.
Okay, Vic, let's go.

He starts off, with Vic beside him. Then stops.

BLOOD (FILTER) CONT'D.
Take off the .45 and leave it.

VIC
It's empty.

BLOOD (FILTER)
All the more reason.

VIC
I feel empty without it.

BLOOD (FILTER)
Force yourself. Be a man.

Vic drops it, and starts out. Blood stops. He goes back to Spike and she leans over as he speaks to her. Vic is clearly trying to hear what's being said, but cannot.

116 SHOT PAST VIC TO BLOOD

as the dog finishes saying whatever it is he's said to Spike, she nods, and the dog trots over to Vic. He keeps going, toward the rim of the bowl, and Vic runs after him as CAMERA TURNS TO GO WITH.

117 WITH VIC & BLOOD - ARRIFLEX

as they go over the rim, and start down. CAMERA CLOSE WITH THEM.

VIC (FILTER)
What was that all about?

BLOOD (FILTER)
Just some last minute instructions on how to protect the area while we're gone.

VIC (FILTER)
Why don't I believe that?

BLOOD (FILTER)
You're a basically suspicious type.

VIC (FILTER)
Y'know, ever since you been with that chick you've gotten really sneaky.

BLOOD (FILTER)
I am still the most loyal and daring creature in the known universe.

VIC (FILTER)
And humble to a fault.

BLOOD (FILTER)
Humble won't buy it when we're talking to Fellini.

Vic stops. Blood keeps going, realizes Vic has stopped, and comes back to him.

BLOOD (FILTER) CONT'D.
Now what's the matter?

VIC (FILTER)
You want me to go down there and talk to Fellini?

BLOOD (FILTER)
And maybe twenty others.

(CONTINUED:)

117 CONTINUED:

VIC
(aloud)
Fellini hates me. He's been trying to kill me for two years.

BLOOD (FILTER)
That's only because he doesn't understand what a wonderful person you are.

VIC
You're tryin' to get me slaughtered!

BLOOD (FILTER)
Gird thy loins, stalwart one.

VIC
Knock off that crap! I ain't going down there.

BLOOD (FILTER)
I'm sure Spike will understand.

Vic stares at him a long moment, then snarls and starts walking down the hill again. Blood chuckles in V.O. and follows him. CAMERA HOLDS THEM as they walk swiftly away down the slope and we

DISSOLVE TO:

118 PARLEY AREA - ON THE PLAIN - DAY

High noon. The bulk of the buried warehouse rising behind the gathering of solos and rovers sitting in a big circle. CAMERA PANS AROUND so we can see each representative, including two tough-looking women sitting individually at two poles of the compass, the men a little apart from them. The group is perhaps thirty in all. Mean, young, dressed individually. And FELLINI, wearing his Napoleon style admiral's hat with the cockatoo feathers, his cape, his high boots, his ragtag finery. He is far older than anyone there, perhaps forty, perhaps fifty, but looking old and crusty and meaner than spit. Everyone else there is alone or with a dog. Only Fellini has three SIDE-BOYS with him; they are bare-chested, ripplingly muscular, tanned and stupid-looking. But super-spit mean. CAMERA COMES TO FELLINI and HOLDS so we can have a good long look at him, just as his face breaks into an evil, gap-toothed smile.

FELLINI
(mock jocular)
Well, well, well. Look who's here! Hello, boy! Good to see you again! Come on in and sit yourself down!

119 REVERSE ANGLE - WHAT FELLINI SEES - HIS POV

Vic coming in across the no-man's-land to the circle that has been set up. Blood at his side. The other rovers turn to look. One of them, STARKIO, a black rover with a livid scar down his face and all dressed in black, a boy of perhaps seventeen, with a Great Dane beside him, rises and moves out a few steps to greet Vic as he comes in. They shake hands solemnly, indicating they have met before and are friends, if not allies. Starkio comes back to the circle and Vic sits down beside him.

120 PAST VIC - FAVORING FELLINI

as the solo checks out the small traveling litter-chair in which fat old Fellini sits, and the two brass-bound sideboys with him.

FELLINI (CONT'D.)
I should've known, boy. It must of been you and that dingo-dog of yourn that got up this meeting.

VIC
I see you're still cheating on the rules, old man.
(beat)
Way I heard it, each roverpak or solo sent one man and a dog.

FELLINI
Wellll...I'm an old, tired man, little fellah, and it's hard for me to get around without I'm helped by these boys. You know how it is.

VIC
I know _just_ how it is, jelly-belly.

BLOOD (FILTER)
Vic! Careful!

FELLINI
Missed you, boy! Downright missed you. Did'ja enjoy all that food you stole from me?

VIC
The food _and_ the ammunition.

FELLINI
You know, boy, you cost me two good riflemen.

(CONTINUED:)

120 CONTINUED:

VIC
Oh? The second one died, too?

FELLINI
You shoulda heard him screamin'
all night for a coupla nights
till I had Victory here put him
out of his misery.

He nods his head toward the taller of the two muscular sideboys. VICTORY is a behemoth. No neck, just a bull head sitting down on his shoulders, muscles oiled and rippling in his shoulders and back.

VIC
Everybody says what a thoughtful
guy you are, Fellini.

Another of the emissaries, CRICKET, speaks up.

CRICKET
How long is this crap gonna go on?
I thought we came here to talk?

Another solo, BATTLE, joins in.

BATTLE
My dog told me this was an open
parley. We gonna have to sit out
here in the sun and listen to you
two jerks fight?

BLOOD (FILTER)
Okay, Vic. Just repeat what I tell
you.

VIC (FILTER)
Can any of them tune in on us?

BLOOD (FILTER)
Maybe, but I don't think so.
(beat)
Tell them it's a standoff and we
have to call a truce and work
together.

VIC
I've been doing some heavy thinking
about this situation. We've been
here a month or two already...a lot
of guys have tried to get in and
been burned. So it's a standoff,
and we got to start using our heads.

121 SLOW PAN AROUND CIRCLE

as various solos and rovers speak, and Vic answers them behind Blood's coaching. They should be dressed in individual ways and each have a character trait expressed in their clothing and manner, at director's discretion.

CHARLIE CHAN
Yeah? Well who pays for Benny Takeda?

BRONCO
You shouldn't'a sent him in and he wouldn't'a got blown away.

SWEET ALICE
I don't trust any of you slobs!

(simultaneously)

VORKIMER
My boys can make it on their own, we don't need no truce!

BIG DANNY
I'm solo. Who's to say I join in and get blown up? Huh, who? C'mon!

BLOOD (FILTER)
(his voice can be heard OVER the din as we come in CLOSE on Vic in PAN)
Tell them about rebuilding. And do it right. As if you meant it.

VIC
Listen...listen to me...hey, shut up!

They fall silent. Fellini has a bemused expression as if he has the hoodoo sign on all of them, no matter what they say.

VIC CONT'D.
Maybe the time's come to stop all this solo against rover stuff. Maybe we ought to try to get together so we don't all starve to death or kill each other. This's a good place to start. There's enough food and ammo in there for all of us.

FELLINI
Just one thing wrong with that, boy.

VIC
Yeah, and what's that?

(CONTINUED:)

121 CONTINUED:

FELLINI
I want all of it. And I've got the firepower to take it.

VORKIMER
And there's enough roverpaks here to stop you.

BIG DANNY
And enough solos all together to make sure!

VIC
See? It's nothin' for nobody unless we work out a way to do it. I say we talk it out and work up a system.
(beat)
All you people who want to try, just raise your hand.

Slowly, one by one, the hands go up. All but Sweet Alice and Fellini.

VIC (CONT'D.)
Okay. That's all but two of you. Now we're gonna talk, and if you don't wanna get left out, you talk too. That's called democracy, or majority rule...or somethin'.

Everybody nods as we:

SLOW DISSOLVE TO:

122 DIFFERENT ANGLE ON CIRCLE - SUNDOWN

FAVORING VIC as we see that time has passed and they've obviously been working it out.

VIC
Then that settles it. We go in six at a time, two men...or women... to a team, with sacks. As much as you can carry in one trip, then the next shift of six teams goes in.
(beat)
How about you two?
(to Sweet Alice and Fellini)

SWEET ALICE
Okay, I guess. If my team goes in when The Flamingos go in, just to make sure none of you guys decide to supply women instead of food.

123 2-SHOT ACROSS CIRCLE - FELLINI & VIC

as Vic turns to the fat man.

VIC
What've you got to say, Fellini?

FELLINI
Walll, boy, I guess you've all got me boxed in. So I'll go along with it on two conditions...otherwise I set up a crossfire'll do you _all_ in.

BRONCO
What conditions?

FELLINI
First of all, I get all the pudding. Every can of it.

CHARLIE CHAN
You _got_ to be crazy as a doodlebug, old man.

FELLINI
(disengenuous)
But I _love_ pudding.

BLOOD (FILTER)
Careful, Vic. Stay out of it; let the others negotiate with him. That's a lot of hate for you there.

FLAMINGO
What's the other condition?

FELLINI
(points to Vic)
I want him.

STARKIO
Forget it! We're all even here!

VORKIMER
Whaddaya mean "you want him"?

FELLINI
This boy's been raiding my larder, shooting up my camp, raising hell with my rovers...I want him.

There is much _sotto voce_ ad lib around the circle. Vic and Blood sit _silently_. Vic starts to say something and Blood edges closer, indicating he should be silent.

124 thru 130 SERIES OF RAPID INTERCUTS - ON ROVER & SOLO FACES

as they look at one another and their expressions harden. They have no stake in Vic, no allegiance (except Starkio), and they're not going to screw up their chance to get food without a fire-fight.

FELLINI
We're gonna do it the way this boy says. Everybody who agrees to my pudding and lettin' me have him, just raise your hand.

SHOTS INTERCUT as the emissaries raise their hands.

131 FULL SHOT - THE CIRCLE - DYING SUN BEHIND THEM

as all hands in the circle go up but Starkio's.

132 ON BLOOD & VIC

as Vic watches, starts to object.

BLOOD (FILTER)
Don't object. Just go with it.

VIC (FILTER)
That old honey-dipper'll stake me out and run bayonets through me!

BLOOD (FILTER)
Let it go!

133 ON FELLINI

FELLINI
(joyful)
Well, boy, seems all your parley-people wanna give you up. You <u>mine</u> now, son.

BLOOD (FILTER)
Ask for a one-on-one duel.

VIC (FILTER)
<u>Whaaaaaat</u>!?! Are you nuts?!?

BLOOD (FILTER)
Do it, Vic! I've got it figured.

VIC (FILTER)
I'll just <u>bet</u> you do, dog. You're gonna get me killed yet.
(aloud)
Okay, Fellini; I won't fight it, but how about you give me a decent chance?

(CONTINUED:)

133 CONTINUED:

CAMERA BETWEEN FELLINI AND VIC

FELLINI
What'd you have in mind, boy?

VIC
One to one duel.

Fellini thinks about it for a moment, then bursts out laughing with the nastiest laugh ever heard.

FELLINI
I agree! Duel to the death, haven't seen one of them in years.

VIC
With you, fat man.

FELLINI
(mock startled)
With me? But I'm too old and fat, son. But I got just the guy to replace me.
(beat)
Victory! Do it to him!

And the huge colossus called Victory lumbers out into the center of the circle as Vic scrambles to his feet. The big bruiser (aged eighteen or nineteen) towers over Vic.

As he lumbers toward Vic, with a look of fear and panic on Vic's face we:

FADE TO BLACK

AND

FADE OUT.

<u>END ACT FIVE</u>

ACT SIX

FADE IN:

134 EXT. NO-MAN'S-LAND - PARLEY CIRCLE - EVENING

EXTREME CLOSEUP on a pair of the beadiest, most malevolent eyes you've ever seen. CAMERA PULLS BACK to show these are the piggy little eyes of Victory, standing there with his mightily-thewed arms swinging like scythes. CAMERA BACK TO FULL SHOT and we see that torches on stakes have been set up to mark the big circle. Vic is on the other side of the circle, shirt off, looking puny in the face of the man-mountain Victory. Fellini is drinking a warm beer and loving every minute of this. Starkio is serving as "second" for Vic, and looking terribly worried. Blood sits near.

STARKIO
He got a helluva reach on him.

VIC
How'd I get into this?

BLOOD (FILTER)
Listen...

VIC (FILTER)
It's listenin' to you that put me here. That monster's gonna pull my arms off and beat me to death with them.

BLOOD (FILTER)
Just <u>listen</u>! Keep it going as long as you can.

VIC (FILTER)
If I live that long.

BLOOD (FILTER)
Keep away from him, keep it going, just waste a <u>lot</u> of time.

(CONTINUED:)

134 CONTINUED:

STARKIO
Blood tellin' you somethin'.

VIC
Yeah. He's big on advice.

FELLINI
Gentlemen, why don't we begin?

VIC
(shouts)
Why don't you get your fat gut out here and start, Fellini...?

Victory moves in on him, circling. Vic gulps and moves in the opposite direction, widdershins, trying to keep out of his way. The crowd starts to cheer for blood.

135 ACTION WITH THE DUEL

(NOTE: this segment will, naturally, be handled wholly at director's discretion, entailing input from stuntmen and natural locations. Thus, only specific incident necessary for plot will be indicated here.)

Vic is smaller, but quicker. Victory has trouble getting his hands on the boy. But when Vic goes to punch him, he literally has to leap off the ground to reach Victory's face. Much scuffling in the dirt. Fellini throws the beer can, hitting Vic in the back. Vic turns, and Victory rushes him, grabbing him in a bear-hug, lifting him off the ground. Vic is facing forward and manages to kick backward between Victory's legs, pulling them both off-balance. They go down and Vic squirms loose. He knees the big man in the gut. Both are covered with dirt that sticks to them from their sweat. Vic is good at rolling and coming up feet-first, kicking like a mule. Victory is stunned, Vic moves in, punching him under the heart, in the sternum. But it doesn't seem to hurt the big man very much. He grabs Vic's arm and twists it back up behind him. This looks like the finish. Vic is in bad pain. Shouts from the crowd. Victory has Vic down on one knee, raises his ham-like fist for a punch straight down on Vic's head...a killing blow.

136 WITH BLOOD

as he bares his fangs, snarls and as CAMERA ANGLE WIDENS he leaps. High through the air and right onto Victory's shoulders. He starts biting Victory on the ear. The big man screams, drops Vic's arm and starts batting at Blood. But the dog leaps away and rushes across the circle.

137 FROM FELLINI ACROSS CIRCLE - PAST HIM IN F.G.

as Blood gallops toward him, getting big in FRAME. He jumps right onto Fellini's face, knocking him and his litter-seat over backward. Fellini howls.

138 SERIES OF INTERCUTS
thru
144 TILT-ANGLE SHOTS and SUBLIMINAL FLASHES of Fellini thrashing in the dirt, his cape over his head...

Solos and rovers alike suddenly rushing into the fray...

Starkio locking his hands together and bashing the slowly recovering Victory...

Vic swinging wildly at anyone near him...

Blood dashing about barking, jumping on people, fleeing, finding a new target, wrecking havoc...

Other dogs fighting with each other...

Fellini's second side-boy grabbing Blood by the scruff of the neck, holding him up and away, Blood thrashing...

145 FULL SHOT - FAVORING FELLINI

as he manages to regain his footing, stands up, screaming mad. Three rovers have hold of the twitching Vic, two others sitting on Starkio.

FELLINI
I'll kill him! I'll kill 'em both!

He fumbles in the cape, and from a sewn-in pocket he pulls a pistol. He waves it around, still too furious to get his act together. Everyone is yelling, the din is tremendous.

146 CLOSE ON BLOOD

BLOOD (FILTER)
Vic! Listen! You've got to do this right...

147 ANOTHER ANGLE ON SCENE

FAVORING VIC as he listens. The noise of the crowd and the screaming of Fellini is so loud it does not permit us--or the viewer--from hearing what Blood is telling Vic. But he is clearly listening to Blood's voice, and the ongoing turmoil permits us to understand something is in the wind. Vic nods slightly, then suddenly shouts:

(CONTINUED:)

98.

147 CONTINUED:

VIC
(shouting)
Fellini! Fellini! Go ahead, kill us, shoot us right now!

Fellini is startled, hesitates a moment. The crowd falls silent. Starkio stops squirming under the rovers sitting on him. Blood is sanguine.

VIC (CONT'D.)
I know what you want to do with us! You ain't gonna do it, you pig! You ain't gonna throw us into that warehouse! So shoot us, shoot us now, you stinkin' fat slob! Shoot! Shoot!

Fellini looks perplexed. For all his rapaciousness, this isn't the brightest man in the world. He narrows his eyes and licks his lips. He walks over to Vic and looks at him. CAMERA IN ON THEM. Vic's face is frightened but there isn't the faintest hint of duplicity there.

FELLINI
Boy...you're dead, mark it. Either way, you're a dead thing. But maybe a little later than sooner.

VIC
(tightly)
Get it done, you piss-ant.
(beat)
Just put it up and <u>do</u> it!

FELLINI
You're really scared, ain't'cha, boy?

VIC
Not of you.

FELLINI
And not of being shot, either, I guess. But there's somethin' in that warehouse that scares the hell outta you, ain't there, boy?

VIC
No. Nothing. I never been in there, how could I know what's inside?

(CONTINUED:)

147 CONTINUED: - 2

FELLINI
That's a good question.
(beat)
But I think you do know.
(beat)
What is it, boy?

Vic turns his head away. He won't talk.

FELLINI
(to crowd)
He knows somethin' we need to know. There's a trick here. How come that place's never been broke into? How come such a big thing's never been found before?
(beat)
He knows!

VORKIMER
Make him talk!

CHARLIE CHAN
Make him tell us!

BATTLE
I ain't goin' in there till I find out what's inside!

FELLINI
Okay, boy. Start talkin'.

Vic won't speak. He looks terrified. Fellini turns to the battered Victory.

FELLINI (CONT'D.)
Open him up.

He turns and walks away, putting the gun back inside the cape. Victory passes him, going to Vic, as CAMERA GOES WITH FELLINI. The other side-boy sets up the litter chair and Fellini sits down, looking tense and mean. We HEAR from OFF-CAMERA the SOUND of Victory working Vic over. Fellini watches and it goes on for a few beats, but there is no sound from Vic. Fellini grows impatient, waves his hand. The OFF-CAMERA SOUNDS STOP.

(CONTINUED:)

147 CONTINUED: - 3

FELLINI
He won't talk. He's the meanest little bugger I ever did see. He's been drivin' me crazy for a year.
(beat)
But I know what <u>will</u> make him talk.
(beat, to his other side-boy)
Ratch, bring that mutt over here.

RATCH, the other muscular Fellini-servant, still holding Blood by the scruff of the neck, brings him to the old man. Fellini reaches into the cape again and pulls out the pistol. He cocks it, holding it up to Blood's head.

FELLINI (CONT'D.)
It don't take much, boy.

BLOOD (FILTER)
Tell him, Vic.

Vic is pulled INTO SHOT by Victory. He looks terrible.

VIC
(whispers)
Screamers.

The crowd goes dead. Beat. Beat. Then horrified and dismayed whispers through the crowd. There is ad lib of "I'm not goin' in there" and "You can get burned to a crisp by them things" and "Jeeeezus!"

148 2-SHOT - FELLINI & VIC

as Fellini thinks on it for a moment. He hums to himself, then smiles a rotten smile.

FELLINI
Boy, you gonna be our advance scout.

VIC
(horrified)
No! Please, no!

FELLINI
(to crowd)
No wonder he didn't wanna go down there. He set up this whole damn parley to get <u>us</u> to go down there, hopin' we'd kill 'em off...but <u>we'd</u> of died, too!

149 SERIES OF INTERCUTS
thru
154 FACES of the rovers and solos. Angry, hateful, mean!

CRICKET
You sneaky rotten slime!

SWEET ALICE
Lemme at him! I'll cut his head off!

BIG DANNY
Give him to us!

BRONCO
I never did trust him, he's solo!

FLAMINGO
I want a chance at him!

FELLINI
Hold on, hold on, children! I got just the thing for this boy.

155 2-SHOT - FELLINI & VIC

Fellini puts his face very close to Vic's; malevolent, nasty, and happier than ever.

FELLINI (CONT'D.)
This boy is some swell solo fighter. We gonna put him and his nice little dog down inside there and let them shake up the screamers.

VIC
You been eatin' onions again, Fellini?

FELLINI
Good, boy, real good. You just keep up that sense'a humor. You gone need it.
(beat, authoritative)
Get him a good gun and a coupla racks of loads. Maybe he can stay alive down there long enough to do us some good.

VIC
(scared)
No! No, Fellini, don't do it! Shoot me now!

Fellini laughs in his face, and waves everyone to getting things ready. People move off toward their camps as Vic and Blood are hustled off into the darkness and we

DISSOLVE TO:

156 ROOF OF THE WAREHOUSE - NIGHT

Lit by torches, with a gang of rovers and solos all dressed in motley, wearing scarves and jackets to keep the cold off their bones. The wind HOWLS. It is eerie, the licking flames of the torches the pale illumination for the entire scene. No moon. And Victory and Ratch, Fellini's side-boys, bashing in the last of the roof-hole with mauls and pickaxes. They have opened a gaping wound in the warehouse. Vic is being held by two rovers, another has Blood in his arms. Both are quiet, waiting. One of the rovers, Vorkimer, has a Thompson submachine gun and two bandoliers of slugs for a 30.06; another has a sack (which, we will discover, holds circular drums of slugs for the submachine gun); and another has the 30.06--which we assume will be given to Vic when he has been dropped into the warehouse.

BIG DANNY
Who's got that rope?

CHARLIE CHAN
Whose idea was that old chopper?

He points to the Thompson held by one of the rovers.

FELLINI
Now, now, young fellahs, don't get all impatient.

FLAMINGO
It was _my_ idea, stupid. It works real good if you gotta take out a lotta meat all at one time.

The remark breaks her up and she laughs raucously. No one else seems to think it's funny.

CHARLIE CHAN
Just don't give it to him till he's down there...and not that rifle, neither.

BLOOD (FILTER)
The quality of grammar in this group is truly antëdiluvian.

VIC (FILTER)
I could learn to hate you.

BLOOD (FILTER)
It only burns for a little while.

BIG DANNY
(screams)
Who's got that miserable rope, huh? Huh?

(CONTINUED:)

156 CONTINUED:

VIC (FILTER)
I'm not going down there!

BLOOD (FILTER)
I don't notice anyone offering you the option to refuse.

VIC
(yelling)
The screamers'll kill me!!!

FELLINI
Not too quickly, I hope.

BIG DANNY
You're makin' me crazy! Who's got the rope?

Cricket comes up with the rope. Big Danny grabs it from him, looking mightily pissed. He comes to Vic, ties it around Vic's waist, signals to the rover holding Blood, who brings the dog to Vic and hands him to the solo.

VIC
I'll get all of you for this!

SWEET ALICE
Tell it to the screamers, solo.

They march Vic to the hole. He fights ever step of the way, howling and punching. They drag him to it and Victory lifts him.

FELLINI
So long, boy. You been fun but we got to say bye now.

He nods to Victory, who positions Vic over the hole while half a dozen others hold the rope. He lowers Vic into the hole in the roof and as Vic begins to disappear, they play out the rope.

VIC
(yelling)
I ain't finished yet!

FELLINI
Sure had us fooled, boy!

Everyone laughs as Vic's head, and Blood's, vanish down into the hole.

CUT TO:

104.

157 VERTICAL SHOT - STRAIGHT DOWN ON VIC & BLOOD

as they disappear down the hole, twisting around and around on the knotted rope. CAMERA PULLS BACK AND UP to include the rovers paying out the rope, then the shape of Fellini on the roof, his cape blowing wildly in the wind, then the full crowd and the entire roof. CAMERA UP AND AWAY to show us the entire warehouse and the no-man's land and the camps with their eerie fires flickering in the wind.

CUT TO:

158 INT. WAREHOUSE - VERTICAL ANGLE - UPSHOT

with the fitful light from the torches on the roof casting meager illumination, we see Vic and Blood overhead, coming down toward us, twisting on the rope. As they APPROACH CAMERA the ANGLE FLATTENS to a MEDIUM SHOT on them.

FELLINI
(voice from above)
You down, boy?

VIC
Throw me those guns, Fellini!

BIG DANNY
Look out! Get away from under the hole. Here they come.

Vic and Blood (whom he has set down) retreat a short distance. CAMERA TITLTS UP SMOOTHLY as a sudden pinwheel of light falls through the hole and crashes down. It is a flaming torch.

VIC
What the hell'd you do that for? You tryin' to tell them screamers where I am?

FELLINI
You bet we are...ain't that why we put you down there, boy?

BIG DANNY
Shut up, Fellini!
(to Vic)
It's so you can see the guns when I drop 'em. Look out. Here they come.

And down come the Thompson, the 30.06, the sack of drums for the submachine gun, and the two bandoliers of ammo for the 30.06. Vic runs to the pile, rips open the sack, pulls out a circular drum of slugs for the machine gun, slaps it in, and without a moment's hesitation aims up at the hole and fires off a long burst, then another. There is silence for a moment, then Fellini's rotten laughter.

159 CLOSE ON VIC

as he stands in the darkness only barely, shadowly lit by the torch on the floor, and he listens to Fellini ridicule him. His face tenses and his lips skin back from his teeth.

FELLINI
(jocular)
Missed us, boy. That's why we didn't give the stuff to you up here. That's why we sent it all down unloaded.
(beat)
Better not waste that ammo, son; you gonna _need_ it when you see that green light comin' for ya.

SWEET ALICE
Have fun, solo. We'll be back tomorrow sometime...see how you did.

160 ANOTHER ANGLE ON VIC - SHOOTING UP PAST HIM

to the hole, as the light dims and vanishes. CAMERA TILTS BACK DOWN to HOLD Vic and Blood.

VIC (FILTER)
(softly)
I'm scared, Blood.

BLOOD (FILTER)
(softly)
I know, Vic. Take it easy. It's going to work out, I promise you.

VIC (FILTER)
We'd better find a good place to hide. They must know where we are by now..._damn_ that Fellini!

BLOOD (FILTER)
Follow me, I'll find the perfect spot.

161 WITH THEM - ARRIFLEX

as Vic, with the 30.06 slung over his shoulder along with the bandoliers, the sack hung from his belt, and carrying the Thompson at the ready, follows Blood. The boy carries the torch and as CAMERA ANGLE WIDENS to follow their path
(CONT'D.)

(CONTINUED:)

161 CONTINUED:

(CONT'D.)

we see the huge warehouse around us. It rises up into utter darkness, with beams and catwalks, and enormous stacks of goods piled atop one another. Apart from dust and desert sand that has drifted in, it is untouched by time or the war. It was apparently buried intact. They move down a corridor between huge cartons marked with the names of the items they contain. They GO AWAY FROM US in ARRIFLEX.

162 thru 168 SERIES OF TRACKING SHOTS - ARRIFLEX

through the warehouse, the boy following the dog and the dog moving as if he knows exactly where he's going.

169 SHOT ON DOORWAY

as Vic and Blood come into SHOT IN F.G. LARGE. There is a flickering light through that doorway. Vic stops.

VIC (FILTER)

Light. Screamers!

BLOOD (FILTER)

Come on.

VIC (FILTER)

But you led us right to them!

Blood goes on ahead, through the doorway. Vic hoists the Thompson into his armpit, pulls back the spring-bar that puts the weapon on automatic fire, and follows slowly. (See photo and description of weapon below.)

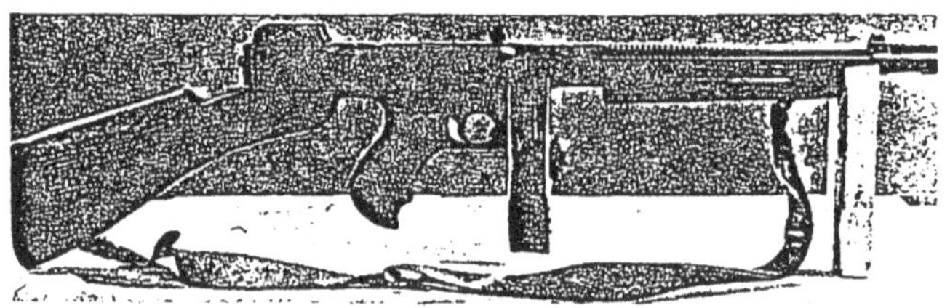

Thompson submachine gun M1A1. (*U.S. Army.*)

Thompson submachine gun A weapon designed by Gen. John T. Thompson (1860–1940), Director of Arsenals in the United States during World War I. The first prototypes were developed in 1918. There are several models of the Thompson, with the Models 1921 and 1928 manufactured by Colt, and the M1928A1 and the M1 series manufactured by Auto-Ordnance and Savage. The Model 1921 is a retarded-blowback-operated weapon with selective full automatic and semiautomatic fire. The cyclic rate of fire is 800 rounds per minute, and the .45 cal. ACP cartridge provides muzzle velocities of about 920 fps. The length of the weapon (with stock and compensator) is 33.75 in., and it has a barrel length of 10.50 in. without compensator. Available for use with this weapon are 18-, 20-, and 30-round box magazines and 50- and 100-round drum magazines. The weapon weighs 12 lb with a 20-round magazine. The Model 1927 is a Model 1921 with an action that permits semiautomatic fire only. The Model 28 is basically a Model 1921 with provisions to reduce the rate of fire from 800 rounds per minute to less than 700 and with simplifications to allow mass production. When this weapon was adopted as standard with U.S. forces, it became known as the "Thompson .45 cal. submachine gun M1," and finally as the "M1A1."

(CONTINUED:)

169 CONTINUED:

CAMERA TRUCKS IN STEADILY BEHIND VIC as he goes through the doorway. The light inside is from a torch. There is someone in there, moving around. Vic jams the torch into a space between cartons, lifts the submachine gun and is about to fire, when the person in the shadows turns around.

SPIKE
Took you long enough to get here.

Vic is dumbfounded at the sight of Spike. She has a dozen or two cartons opened...food, ammo, bottled water, everything they could possibly want for a six month hike.

VIC
What the...

BLOOD (FILTER)
It was necessary to divert their attention while Spike sneaked into the area and burned open the wall of the warehouse, with the laser rifle.

VIC
You almost got me killed by that big freak Victory, and took a chance I'd be shot by Fellini? Just so she'd have it clear?!?

SPIKE
How'd he do in the fight, Blood?

VIC
I damn near got killed, that's how.

BLOOD (FILTER)
Spike, how are we set for supplies?

SPIKE
More than enough of everything.

VIC
Where are the screamers?

BLOOD (FILTER)
There are no screamers.

VIC
But you let me believe...

(CONTINUED:)

169 CONTINUED: - 2

BLOOD (FILTER)
It was necessary that you think the place was full of them, or you might not have seemed terrified enough to fool Fellini.
(beat)
It's called the "tar-baby in the briar patch" gambit. Many thanks to Uncle Remus, an early 20th Century battle tactician.

VIC
Why you low, miserable, eggsucking...

BLOOD (FILTER)
Are we ready to go, Spike?

SPIKE
I've got everything packed in these sacks. He and I can load up on our backs. One of us can carry you up the rope.

VIC
You two are the most sneaky...

BLOOD (FILTER)
(authoritatively)
Not now. When we're out of this, <u>then</u> you can upbraid me for my duplicity.
(beat)
Right now, we'd better load up and get going.

Vic throws his hand up in exasperation. He'd throw up the other one, but it holds a Thompson. He wanders around a moment, trying to get his temper under control, then goes to Spike and just stands there. She grins at him.

SPIKE
My hero.

VIC
(angry)
Just load me up and shut your face!

Still grinning, she turns him around and starts to fit the sacks with their attached ropes to the back of him. He is nearly bent double with goods, but suffers in silence. Then he does the same for her. Once loaded, Spike picks up the laser rifle and starts toward the doorway with her torch. Vic takes his torch and, with Blood, follows.

170 thru 174 SERIES OF PANS & TRUCKS - THRU THE WAREHOUSE

WITH THEM as they move down corridors and through rooms to the place where Spike entered the building.

SPIKE
I picked a spot all the way around on the far side, just to be safe.

BLOOD (FILTER)
You did very well indeed, Spike. My congratulations.

VIC
(ruefully)
Yeah, just peachy-keen. I'm sorry I was loafing around and couldn't help.

BLOOD (FILTER)
We each do what we're best suited to do, Vic. Get used to it.

VIC
I'll <u>never</u> get used to it.

175 EXIT ROOM - ON DOORWAY

as they enter. Spike lifts her torch and they see a long knotted rope hanging down. It disappears into darkness high above them. We cannot see the hole she burned out.

SPIKE
Up there. It's a good long climb.
(beat)
You want me to carry you, Blood?

VIC
I can carry him. You just get your butt up there and stand guard on the outside. They're probably all around, watching for screamers to come out.
(beat, mirthless)
Screamers! Hah!

Spike starts up the rope. Vic unbuttons his jacket and bends down with difficulty because of the sacks on his back. He picks up Blood and awkwardly manages to stuff him inside. Blood's head and forepaws protrude. He holds the wildly swaying rope and CAMERA TILTS UP to show Spike vanishing into darkness above them.

(CONTINUED:)

175 CONTINUED:

VIC
You really set me up for this one.

BLOOD (FILTER)
We were in a bad place, Vic. I don't have to rehash it with you. It was one of the few ways I could think of to get us fat again.

VIC
I'd like to know what the other ways were.

BLOOD (FILTER)
There were four of them...each one more chancey and dangerous than this one.

VIC
You've got too many smarts for my skin.

BLOOD (FILTER)
Is it my fault I suffer from aristophrenia?

VIC
That's a new one; I never heard you use that before.

BLOOD (FILTER)
(chuckles)
It's the condition of having a superior intellect.

VIC
I should have known...uh...uh...

BLOOD (FILTER)
What's the matter?

VIC (FILTER)
I don't want to argue with you, Mr. Superior Intellect, but if you look around back there, do you see what I see?

Blood cranes his head around Vic's chest and CAMERA GOES WITH HIS POV and we SEE the damnable green glow of three hideous SCREAMERS in the doorway. They are standing, silently, watching the boy and the dog. At that moment, from above, comes Spike's VOICE O.S.

SPIKE'S VOICE O.S.
Okay! I'm up! Come ahead!

176 FULL SHOT - FAVORING VIC

as the screamers stare at him, and he stares at the green radiation victims. A low MOANING comes from them, and one of them starts forward. Vic, almost without thinking, throws the torch. It hits and spatters flame all around the screamer, who falls back, now howling in that characteristic SOUND we have come to know and be chilled by. In a moment, the tinder-dry cartons have caught fire and a sheet of flame leaps up. Vic jumps and gets on the rope. He starts pulling himself up. One of the screamers breaks through the fire and, flaming himself, grabs the rope. The rope catches fire.

177 WITH VIC - ARRIFLEX

as he pulls himself hand-over-hand up the rope, the fire coming up behind him. Up and up as CAMERA GOES WITH and the flames below rise and spread, the screaming of the damned radiation victims rising in a terrifying symphony.

CAMERA STAYS WITH HIM as he goes up. He is sweating, can barely make it with the combined weight of food, ammo, submachine gun and Blood weighing him down. He slips back a few feet, burning his hands which WE SEE IN CLOSEUP.

178 SHOT FROM ABOVE - DOWN ON VIC

with the fire illuminating everything below, and Vic coming up through it. His face comes UP INTO CLOSEUP and we know he won't be able to make it. His hands in EXTREME CU can be seen to be slipping with sweat, and just as he's about to let go, a hand reaches down INTO FRAME and grabs him.

179 FROM BELOW - ON VIC

as Spike's hand grabs him and yanks him up. He manages to fling himself a foot up the rope and grab onto the edge of the hole in the wall. Then his shoulders go in, his upper torso, and his legs squirming through.

180 EXT. WAREHOUSE - NIGHT

as Vic emerges high up on the wall of the warehouse, through a hole with melted sides, like a giant running sore. He comes over the lip, hangs there a moment, then slides down the rope on the outside. Just before he reaches the ground, where the rope is being held by Spike, Blood wriggles free and jumps out of his jacket, onto the ground. Vic slides down and falls to the ground, exhausted. At which point SHOTS RING OUT and we realize they have been spotted.

VIC
Oh my God...I'm tired...

(CONTINUED:)

180 CONTINUED:

BLOOD (FILTER)
Later you can be tired!

SPIKE
Let's get the hell out of here!

She starts firing the laser rifle off in the direction of the shots. But before Vic can get to his feet, there are half a dozen rovers coming at them out of the darkness. Then Spike's laser rifle gives out, exhausted after all these years, and she's weaponless. Vic is on his feet, knocking her down with a body-block, and from one knee he sprays the darkness with the Thompson. There are HOWLS from the darkness and the SOUND of people running away.

BLOOD (FILTER)
Over here, this way! Follow me, it's clear.

And then all three of them are running for their lives, as CAMERA HOLDS on them going away into the darkness and we

DISSOLVE THRU TO:

181 SEASHORE SETTING - EARLY MORNING

The sea is coming in with a soft tide. A smokeless fire is crackling. Mist and fog are rolling out. Everything outside the circle of three figures around the fire is soft blue and peaceful. CAMERA COMES IN to HOLD them.

SPIKE
(to Vic)
Did I say thanks for knocking me down?

VIC
(surly)
Forget it. We're even.

SPIKE
You still sore about our fooling you?

VIC
Hell no. How could I be sore about you two getting me into a fight that could've gotten me crippled, putting me up the barrel of Fellini's gun, risking my neck with screamers?

(CONTINUED:)

181 CONTINUED:

BLOOD (FILTER)
I think we should head East, see if we can find a place where somebody's started raising crops.

VIC
Here we go with "over the hill" again.
(beat)
And you can forget that "we" stuff.
(to Spike)
I still think you're a dippy chick, and crazy as a cockroach. You're too mean for me, lady.

SPIKE
(to Blood)
Tell it I'm not that fond of it, either. Tell it that it messes up too often.

BLOOD (FILTER)
She says to tell you she isn't that fond of you, either, that you...

Vic gets to his feet, shouldering the packs of food and ammo. He starts to stalk away.

VIC
That's it! I'd rather drown than have to put up with you!

Spike and Blood look at each other. She smiles. Then they get up, she shoulders her share, and they start off after Vic, who is already down the beach. CAMERA HOLDS THEM as we HEAR BLOOD'S VOICE OVER, diminishing in volume as they walk away.

BLOOD (FILTER) V.O.
As long as we're all going in the same direction, why not run through a bit of history?
(beat)
I'll bet neither of you ever heard about a very interesting scandal in American history. Well...once upon a time there was this big building called The Watergate, and there was this strange old man called...

CAMERA HOLDS their retreating forms as we

FADE TO BLACK

and

FADE OUT.

END ACT SIX

The Wit and Wisdom of NBC Broadcast Standards

by Jason Davis

Assuming you're doing this correctly, you've just read Harlan Ellison's first draft of *Blood's a Rover*, which was submitted to his studio and network colleagues on 7 April 1977. I'm still not entirely certain why the folks at NBC thought this source material would be viable for their primetime schedule 41 years ago; I'm still astonished they aired—albeit, edited for content—the Bryan Fuller-adapted version of *Hannibal* just a few years ago. Nevertheless, NBC received the pilot script, and pressed on...*but they had notes.*

"Although this story is in the science fiction genre," the Broadcast Standards report began, "there is potential in many areas for imitation." With that notion in mind, it was suggested that all the characters be aged up, and that the actor playing Vic could appear to be "eighteen or nineteen as well as sixteen."

Following that initial caution, a further two pages highlighted NBC's omissions and revisions: The dead rover in scene 14 mustn't be in a "grotesque position," and his eyes were to be closed. The *f* in Vic's "Oh, f— buzz off!" was too much, and had to go. The words *ramadoola* and *varks* required definition before their use would be allowed. All instances of violence were to be shot as evasively as possible, with plenty of coverage in case the director's idea of evasive and the network's diverged. All uses of *crap* were to be omitted, as were "bat-droppings," and all the instances of Vic's aborted profanity; even unfinished expletives must be expunged. The notes concluded with a third page cataloging 23 "expletives and irreverent references to the Deity" which were to be removed, most of which were variations of *damn*, *hell*, and the crowd's divine-wrath-inducing "Jeeeezus" in scene 147.

Finally, it was pointed out that the US Constitution limits the President's term of office to two four-year terms. "Unless Vic is supposed to be ignorant of this fact, you may wish to review his reply." This refers to Vic's recitation of the presidents, which follows the then-incumbent Jimmy Carter with "Brown, Kennedy, Kennedy, Kennedy..." Someone should explain to our friend at the network that it *is* possible to have two presidents with the same surname; the notion of a ex-California governor succeeding Carter—on the other hand—is *complete* fantasy.

Oddly, there's nothing in the censor's notes about Spike's act of cannibalism, though it vanishes from the final draft. Presumably, that objection was handled via an in-person meeting, rather than in mimeographed memos.

Prior to Broadcast Standards reviewing the originally submitted 7 April teleplay, Ellison revised the first two acts—the material that appeared in prose as the short story "Eggsucker"—on 10 June 1977. With NBC's notes in hand, he revised the remainder of the teleplay, producing the 13 August 1977 draft that follows.

When, in early 2014, I presented my notes on the various Vic-&-Blood-related material in the files of The Lost Aztec Temple of Mars to Harlan, we determined that the first-draft teleplay better represented author's view of the post-apocalyptic world of the solos and roverpaks. The final draft—which NBC eventually passed on, of course—appears here for the first time.

First Draft Teleplay
14 May 77

Revised Acts 1 & 2
10 Jun 77

Final Draft Teleplay
13 Aug 77

"BLOOD'S A ROVER"

by

Harlan Ellison

Pilot Teleplay

based on

the award-winning novella
and film

A BOY AND HIS DOG

created by

HARLAN ELLISON

"BLOOD'S A ROVER"

ACT ONE

FADE IN:

1 BLACK FRAME - TITLE FLASHES SUDDENLY IN BRIGHT YELLOW

WORLD WAR III

1950-1983

33 YEARS

2 FULL SHOT (STOCK) - A CITY

High buildings, grassland, trees, an idyllic scene as we might see it today.

SUPERIMPOSE: H-BOMB EXPLODING

The blast fills the screen, everything goes into RED OUT.

3 BLACK FRAME - TITLE FLASHES SUDDENLY IN BRIGHT RED

WORLD WAR IV

2001

5 DAYS

4 FULL SHOT - DESERT - THE CITY AFTER THE BOMBS

We should distinctly understand that this is the same city we saw in Scene 2. Now utterly gone. SUPERIMPOSE: TITLE OVER IN RED FADING TO YELLOW.

2024

JUST ENOUGH WORLD FOR
THE QUICK AND THE DEAD

TITLE FADES OUT and CAMERA COMES DOWN to:

5 EXT. BLASTED WASTELAND - DAY - EXTREME LONG SHOT

This is a land that has been pounded by calamity. Barren, stark, high-contrast gold and black. Desert that was very likely a city once... we can see obviously man-made shards of Brancusi-like metal thrusting up spindly arms and angles from the hard-packed ground. The rear end of a buried car juts its silhouette into the dawn sky. A red, molten ball of sun rises over the horizon.

(CONTINUED)

5 CONTINUED

And topping a rise, coming toward us, two figures in sharp black relief against the low sky. One seems to be a human the other a dog. LARGE IN F.G. we see the barrel of a rifle aimed toward them.

ROVER #1 (V.O.)
(whispering)
Where did they come from?

ROVER #2 (V.O.)
(whispering)
Shhh, if that dog's a teeper
he can ping us at this distance.

ROVER #3 (V.O.)
(whispering)
They'll find the booze... they're
right over it!

ROVER #1 (V.O.)
Dinky's down there... he never
come up...

ROVER #2 (V.O.)
I said: shut up! If they get
close, I'll blow 'em away!

As the boy and the dog reach MID-B.G. the CAMERA PULLS BACK to show us three extremely raggedy boys (16, 17, 18 years old; tough juveniles) lying out on their bellies. The rifle is aimed at the pair moving toward us. The one with the rifle wears cartridge belts of bullets crossed on his chest, patched combat fatigues too big for him. One of the others has on a dented crash helmet such as the kind worn by today's stock car drivers, tied to his head with a bandana; he carries a metal and plastic crossbow; the third boy has a tire iron; he wears a WWII-style "pot" helmet and a pair of ancient aviator goggles in la Lucky Lindy; one of them has his feet wrapped in rags, burlap, cardboard, tied together with friction tape.

As the boy and dog ramble toward us, the boy pausing from moment to moment to kick at the dirt, as if hunting for something buried in the ground, we

CUT TO:

6 CLOSE SHOT ON VIC AND BLOOD

He is of indeterminate teen-age, but a very tough-looking, hardened kid for that age. He wears a forage cap, has a rucksack on his back, a thong sack slung from one shoulder; a .45 holstered on his hip;

6 CONTINUED

a bolo knife in an oiled sheath just showing over his right shoulder; twin crossed cartridge belts of bullets for the 30.06 hunting rifle with the telescopic sight he carries at port arms, but the loops are all empty in direct comparison to the Rover in Scene 5, whose belts are filled with bullets; a can opener on a thong around his neck; heavy hiking boots; and a ragtag wardrobe that is topped off by a Howdy Doody T-shirt revealed under his own open battle jacket. We TRUCK WITH VIC IN CLOSEUP for a few steps till he realizes Blood isn't with him, then HOLD as he turns and SHOOT PAST and DOWN to Blood lying behind him half a dozen paces on the desert.

BLOOD is a shaggy somewhat-cockeyed-looking Puli. He lies belly-down on the desert, as low as he can get.

VIC
You pinging something, Blood?

CAMERA DOWN to CLOSE on dog. We HEAR OVER a soft metallic vaguely electronic PINGING sound, as of search equipment making a sounding. CAMERA IN CLOSER so we know the SOUND OVER is coming from Blood.

BLOOD
(filter)
I'm picking up three rovers... and something else...

CAMERA BACK to include them both. Vic now looks around warily. The dog keeps low to the ground.

VIC
Got a location?

At that moment, the Rover with the rifle opens fire. Vic falls on his face right beside Blood.

BLOOD
(filter)
Yeah. Right over there.

Bullets (puff) into dirt all around them. Vic rolls, gets to one knee and launches himself at a low dune nearby. CAMERA WITH HIM as he goes over the top and slugs SPANG into the dirt where he was a moment before.

7 ANGLE ON VIC BEHIND DUNE

as Blood comes rolling over the top to bundle against him. Three shots in rapid succession geyser the top of the dune.

(CONTINUED)

7 CONTINUED

BLOOD
(filter)
What's a rover pak doing out here in the middle of nowhere?

VIC
I'll stay here. You go ask them.

But Blood is down on his stomach again PINGING as we heard before. Then -- as shots patter around the dune -- his head comes up and he looks toward his left, beyond the dune. He scuttles away.

VIC (CONT'D)
Hey, where y'goin? I've only got five slugs left.

BLOOD
(filter)
Hold it together... I think I'm picking up...

And he's gone. Vic looks panicked and we FREEZE-FRAME his face as we FLASH:

MAIN TITLES OVER

and HOLD FREEZE-FRAME through TITLES to RESUME ACTION:

8 thru 11 SERIES OF VIGNETTE SHOTS - ARRIFLEX

Vic ducking and rolling as bullets spatter everywhere. Blood poking his head back over dune as Vic sees him. Vic crawling flat along ground toward Blood.

Vic rolling over dune to other side, looking for Blood who has vanished, crawling a little further and then, in the dune's shadow so it could not be seen, falling headfirst into a hole, and disappearing.

CUT TO:

12 INT. BURIED SALOON - ON CEILING

as Vic comes falling through in a shower of dirt and broken ceiling parts. He FALLS INTO CAMERA and CAMERA BACKS WITH him as he crashes to the filthy floor amid shattered bottles and rotted plastic booths. The walls of this cocktail lounge have been done in panelled glass and everything is reflected back a thousand times so one cannot tell which is the real image and which the dusty reflection. Part of a tacky hand-lettered banner on the wall reads STARDEW LOUNGE WELCOMES YOU TO HAPPY HOUR.

(CONTINUED)

12 CONTINUED

Vic lies upside-down on his back, legs in the air, at the base of a mound of sloping dirt and ceiling, fallen in.

13 ON VIC - UPSIDE-DOWN

as he groggily shakes his head, we HEAR BLOOD OFF-CAMERA.

BLOOD (V.O.)
(filter)
What an entrance! What grace, what form what a klutz!

Vic looks to his right and CAMERA FOLLOWS to SHOW:

14 VIC'S P.O.V. - WHAT HE SEES

Blood, sitting atop a ruined juke box, (modernistic, circa 2001) looking complacent and staring at his partner. The mirrors in ceiling and walls cast back a thousand images of the dog. CAMERA BACK to include VIC.

VIC
How would you like the butt of my rifle up your nose?

BLOOD
(filter)
This is a way to talk to man's best friend after he saves your life? Tsk-tsk, Vic, I'm hurt, deeply hurt.

VIC
(wincing)
So am I...

And he pulls a shard of broken glass from under him. He slides himself down out of the dirt, and gets up, rubbing his butt.

VIC (CONT'D)
I'll be damned. A saloon. So <u>that's</u> why they were shooting at us.

BLOOD
(filter; sternly)
I've spoken to you about foul language on numerous occasions, Vic. Coarse words...

(CONTINUED)

14 CONTINUED

VIC
(finishes)
...are the sign of a sterile imagination. Yeah, I know.

He looks around. CAMERA ANGLE WIDENS to include a dead rover lying against the bar.

VIC (cont'd)
Was *he* the other thing you pinged?

BLOOD
(filter)
I'd say he died just about the time I fell in here. He looks to have been a scout for our friends up there.

VIC
(warily)
What killed him?

BLOOD
(filter; laconic, licking himself)
Probably that big rattlesnake.

Vic's eyes widen and he looks more closely through the murk and reflections as CAMERA COMES IN on the leg of the dead rover, DINKY, as a huge snake comes out slithering to coil itself, rattling terrifyingly. It is a strange, mutated snake, because it glows a bright orange.

15 FULL SHOT

as Vic leaps up, grunting with disgust. He grabs his rifle, jumps sidewise as the snake strikes and OUT OF CAMERA bats the thing. He clubs it to death but we only see his movement, not the actual clubbing. He stops, breathing heavily. He looks at Blood ruefully.

VIC
Y'know, you've got a real morbid sense of humor.

BLOOD
(filter; changes subject)
Is there anything here that we can use to barter for ammunition or food?

Vic wanders to the bar. There are unopened bottles against the fractured mirror.

(CONTINUED)

15 CONTINUED

VIC
Plenty. This stuff is terrific.

He starts stuffing bottles of liquor in his ditty-bag and his rucksack. FOCUS ON BLOOD as he starts PINGING. Vic looks at him.

VIC
(continuing)
They sniffing around up there?

BLOOD
(filter)
Looking for their friend...
looking for us.

At that moment, dirt falls into the hole and patters down the slope. A face appears in the ceiling hole, blotting out what little sunlight has filtered down into the mirrored saloon. Vic raises his rifle, is about to shoot.

VIC
I've only got five slugs left.
You better get behind something.

BLOOD
(filter)
Hold it. I've got an idea.
Uncork one of those bottles and
pour some in an ashtray.

VIC
Are you nuts? This stuff is
valuable!

BLOOD
(filter)
Is it dearer to thee than life,
oh mouth-that-walks-like-a-man?
Pour! And get out our bar of soap.

Vic stares at him, then uncorks as we

DISSOLVE THRU TO:

16 INT. UNDERGROUND SALOON - ANOTHER ANGLE -

FAVORING CEILING and the HOLE IN THE DIRT AND THE RUBBLE-- as it is kicked in. The slope of fallen-in dirt that permitted Blood exit and entrance is added-to by the dirt falling on it. Blood and Vic are nowhere to be seen, but the piles of rubble may well be concealing them. We HOLD on the ceiling as a face appears. It is ROVER #2, the one who held the rifle in Scene 1. The face withdraws quickly.

(CONTINUED)

16 CONTINUED

Then comes back for a longer look, the rifle protruding into the hole. When there is no shooting, the face withdraws and after a moment Rover #1 swings his legs in and drops, sliding down the dirt mound. He holds his crossbow ready. He is followed by Rover #3, the one with the tire iron. A third face appears in the hole, framed by sunlight, but Rover #2 is clearly being left up there to cover their back with the lone long-distance weapon, the rifle, and to hold a tactical position down on the room below.

17 WITH THE ROVERS

as they bound to their feet, swinging in all directions. No one there. They look around warily: maybe this <u>wasn't</u> where that solo and his dog went. Suddenly there is a terrible MOAN from the darkness.

They swing around and around. But the face in the hole up there is blocking their light. Rover #1 waves Rover #2 out of the hole and sunlight pours down. Now we see Vic, lying beside the dead man, almost cuddling him. It is a sight at once frightening and (because we know Vic isn't wounded) funny. Vic moans again. Horribly.

The Rover with the crossbow aims down at him, ready to shoot him, and Vic raises a trembling finger, pointing behind them. His face is grotesquely twisted.

VIC
(groaning)
Look out... m-mad d-dog...

They swing around.

18 REVERSE ANGLE - ROVER'S P.O.V. - WHAT THEY SEE

Blood, with soap all over his face, fangs bared, crouched there suddenly growling maniacally.

19 MED-CLOSE SHOT - FAVORING ROVERS

as stark terror flushes their faces.

20 ON VIC

VIC
R-run for your life! I'm a
gonner... he got this guy, too...
Ohhhhhh...!

21 SAME AS 19

on the rovers' faces, as CAMERA PULLS BACK to include Blood, reflected a thousand times in the mirrors, barking ferociously and drooling. He snaps and snarls and rushes in among them, so he is in their line of fire, between them.

ROVER #3
Shoot him! Shoot him!

ROVER #1
I can't...he's in between us...
which one is he...?

Rover #1 takes aim at Blood and lets fly with the crossbow just as Blood jumps for them. The bolt misses the speeding dog and buries itself in the front of the modernistic juke box. This is a flashy-looking machine, obviously employing circuitry different from a contemporary juke box, and it suddenly lights up. There is a BLAST OF FANFARE MUSIC that startles everyone, and then a WOMAN'S VOICE booms out.

JUKE BOX WOMAN
(warm, but metallic)
Hi, ginchies! Whaddaya wanna hear?
(beat, repeat)
Hi, ginchies! Whaddaya wanna hear?

This lunacy continues throughout the remainder of the action.

Blood is now leaping and snapping all over the rovers. The one with the tire iron smashes here and there, hitting the mirrors, but missing Blood. Finally, his panic gets him.

ROVER #3
I'm gettin' outta here!

ROVER #1
After me!

He starts scrambling for the hole and it galvanizes the second rover, who almost knocks #3 down in his attempt to scramble up the dirt mound. #3 kicks him and down goes #1... as #3 practically flies up the mound and out the hole. Rover #1 is stuck there on his back, and Blood puts on a terrific performance, drooling and fanging and jumping at him. Vic continues to moan.

Rover #1 gains his feet and bolts up the mound, and struggles through the hole, kicking out at Blood who is nipping at his boots.

(CONTINUED)

21 CONTINUED

Vic struggles out of the corpse's embrace, as Blood rushes up the slope of the dirt mound and jumps through the hole in the ceiling. Vic dashes after him.

22 EXT. DESERT - FAVORING HOLE IN GROUND

as Vic comes up through the aperture. There goes Blood after the three rovers, who are screaming and running for their lives. Vic gains the surface and stands up. His thong sack clanks: the bottles. His rucksack bulges prominently. He watches Blood for a moment until the dog screeches to a halt and watches the three rovers disappearing in the distance. Then the dog lopes back to Vic.

BLOOD (FILTER)
A demonstration of how my noble ancestors made the saber-tooth tremble.

VIC
You look stupid with that soap on your jaw.

BLOOD
(filter)
And you looked just swell cuddling that corpse.

VIC
I could have picked them off when they came down through the hole.

BLOOD
(filter)
And wasted some of the few bullets we had left. Intelligence is always a better weapon than violence.

VIC
Okay, okay. Gimme some slack.
(beat)
Let's go get some ammunition.

They start to walk away from CAMERA.

BLOOD
(filter)
That's what I adore about you, Albert. You learn so quicly.

And they walk away as we

LAP-DISSOLVE TO:

23 EXT. CRATER CITY - EVENING - EXTREME LONG SHOT - MATTE

LAP-DISSOLVE HOLDS Vic and Blood from preceding scene, walking away from us as the image fades and LONG SHOT fades in of them walking toward us through a rubble-strewn city filled with bomb-craters, a scene of desolation and ruin (rear projection).

LAP-DISSOLVE THRU TO:

24 EXT. CRATER CITY - NIGHT - AT THE WHARF

The black ribbon of the River stretches out there, with more rubble on the other side of the shore, indicating another city that has died. But the wharf has been maintained in good order. Possibly by the roverpak that lives on the huge garbage scow out there in the middle of the water. We see all this as CAMERA PULLS BACK from a hand-painted, crude sign that shows a gun and a scow and a skull-and-crossbones and the numbers 82. The sign is at the entrance to the wharf. Vic and Blood come sauntering into the frame.

The boy and the dog walk out onto the wharf, toward the end where a lantern and a big old ship's bell hang from an iron post. It is a moonlit night. We can see the scow out there clearly against the black water. A lantern flickers at the stern.

Vic grabs the rope hanging from the bell and rings the big brass clapper. The sound rushes off across the river.

They wait a beat, then another lantern appears out there on the scow. Vic cups his hands and yells.

VIC
(yells)
Hey, Skipper! Walter!

A VOICE (probably amplified by a megaphone of the Rudy Vallee variety) calls back. It is a mean voice.

SNAKE
(faintly, over water)
Yeah, who is it? Whaddaya want?

VIC
(yells)
Tell Skipper and Walter it's Vic and Blood.

SNAKE
(faintly, over water)
What kinda loads you need?

(CONTINUED)

24 CONTINUED

VIC
(yells)
Thirty-ought-six dum-dums and forty-five automatics.

SNAKE
(faintly, over water)
Whaddaya got for barter?

VIC
(yelling)
Nine bottles of liquor! Good stuff!

There is a longer beat, several seconds, as they (and we) wait. Then:

SNAKE
(faintly, over water)
Stay where we can see you, in the light! We'll send the skiff!

25 WITH VIC AND BLOOD

as Vic drops down, feet dangling over the edge of the quay. Blood circles him, then comes to sit beside him. Both look out across the water, where we see activity around the scow.

BLOOD
(filter)
Just so it shouldn't be a waste of time while we're waiting, name me the Presidents of the United States after Franklin D. Roosevelt.

VIC
(distracted)
Don't want to.

BLOOD
(filter)
What's the matter, brain in repose?

VIC
(suddenly very sad)
Get off me.

BLOOD
(filter; jollying him)
Come on, take a crack at it. I'll get you started: Truman, Eisenhower...

(CONTINUED)

25 CONTINUED

Vic is ignoring him, kicking at the water, clearly unhappy. Blood pauses, then in a much tighter, stricter, more schoolmasterly voice, pushes him again --

BLOOD
(continuing;
filtered, annoyedly)
Truman...Eisenhower...

Out there on the water we HEAR the SPLASH of the skiff being dropped overside. More movement. But here, on the wharf, Vic suddenly snaps his head around and glares at Blood, and answers him in vicious tones:

VIC
(angrily)
Crunch off, Blood! Truman, Eisenhower, Kennedy, Johnson, Nixon, Carter, Brown, Kennedy, Kennedy, Kennedy! I told you I didn't want no lesson now!

BLOOD
(filter; easily)
Any lesson, watch your grammar; and you forgot Ford.

VIC
(yells)
Lemme alone!

And he gets up, and walks away along the quay as Blood watches. He stops at a piling and sits on it. Blood waits a moment, then pads after him.

BLOOD
(filter; gently)
Hey, what's the trouble, kiddo?

Vic is silent a few beats, then speaks sadly.

VIC
Nuts. I don't know. Just feeling very crummy. No women for almost a month, all this running and jumping just to stay ahead of Fellini and his roverpak, or some crazy solo with one slug too many... all this history and junk you keep telling me till my head hurts. Every day's just like every other day, just hustling for food.

(CONTINUED)

25 CONTINUED (2):

Blood jumps up on the next piling, and looks at Vic.

BLOOD
(filter; gently)
I think I've picked up a flea behind my right ear. Would you mind doing me a scratch?

Vic reluctantly moseys over, idly begins to scratch Blood behind the right ear. They continue to stare out at the skiff coming toward the pier.

BLOOD
(filter)
Listen: this is only temporary. One day very soon, someone's going to settle down and start planting food right in the ground so you can eat any time you want. And they'll put up a stout wall to keep out big roverpaks like the one Fellini runs, and after a while someone else will join them, and after a while it'll be a real settlement.

VIC
Bull. More of that mythology you're always trying to tell me.

BLOOD
(filter)
It will happen! It may already be happening somewhere. The war's been over for forty years. Humans have a tribe instinct; if we could just get away from this area, look around, you'd see I'm right. You keep hearing rumors all the time from the minstrels that pass through... don't you?

VIC
It's all ramadoola. Bull.

BLOOD
(filter)
Maybe not.

VIC
(angrily)
That's your idea of Heaven, ain't it? "Over the hill."

(CONTINUED)

25 CONTINUED (3):

BLOOD
(filter)
"Over the hill" is as good a name for Heaven as any other.

The skiff pulls in at the dock, with three rovers in it. Vic shoves off from the piling and walks toward the wharf end again.

VIC
(filter)
Yeah, well, "over the hill" my butt, dog. We're never gonna see it!

26 SHOT PAST ROVERS IN SKIFF TO DOCK

as Vic strolls toward them, Blood padding alongside. There are three members of the 82nd Airborne in the little boat, with a lantern hanging from the stern on a pole, like a Venetian gondola. All three rovers carry pump shotguns, leveled at Vic and Blood.

SNAKE
Hold it.

Vic stops.

SNAKE
(continuing)
Drop the rifle, nands way out onna side, get down on yer face and spread.

Vic just stares at him.

BLOOD (V.O.)
Oh boy.

The three pump guns lock down on Vic.

SNAKE
I said: spread!

Vic moves several slow steps forward. He makes no move to comply.

VIC
Listen, buddy: Skipper and Walter know me and sent you over, and that means I'm okay, so move your butt so we can get in.

In response, all three shot guns emit the sound of their hammers being pulled back. The beat goes on...

(CONTINUED)

16.

26 CONTINUED (4):

BLOOD
(filter)
God save me from idiots who have to do their machismo number.
(beat)
My wonderful self is about to be killed very dead.

HOLD THE SHOT beat beat beat as we:

FADE TO BLACK

and

FADE OUT

END ACT ONE

ACT TWO

FADE IN:

27 EXT. DECK OF SCOW - NIGHT - SHOOTING DOWN - ON SKIFF

as it pulls alongside. A ladder is lowered. Vic grabs Blood under the belly and climbs up one-handed.

SNAKE
(from below)
Can't that eggsucker climb up hisself?

There is nasty, ridiculing laughter from the rovers in the skiff and on deck.

BLOOD
(filter)
Calling a noble canine "eggsucker" is about as actionable an insult as I care to imagine.

VIC
(filter)
You can explain it to me later. Right now, cool it. We need the bullets.

CAMERA RISES TO HOLD VIC as he goes over the taffrail. Two more rovers with bren guns meet him. Snake and his partners come up behind him.

28 ANOTHER ANGLE ON DECK - WITH VIC

Snake gestures with the shotgun as Vic drops Blood. The gesture is toward a superstructure erected on the mid-deck. It is a house of spare bare boards, oil drums, something that looks like the remains of a quonset hut. It is a gimcrack residence the Seven Dwarfs might inhabit. Vic and Blood start for it in the shadowy dimness. The five 82nd Airborne rovers follow, guns leveled.

They approach the entrance to the superstructure, and the door flies open. A short, swarthy, very jolly-looking man who could be thirty or forty stands there. It is SKIPPER.

SKIPPER
(volubly)
Vic! Hey, c'mon in!

(CONTINUED)

28 CONTINUED:

VIC
(dourly)
Hiya, Skipper. Good to see you again. How's chances of your getting this clown with the shotgun to back off?

SKIPPER
Snake! Damn it, this solo's a friend of mine.

SNAKE
He gimme trouble. Him an' that little eggsucker.

BLOOD
(filter)
That's twice! Aren't you going to defend my good name?

VIC
(to Snake)
Hey, pinhead: don't call my dog no eggsucker.

Skipper sees trouble, and grabs Vic, brings him inside. Blood rushes through quickly. Snake and two others follow.

29 INT. SCOW - FULL SHOT

A larger room than it seemed outside. Found materials furnish the place. Bunk beds with people sleeping in them, a fireplace made from bricks and a length of old stovepipe. A chicken turning on a spit in the middle of the room. It is very dim and smokey, like an Altman film of primitive life. The fire is tended by an old crone. We note that the people here, the members of the 82nd Airborne, are much older than most of the boys we've seen in roverpaks. These people are actually in their mid-twenties, but the life has weathered them, made them look old and haggard. A long, lean man with a patch over one eye, wearing a fedora with a feather in it, sits in a rickety rocking chair. He is WALTER, Skipper's partner.

VIC
Hello, Walter.

WALTER
Let's see the barter.

(CONTINUED)

29 CONTINUED:

BLOOD
(filter)
Big on hospitality, aren't they?

Vic begins unloading the ditty bag. He pulls out two bottles of liquor and hands them to Skipper, who hands one to Walter.

VIC
Seven more like that.

WALTER
This's been opened.

VIC
Needed a couple of drops to save my life this afternoon. Just a few drops.

SKIPPER
Looks good to me, Walter.

WALTER
Jus' fine. Got a boot, Vic?

Vic nods, shrugs out of his rucksack and fishes around in it till he comes up with a western-style boot, cut off halfway up the side. He hands it to Skipper.

30 WITH SKIPPER

as he hefts the boot, and shakes it. It clatters from things inside.

SKIPPER
How much brass you got in here?

VIC
About thirty .45 casings, and maybe forty of the 30.06 shells.

SKIPPER
We'll give you fifteen for the pistol and twenty for the rifle.

Vic stands up, takes the bottle from Skipper.

VIC
When was the last time you had booze?

WALTER
Twenty-five and twenty-five.

(CONTINUED)

30 CONTINUED:

Vic takes the second bottle, shoves it back in the thong bag. Blood is already at the door.

VIC
Tell 'em not to hoist up that skiff.

Skipper, laughing, takes the second bottle back.

SKIPPER
Okay, okay. Full reload.

He hands the boot full of brass to a little boy of about ten, PIDGE, and slaps Vic on the bicep. Vic shies away, he doesn't like being touched, not even by a "friend."

SKIPPER (CONT'D)
(to Pidge)
Pidge, take this to the shop. Tell Coop to reload 'em all.

The little kid goes out a door into a corridor that must lead back to the stern, to the shop. Vic hands Skipper the other bottles.

WALTER
That'll take a while. Sit and tell us what it's like on the land.

Skipper sits on the floor, the seven bottles of liquor by his side, one in his fist. Walter holds the ninth one. Vic nods, sits down on an empty crate vacated by a very little kid of perhaps nine or ten. Blood comes over and settles down uneasily on his stomach beside Vic.

31 HIGH SHOT - THE ROOM

as the dingy and haggard denizens of the scow begin to circle in on Skipper and Walter, like zombies closing in on a voodoo altar. Vic looks around uneasily. Skipper lifts the bottle and smiles at it.

SKIPPER
You know how long it's been...

And then he realizes all the crones and old men are in too close. He snaps his head around, seeing them all.

SKIPPER (CONT'D)
Snake!

And Snake is there with his pump gun, jamming it into the crowd, pushing them back, shoving them away from the booze.

(CONTINUED)

31 CONTINUED:

They are listless and don't fight too much. House pets. But they keep circling back.

SNAKE
(to Skipper)
Better give'm one.

Skipper doesn't want to. He wants it all for himself and Walter. But he looks at Walter, who nods. Skipper tosses a bottle to Snake, who hands it to the closest of the old men, who scuttles off into a dark corner, taking everyone with him. Snake stands there waiting. He is clearly a man who will one day usurp power. Skipper and Snake eye each other for a long moment, then he hands a bottle to him. Snake goes to the wall, pulls the cork and starts drinking. Walter is already guzzling. Vic just watches.

SKIPPER
(taking a long slug)
Ahhhhh... fire'n'brimstone!

Then he sees Vic watching. Reluctantly, he offers the open bottle. CAMERA HAS COME DOWN SLOWLY to FULL SHOT favoring Vic and Skipper, with Walter still visible... watching.

BLOOD
(filter)
Careful!

VIC
No. It's for you.

SKIPPER
C'mon, have a slug; we'll have a party till you get your ammo.

VIC
Not for me. I don't like the taste.

Skipper shrugs. He half-turns and clinks bottles with Walter.

DISSOLVE TO:

32 ANOTHER ANGLE ON SCENE - LATER

Even murkier. But we can tell Skipper and Walter and Snake are drunk. Vic sits very straight and alert on the crate, just watching, as the 82nd Airborne gets smashed.

(CONTINUED)

32 CONTINUED:

BLOOD
(filter)
There are few things in this life as nasty-looking as a human filled with alcohol. They call it hung-over, and if one need any proof that we members of the canine species are smarter than humans, one need only point out that a dog with any self-respect will not touch the filthy stuff.

Skipper extends a tin cup toward the dog.

SKIPPER
(slurred)
Hey, doggie... have'a drink?

Blood lifts his nose and turns his head away. Affronted.

SKIPPER (CONT'D)
Wassa madder, he don't wanna drink with us? Too good t'drink with us? Dog ain't s's'posed to drink with us? What's he think, I'm an old man he don' wanna drink with us?
(beat, surly)
I'm as good's I ever was, tough as any'a them snotnose punks!

BLOOD
(filter)
Careful, Vic. They're getting mean.

VIC
(filter)
I can handle them.

SNAKE
(drunkenly)
Whassa matter with the li'l eggsucker?

BLOOD
(filter)
That's three.
(beat)
I'm going for a walk. I can bear this vile display no longer.

He gets up and strolls through the door into the corridor leading to the shop. Behind him there is laughter of ridicule.

33 WITH BLOOD

as he wanders down the corridor composed of old crates nailed together. From ahead of him we HEAR the SOUND of sizing die machines and reloading presses.

BLOOD (V.O.)
If one's "master" cannot, or will not protect one's honor, then perhaps a noble and talented sniffer ought to find a new relationship.

34 INT. SHOP - ON DOORWAY - LOW ANGLE

as Blood comes in through the opening. The shop is set up with ancient machines: a Lyman reloading press, primer seater, powder scale, Saeco sizing die, C-H Tool & Die Corp. bullet swaging die set, canneluring tools, lathes, etc. Piles of shavings litter the floor. Half a dozen 82nd Airborne rovers are working reloading Vic's ammunition. Blood pads about, looking at this and that, amid the noise, till a big, muscular kid of perhaps eighteen, COOP, looks down, sees the dog, and throws a piece of metal at him.

COOP
G'wan, get outta here, you damned eggsucker!

Blood shies from the throw and rushes back down the corridor.

BLOOD (V.O.)
That's it! I've had it! The next miserable human who calls me a foul name is going to go to his grave with my teeth in his throat!

35 SAME AS 31

as Blood comes back into the "main saloon" of the scow. If everyone was smashed before, they look like death warmed over now. There is nothing appealing about this. Anyone who might ever contemplate drinking, seeing this scene, should be repelled. Vic is lecturing on "life on the land."

VIC
(pontifically)
So things're getting tighter out there. Most of the fast easy food you can dig up is gone. Fellini has the biggest roverpak, and he's scared off most of the solos. He hates me... I keep gettin' to the buried food before he does...

(CONTINUED)

35 CONTINUED:

VIC (CONT'D)
An' sometimes I just swipe it from him once they've dug it up.

BLOOD
(filter)
The Lone Ranger rides again.

He settles down by the bulkhead.

VIC
Fellini's got that big slave wagon, and all them kids pull it.

Blood is near Snake, he suddenly realizes...as Snake kicks out to shove the dog further from him. Blood reluctantly scoots over a few feet. They appraise one another.

VIC (CONT'D)
He's really organized. About two dozen top guns hanging around all the time. Won't be long now.

SKIPPER
What won't be long now?

VIC
Till he takes over the city.

They all seem startled. Everyone is listening-up hard. Like one of those commercials for the stockbroker in which all movement and sound stop as everyone leans in to catch the eavesdrop. It should be made clear by their perplexed expressions that they have no sense of history; that the past is one minute gone and that because they have no sense of imagination they cannot conceive of the future.

WALTER
I don't understan'.

VIC
(warms to topic)
He can't let any solos find ammo or food; he needs all he can get to feed his people. It's those troops that keep some solo like me from getting close enough to put a bullet in his fat head.
(beat)
He can't feed 'em, he loses 'em; and he loses 'em... he's just another fat old man.

(CONTINUED)

35 CONTINUED (2):

SKIPPER
Yeah, but what's that got to do with us? We ain't solos. We're organized. We know where the mine is to get the powder for the loads. Nobody can get to us here ... an' they need us to do the reload of their brass.

VIC
(laughing)
Dream on, Skipper. Fellini doesn't need you. He could torture the mine location out of you; so he doesn't _think_ he needs you. Same thing.

36 ON BLOOD

as he raises up his head and looks at Vic.

BLOOD
(filter)
Careful, Vic. Stupid people resent smart people.

37 ANOTHER ANGLE - FEATURING VIC AND SKIPPER

But Vic is too smugly involved for paying attention. He doesn't respond to Blood's warning, but keeps talking.

SKIPPER
Yeah, but the _other_ roverpaks need us. We don't need Fellini's business to stay alive.

VIC
(braggartly)
For how long, man? As soon as Fellini cleans out or scares off the solos in the area, then he'll start taking over the roverpaks.

WALTER
(warily)
How do you know all this? Some minstrel lay it on you?

(CONTINUED)

37 CONTINUED: 37

VIC
(puffing up)
I just figured it out. As Santayana said in The Life of Reason, 'Those who cannot remember the past are condemned to repeat it.' That's a book; I've read books; that's history; I've studied history. I know that's what'll happen.

BLOOD
(filter)
That tears it. We've got trouble.

There is nervous agitation in the room as rovers slowly reach for their weapons as they watch Skipper and Walter move back away from Vic as if he were a pariah, a leper. There is a deathly hush in the place, just the hissing and crackling of the open fires. Snake gets to his feet, the shotgun suddenly very much in evidence.

38 ANGLE PAST SNAKE TO VIC ON FLOOR

He is tensed, the gun not quite pointing at Vic, but ready.

SNAKE
(mean)
Where'd you get all that garbage?

Vic suddenly realizes he's in trouble. He licks his lips. He looks around in silence, looking for an alibi, an out, an excuse.

VIC
(trapped)
Uh... uh...
(then suddenly)
I got it all from Blood!

The dog's head snaps up sharply in amazement.

BLOOD
(filter)
Why, you... you... fink!

Snake turns to look down at the dog. His face is the meanest thing anybody has ever seen. Ever.

SNAKE
(viciously)
I wouldn't take all that stupid crap from no stupid eggsucker!

(CONTINUED)

38 CONTINUED:

Blood cannot control himself. His fangs bare. He tenses.

BLOOD (V.O.)
That's it! Nobody talks that way to the noblest creature on Earth! An avenging angel, a death-dealing instrument of destruction, a lone heroic beast defending his honor against the Philistines, a juggernaut of power and pain... launching himself on a mission of vengeance...

All this as he leaps and springs IN SLOW MOTION. The V.O. is swift, fast, running together as if he is thinking it, but his movement, caught in SLOW MOTION, shows him arching up and out, as Snake ducks, Blood sails past through the air... and hits the wall. He falls down, stunned, as we HEAR in VOICE OVER, slowly, stupefiedly...

BLOOD (V.O.)(CONT'D)
How fleeting is grandeur.

39 DOWN ANGLE - WITH SNAKE - TO BLOOD

as the rover throws down on the dog, thumbs back the hammers on the shotgun, and begins to sight.

SMASH-CUT TO:

40 thru 51 SERIES OF INTERCUTS - INSTANTANEOUS

BLOOD LOOKING HALF-CONSCIOUS BUT TERRIFIED.

VIC SUDDENLY GALVANIZED INTO MOVEMENT.

SNAKE'S MEAN LITTLE EYES NARROWING.

VIC OPENING HIS MOUTH TO YELL.

SNAKE'S FINGER TIGHTENING ON THE TRIGGERS.

VIC SLAPPING HIS HAND ACROSS HIS .45'S HOLSTER, UNSNAPPING THE FLAP, GROPING FOR THE GUN.

BLOOD SEEING DEATH.

SNAKE'S FINGERS PULLING TRIGGERS BACK.

VIC WHIPPING UP THE AUTOMATIC.

A BLUR OF LIGHT THAT IS VIC'S GUN FIRING.

EXTREME CLOSEUP OF THE SHOTGUN FLYING THROUGH THE AIR TO LAND IN ONE OF THE OPEN FIRES, SCATTERING CINDERS AND SPARKS.

52 FULL SHOT WITH VIC

as he bounds to his feet, the .45 in one hand, the rifle in the other. We see a dim shape lying against the wall. BUT WE HAVE NOT SEEN SNAKE BEING KILLED OR HIS BODY CLEARLY! All around the room rovers are grabbing for weapons. But Walter sits in his chair and doesn't move. Skipper leaps to his feet. Vic grabs him around the throat with the arm that ends in the hand holding the .45. Vic slings the rifle. He is wearing his rucksack already.

VIC
Freeze, you varks.

He manhandles Skipper over to the fallen Blood, forces Skipper to his knees as he, Vic, gets to his knees, and then, awkwardly, he manages to lift the dog over his shoulder, and with Blood woozily assisting, he forces the dog head-down into the rucksack. Blood's back end sticks out, tail drooping.

53 ANGLE ON VIC - PERSPECTIVE ON ROOM

as we see the mass of 82nd Airborne rovers swaying toward Vic and their captured leader. It is almost a unified movement, a gestalt. They want to do something, but Vic has Skipper pinioned. They edge forward as Vic moves back toward the door; he unslings the rifle again, awkwardly, the weight of Blood on his back giving him trouble balancing. He now uses the rifle to clear rovers out from around him as he goes for the door. He backs against it, then turns Skipper slightly.

VIC
(to Skipper)
Open it.

SKIPPER
(chokingly)
You'll never get another slug
reloaded, man!

VIC
Just open it, Skipper. I've
got no beef with you.

WALTER
(from chair)
Why don't we talk this out, Vic.

VIC
I don't care if you think I'm
stupid; just don't talk to me like
I'm stupid.
(beat, to Skipper)
Open it!

(CONTINUED)

53 CONTINUED:

Skipper reaches around, opens the door onto the deck. Vic edges out, pulling Skipper with him as the rovers move in to fill the empty spaces. Walter does not leave his chair.

FLIP FRAME TO:

54 EXT. RIVER - NIGHT - OVERHEAD SHOT

The OVERHEAD SHOT assumes a FLATTER ANGLE as the skiff goes away from us, toward the darkness. One of the rovers grabs the lantern and holds it up, but all that can be seen is the skiff disappearing in the night until there is the SOUND of a big SPLASH, and then thrashing in the water, and Skipper swims out of the darkness toward the scow.

SKIPPER
Throw me a line, you stupid buncha --

FLIP FRAME TO:

55 thru 62 SERIES OF ARRIFLEX SHOTS - TRAVELING WITH VIC

as he climbs up on the wharf with Blood still upside-down sticking out of the knapsack on his back. He starts running. TRUCKING and PANNING SHOTS with Vic as he runs and runs, trying to get as far away from the wharf and the scow, and the implied threat of the 82nd Airborne coming after him as he can. WITH HIM as he dashes down a main street littered with rubble, as he jumps what is left of a shattered wall, as he dodges into an open doorway, as he emerges from the rear of a blasted building. And every once in a while, on a street, we should SEE a crater that emits an ominous green glow. This need not be explained for now. WITH HIM in his flight till he is HELD IN MED-LONG SHOT at the far end of an alley, running TOWARD CAMERA. He rushes INTO MED-CLOSE SHOT at the end of the alley nearest us, and collapses. He falls down and shucks out of the rucksack, dumping the now-revived Blood out on the filthy pavement amid cans and sheathed knives and clothes and other oddments of survival. He falls back against the wall of the alley, and just breathes hard.

Blood circles woozily for a few beats, getting his legs under him. He sits down in front of Vic, who is sitting against the wall with his aching head in his hands. He says nothing for a while. Then Vic looks up at him.

BLOOD
(filter; embarrassed, but cheery)
How's it going, kiddo?

(CONTINUED)

55 thru 62 CONTINUED:

VIC
(angrily)
Stupid lame-brained short-tempered imbecilic moron dog! Nearly got us killed! Lost us the only armorer in the territory! We're nearly outta ammo and you gotta get insulted, stupid looney lousy... eggsucker!

Blood looks the other way, lifting his nose. Above it. Vic, having vented his spleen, drops his head back into his hands. Blood watches him for a few beats, then speaks very softly.

BLOOD
(filter)
I was getting tired of this town, anyway.

Vic gives him a quick look of disbelief and anger.

VIC
(livid with rage)
Always cute, ain't you? Always got something cute to say! I'm down to four slugs, lower'n I've ever been! You got us dead... that's how cute you are!

BLOOD
(filter; contrite)
Hey, I'm sorry, Vic... take it easy... we'll find a way out of this...

VIC
(raging)
Take it easy?!? You just got us marked lousy with the 82nd Airborne ... and every other roverpak in the territory needs them... they'll put out the word on us... we're gonna be open targets for everybody!

BLOOD
(filter)
Look on the bright side: this is a good chance to go look for 'over the hill.'

Vic picks up a chunk of brick from the alley, and heaves it in his direction. Blood dodges.

(CONTINUED)

55 thru 62 CONTINUED (2):

BLOOD (CONT'D)
(filter)
Okay, so I'm not infallible...
I have feelings, too... when you
feel down and lousy I have to
cheer you up... aren't I entitled
to --

VIC
(screams)
You're not entitled to nothing 'cept
to do your job and keep me alive...
and when you can't do that you're
not worth feeding!

BLOOD
(filter)
Hold it a minute, buster!

VIC
You been makin' a lot of slow moves
lately; you're not worth...

BLOOD
(filter; getting
angry, too)
Look, kiddo, it wasn't all my
fault! I admit I lost my tempter,
but if you hadn't started playing
the big man and showing off your
education...

VIC
(warning)
Watch it, dog!

BLOOD
(filter)
... or if you'd stopped Snake
when he started insulting me,
I might not have run amuck.
It's your responsibility, too:
this is a partnership!

VIC
(chill, mean)
And one of the partners does
all the work. I'm the one with
the hands... I'm the one has to
pull the trigger...

(CONITNUED)

55 thru 62 CONTINUED (3):

BLOOD
(filter; flipping)
I'm a dog, you useless bumbling stupid human! You'd be dead a hundred times over if it weren't for me!

Vic stands up. He looks totally off-the-wall. We can understand that it isn't simply what they've just been through that has done this to him. It's everything they've been through, the constant pressure, the danger, the responsibility of staying alive.

VIC
I can't stand any more of this! I gotta get out of here, I gotta get away...

Blood is on to him now. His own irrational drive is gone in an instant.

BLOOD
(filter)
This is insane, Vic. We've been together two years. We're friends! We shouldn't be arguing like this...

But Vic is spaced. He shakes his head, makes incomplete motions, talks to the wall. He stuffs the goods back in the rucksack and shrugs into it, mumbling all the while.

VIC
(softly mumbling)
I gotta get away... gotta be on my own... gotta get some rest...

Then he walks straight out of the alley, and he's gone. Perhaps in a little while he'll get straight, but right now he's got to get out. Blood just sits there staring after him.

BLOOD
(filter)
I don't believe this.

63 ON BLOOD

as he goes to the mouth of the alley. He looks around the wall carefully.

BLOOD (V.O.)
Oh no.

(CONTINUED)

63 CONTINUED:

ANGLE ELEVATES to HOLD the street. Vic is striding right down the middle, stalking forward with that tilted-forward manner of someone almost shell-shocked... blind to danger... blind to everything! In plain sight, no cover, no attempt to protect himself! And he's heading directly toward one of those glowing green craters.

BLOOD
(filter; softly)
Vic... look out...
(building)
Screamers, Vic... in the craters...
(louder)
Vic... look out... stop...
(shouting now)
The radiation glow... the green glow... Vic, can't you see it... Vic! Vic! Look out...

He starts running, almost without conscious volition, down the street, unprotected, full out, trying to catch up with Vic way ahead of him, his FILTER VOICE OVER:

BLOOD (CONT'D)
(filter)
Stop! Stop, you fool! If it touches you you'll die... screaming... stop! Vic, turn... go back...

VIC
(filter; mumbling)
Gotta get outta here...

BLOOD
(filter)
Look out, look out! Dodge, stop, go back... you're going to die...!

64 DOLLY SHOT - IN FAST WITH BLOOD

as he runs full out. Now we ZOOM IN on the crater and see a hand clawing at the edge of the crumbling pavement in the street. It is scabrous and glowing faintly green. Blood is still yelling as we PULL BACK FAST as Vic goes away from us, BACK TO BLOOD who is running as fast as his little legs will carry him. He is almost upon Vic, as Vic nears the edge of the crater. Blood leaps, hits Vic in the back, knocking him sidewise, but the force of the jump carries Blood over the edge, right over the bulk of something indistinguishable, but clad in rags, and quite hideous to see, even though we can't tell what it is.

65 INT. CRATER - ARRIFLEX - WITH BLOOD

as he hits the bottom, doesn't stop for breath, goes scrabbling up the other side and out and down the street, full tilt. Behind him we HEAR the SOUND of FEET RUNNING.

66 TRACKING SHOT - STREET

as BLOOD RUSHES PAST going a mile a minute. HOLD CAMERA as Vic comes rushing behind him.

67 EXT. STREET CORNER - MEDIUM SHOT

as Blood runs into the FRAME, looks behind him, sees Vic, and collapses in the gutter. He falls on his back, lets in the air, and we HEAR HIM panting ferociously.

Vic runs INTO FRAME and flops down on the curb.

They lie that way for a few beats. Then Blood gets to his feet. He stares at him.

BLOOD
(filter)
That was stupid of you.

VIC
(wearily, softly)
I'm sorry, Blood.

BLOOD
(filter)
That's okay, kiddo. Come on, let's get out of here... go somewhere you can sleep a while.

He gets up. But Vic doesn't move.

VIC
I don't know what's the matter... I'm just beat... tired of fighting, tired of being scared all the time...

BLOOD
(filter)
Take it easy. It'll get better. All we have to do is stick together.

VIC
You better go find somebody new to run with.

(CONTINUED)

67 CONTINUED:

BLOOD
(filter)
What are you talking about it!?!
We're partners. Now get up and
let's go... we're unprotected out
here.

VIC
It's all done, Blood. I'm out
of it now. You go on...

BLOOD
(filter; getting angry)
Stop feeling sorry for yourself!
Get on your feet and come on.

VIC
(filter; wearily)
Get away from me. Lemme alone.

BLOOD
(filter)
I saved your miserable life, you
ingrate!

Vic picks up a rock.

VIC
I said: get away from me, go
find someone who's got a chance.
I can't cut it any more.

BLOOD
(filter)
Wouldn't you be just as happy
with some sense?

Vic hefts the rock.

BLOOD (CONT'D)
(filter)
You did that once. Don't do
it twice, man!

Vic throws the rock at him, and again Blood dodges and it misses.

VIC
We're quits, dog... two years
is enough... If I'm gonna die,
I'll do it alone.

Blood walks off a pace or two. He stops and turns back and stares.

(CONTINUED)

36.

67 CONTINUED (2):

BLOOD
(filters)
Take care of yourself, kiddo.
(beat)
Boy, I hate to see me go.

And he walks away, head down, into the darkness, leaving Vic staring after him. COME IN CLOSE on VIC and we SEE HE is crying softly. But he looks weary, exhausted, beaten. And we

FADE TO BLACK

and

FADE OUT

END ACT TWO

ACE THREE

FADE IN:

68 EXT. ROCKY SEACOAST - MORNING - HIGH MEDIUM SHOT

as CAMERA COMES DOWN on a single person, behind a big boulder, holding a .22 fitted with a scope. It is a young woman, SPIKE. Behind her on the ground is a small pile of cans and several bandoliers of bullets. She is dressed in camouflage suit and her dirty long hair is bound up in a knot at the back of her head. She wears dark-tinted sunglasses. We HEAR a SHOT and a ricochet spangs off the top of the rock behind which she hides. CAMERA DOWN TO CLOSE on Spike.

She pops up, bangs off a shot and ducks back.

Another shot comes at her. She starts to pop up and get off another shot, when we (and she) HEAR A VOICE.

BLOOD
(filter)
I wouldn't do that if I were you.

She drops back, spins around, swings the rifle.

69 PAST SPIKE - HER P.O.V.

just the cliff and the sea and that's it. No one. She does a full 360° appraisal, and then goes back to her original position, looking worried.

BLOOD
(filter)
Now if you count to seven slowly, and then track left to 10:00, you might get one.
(beat)
Go ahead, try it. Now count to five.

We see her counting slowly, then up on one knee, and snapping off a shot. From the distance, where more rocks are piled, we HEAR a howl of pain.

SPIKE
(aloud)
Who's there? Who are you?

BLOOD
(filter)
Your fairy godfather; come to save you.

(CONTINUED)

69 CONTINUED:

A couple of shots spang off the rock.

SPIKE
I can't see you.

BLOOD
(filter)
I'm here, don't worry about it.
What's your name?

SPIKE
Spike. Who're you?

BLOOD
(filter)
You can call me Blood.
(beat)
They're trying to flank you, by the way. One coming around from the left, the other over that rise on the right.

Spike looks around frantically. Trapped.

BLOOD
(filter)
Try the cliff.

Spike gathers up her stuff, shoves it into a rucksack, slings the bandoliers, and crawls on her stomach to the cliff.

70 ANGLE DOWN CLIFF

she slithers over the side. There is a small ledge there. She gets down onto it.

BLOOD
(filter)
Keep going to your left. I'll meet you at the cave about a quarter of a mile up the beach.

Then silence. Spike crouches on the ledge.

SPIKE
Hey! Hey, where are you?

No answer. She keeps going as CAMERA TRACKS HER LEFT. Down the little ledge, to a path, down the path, and then off into the distance as we:

DISSOLVE TO:

71 INT. CAVE - DAY

right near the sea. Spike comes trudging across the sand, and sitting on his haunches in the middle of the mouth of the cave is Blood, panting prettily. Spike comes up to the cave, not too close, rifle ready, waiting for Blood's master to show himself... but there's only the dog.

BLOOD
(filter)
What've you got to eat?

She stares at him in wonder.

BLOOD
(filter)
I'll take anything but beets. I haven't had a square meal in three days. What I mean to say is, lady, can you spare a meal for a terrific sniffer like me?

She comes to him, squats down, still cautious.

SPIKE
You saved me up there?

BLOOD
(filter)
Modesty forbids my answering that question.
(beat)
Hunger forces the truth from me. It was I.

SPIKE
But I can hear you. Inside my head.

BLOOD
(filter)
It's called teeping; that's slang for telepathy. Very rare these days. You're clearly an exceptional person: I can talk to you.

SPIKE
I've _heard_ about skirmisher dogs, and I even saw one working with a roverpak once. But --

BLOOD
(filter)
Listen, kiddo: I'd love to discuss the state of the world with you, but I'm _really_ hungry.

(CONTINUED)

71 CONTINUED:

SPIKE
(cautious)
Is that why you helped me up there? So I'd feed you?

BLOOD
(filter)
I've always mistrusted humanitarians.

SPIKE
(totally confused)
Huh?

BLOOD
(filter)
Forget it. The answer is yes, I helped you in hopes you'd spring for a meal. Anything wrong with that?

SPIKE
No one ever helped me before.

BLOOD
(filter; a little sadly)
Yes, I can imagine. Well, a new day is dawning. There'll be a lot of that going around.

Spike shucks out of the rucksack, starts digging around for food. She continues talking to Blood.

SPIKE
You talk funny. But you're a smart pup.
(beat)
How does this talking-in-the-mind work?

BLOOD
(filter; checking the cans)
Do you know what you've got there?

SPIKE
Not much. I'm fat on ammo, but real thin on food.

BLOOD
(filter)
No, I mean do you know what's in those cans?

(CONTINUED)

71 CONTINUED (2):

She looks bewildered.

SPIKE
Food.

BLOOD
(filter)
Do you know what kind of food?

SPIKE
How am I supposed to know till I open them?!

BLOOD
(filter; quietly)
Read what's left of the labels.

She looks even more bewildered. She turns the cans in her hand, assaying the decaying labels. It is obvious: she cannot read. Blood comes to her, looks over her arm.

BLOOD (CONT'D)
(filter)
That one is corned beef hash. This one is crushed pineapple. That one has no label, so I don't know what it is.

She stares at him in amazement. A dawning interest in him grows as we study her face, seeing the cunning of the wily predator.

SPIKE
You work with a roverpak?

BLOOD
(filter)
No. I'm solo.

SPIKE
Where's your master?

BLOOD
(filter; haughtily)
I'm my own dog. I go where I choose.

SPIKE
Don't try running that one past me, dog. Nobody makes it by herself out here.

(CONTINUED)

71 CONTINUED (3):

BLOOD
(filter)
You seemed to have done it. How old are you?

SPIKE
(bothered)
I don't know. Older than twenty, I know that much.

She shows him the butt of her rifle. It has notches cut in it.

SPIKE (CONT'D)
I tried to keep track. Every time the big rains come, I cut another notch. But I missed a few at the beginning.

BLOOD
(filter; sadly)
I've never known a female solo this close. It must be extremely difficult for you.

SPIKE
(tightly)
I get by.

BLOOD
(filter)
Why don't you join a roverpak of females?

SPIKE
I don't like being with people.

BLOOD
(filter)
Why don't you open those cans, I'll go find some firewood and we can eat.
(beat)
Then we can talk some more.

He starts to trot away. She calls out to him.

SPIKE
You didn't run it past me, dog. I still want to know what happened to your boy.

She watches him as Blood trots off down the beach looking for driftwood, as we:

DISSOLVE TO:

72 INT. CAVE - DAY

It is dim and shadowy in the cave, eerie with the flickering shapes cast on the water-worn walls by the small driftwood fire. Spike and Blood are eating.

BLOOD
(filter)
It's been a long time since I had corned beef hash. It's delicious.
(beat, wistfully)
I had it once with a fried chicken egg on it.

SPIKE
Where did you find a chicken?

BLOOD
(filter)
There was a roverpak that called itself The Black Gang. They raised them, used them for barter. Vic traded off three cans of --

SPIKE
Vic?

Blood is silent. He keeps eating.

SPIKE (CONT'D)
Who was Vic?

No answer. Spike puts down her food, moves toward the dog, moves to touch him. Blood bares his fangs. She stops but doesn't pull back.

SPIKE (CONT'D)
Okay, no touching yet.
(beat)
Listen, Blood: I get the message you cut out on whoever was running your show... and you're looking for a new tie-up.

BLOOD
(filter)
I'm not sure entering into a working relationship with a solo female is a good idea. You're a little scarred: looks as though you've had some bad fights. I look for the kind of solos who <u>inflict</u> scars like that.

(CONTINUED)

72 CONTINUED:

Spike's face gets hard. She looks at him, but she's seeing a great many days and nights stretched out behind her.

SPIKE

If I had a mother and father, they had me and dropped me before I got old enough to know them on sight.

(beat)

I belonged to a roverpak for a while, till some creep saw I was getting big enough for his kind of fun, and I cut his throat and took his .22 and got out at night. I've been on my own a long time, no roverpak, no dog, no nothing but me. I'm good at it.

(beat)

Yeah, I've got scars. But the ones that gave 'em to me are dead, and I've never been raped.

Blood sits and stares at her for a long moment, then speaks very thoughtfully.

BLOOD

(filter)

Vic and I were mates for two years. We split up. He's gone. I'm available. Maybe you'll do.

She smiles. He edges closer.

BLOOD (CONT'D)

(filter)

There's maybe a flea behind my right ear. Care to scratch him for me?

She smiles more widely, reaches out and tentatively touches him. He moves closer. She scratches as we:

DISSOLVE TO:

73 GRASSLAND AREA - EVENING - FEATURING FARMHOUSE

as CAMERA COMES DOWN on Spike and Blood crouching behind bushes. It is an old farmhouse, and they're about 100 yards in front. There is a sudden SHOT from the house, and as they watch the CAMERA ZOOMS IN to HOLD in MEDIUM CLOSEUP an old, wrinkled, grizzled man with an ancient rifle.

PARTRIDGE

(screams)

No food! No food! Get outta here!

(CONTINUED)

73 CONTINUED:

He is wild, almost a crazed hermit. CAMERA PULLS BACK to Spike and Blood. They flatten as another SHOT comes.

74 EXT. CLOSEUP - SPIKE

There is a tension there, a tough streak that shows she has no patience for all this. CAMERA ANGLE WIDENS to include BLOOD.

BLOOD
(filter)
I don't like what you're thinking.

SPIKE
Then stop reading my mind.

BLOOD
(filter)
It's just stupid what you want to do.

SPIKE
(nods her head to their left)
You see that hole?

Blood looks left as CAMERA SWINGS WITH HIM to show us a huge, smoking hole in the earth and the blasted stump of a small tree.

75 ON SPIKE - TO BLOOD

SPIKE
Well, I don't know what made that hole when he fired at us, but whatever it is...

BLOOD
(filter)
It's a laser rifle. Developed in the Third War.
(beat, musing)
Didn't think there were any left aboveground.

SPIKE
Yeah, well, it was that crazy old man's bad luck to come down on us... if he'd just let us take a little food...

(CONTINUED)

75 CONTINUED:

BLOOD
(filter)
As you say. He's crazy. And so are we if we try to take that laser out of there. Let it go.

SPIKE
I'm hungry. Sit and watch if you like.

Blood starts to say something, but she's up and off, looping out and away to the far right, off the line of sight of the farmhouse. The old man keeps screaming.

76 ARRIFLEX - WITH SPIKE

as she runs. CAMERA STAYS WITH HER but we can HEAR the VOICE OF BLOOD OVER.

BLOOD
(filter)
Spike! For crine-out-loud! He may be old and crazy, but he's got to be good to've stayed alive this long!

No answer. (She doesn't know yet that she can speak to Blood without speaking.) She rushes through the underbrush, doubles back on the house, finds an ivy-overgrown trellis to one side, hits it softly at a dead run, dropping her rifle. She now has a hunting knife between her teeth. Up she goes.

77 WITH BLOOD - SHOT LONG TO HOUSE

as Blood in F.G. sees Spike on the shattered roof. She pries up a board and drops out of sight. There are half a dozen beats of silence as Blood starts out, a shot sends him back to cover.

BLOOD
(filter)
Spike! Spike! What's happening?

There is a YELLING from the house, and then another VOICE YELLING and we cannot tell which is which. Then CAMERA ZOOMS PAST BLOOD to the HOUSE as one of the windows is blown out. CAMERA BACK FAST as Blood takes off.

78 CAMERA WITH BLOOD - ARRIFLEX

as he rushes to the house. CAMERA HOLDS as he runs around and appears coming from the other side. There is a storm cellar housing that rises up almost to the bottom of the blown-out window. Blood dashes up the housing and jumps through the empty frame.

79 INT. FARM HOUSE - ON WINDOW - LIVING ROOM

as Blood comes sailing through.

80 REVERSE ANGLE - BLOOD'S P.O.V. - WHAT HE SEES

Rolling around on the floor are Spike and an old man... a very old man... about sixty-five or seventy. It is PARTRIDGE. He is cursing inarticulately, she is yowling, and neither of them has a weapon. They are just grappling and rolling around, knocking over furniture. CAMERA BACK TO INCLUDE BLOOD, who just watches. After a few moments, Spike rolls up on top of the old man and pins his arms. She is about to slug him when he snaps:

PARTRIDGE
Go ahead, you bully, hit me! I already got you on trespass, breaking and entering, unlawful entry, malicious mischief, intentional destruction of property. Oh, I got a good one, a good one here!

Spike is so startled by this lunatic outburst, that she stays her hand.

PARTRIDGE (CONT'D)
(in Latin)
<u>Trespass</u> <u>quare</u> <u>clausum</u> <u>fregit</u>... I'll sue you within an inch of your life for your tortious conduct... pursuant to judgment rendered in the landmark decision of Anslinger Gypsum Corp. vs. Nordinski: 1932, 22 California 211, 32 Pacific 570, also cited in 190 Am Jur 273, 1955...

Spike is dumbfounded.

SPIKE
I don't know what you're talkin' about, you crazy old bugger, but I'm gonna bust your head!

(CONTINUED)

48.

80 CONTINUED:

PARTRIDGE
Go ahead, just go on ahead!
Only makes my case stronger:
trespass vi et armis. Not to
mention calling me names, which
is slander, intentional infliction
of mental distress. Oh, yes
indeed, justice will be done!
I'll have you in court so fast
it'll make your head swim.

Spike looks around at Blood.

SPIKE
Do you know what this old fud is
babbling about?

BLOOD
(filter; amused)
He's going to sue you.

PARTRIDGE
Who you talkin' to, girl?

SPIKE
Shut up, old man!
(to Blood)
What's sue?

BLOOD
(filter)
To bring a legal action, seeking
redress for damages sustained by
the plaintiff.

SPIKE
Now you're talking crazy!

BLOOD
(filter)
How did you wind up tussling
with him?

Spike looks at bit chagrined. She nods her head toward
the fireplace.

SPIKE
He jumped me from behind. He
was hiding in the fireplace.
Pretty nearly blew my head off,
missed me and got the window.

BLOOD
(filter)
Better get off him.

(CONTINUED)

80 CONTINUED (2):

SPIKE
Why don't I just knock him off?

BLOOD
(filter)
I like the cut of his jib.

Snorting derisively, Spike gets off Partridge, and steps away from him. The old man crawls to his feet, looking triumphant.

PARTRIDGE
Knew the threat of the law'd scare you off, you little whippersnapper!

SPIKE
(to Blood)
I think I gotta kill this old coot.

81 ANOTHER ANGLE - FAVORING PARTRIDGE

PARTRIDGE
Occurs to me you're just a tad crazy as a bedbug, little girl.

(beat)
Way you keep talking to thet dog. Prob'ly shouldn't of whomped you so bad. But it's no hard feelin's. I'll see you in court and they can handle all this litigation.
(beat)
No need t'be rude to a guest, though. You et your lunch today yet?

BLOOD
(filter)
Tell him you'd be pleased to stay for lunch. And ask him if he's got something wholesome for your dog.

She looks at Blood as if he's as crazy as the old man.

BLOOD (CONT'D)
(filter)
Go on, go on.

SPIKE
I'd be pleased to have some lunch...

BLOOD
(filter)
Sir.

(CONTINUED)

50.

81 CONTINUED:

SPIKE
(grimacing)
...sir. And do you have an old bone for my dog here?

BLOOD
(filter)
I don't want a bone, confound it! A steak or a plate of eggs with bacon!

PARTRIDGE
I'm sure I can dig up a bone or some meal for the pup. Come along, child.

He starts toward the kitchen, with Spike grabbing up her knife, sheathing it, and following. Blood watches for a moment.

BLOOD (V.O.)
I wonder if Vic has a sister.

Then he follows as we:

DISSOLVE TO:

82 INT. STAIRWELL - SHOOTING DOWN FROM LANDING ABOVE TO LANDING BELOW

ON VIC, who is sitting beside a small fire he's built right there on the tiles. This is obviously in a big, abandoned office building, somewhere in the city where we last saw Vic. He has something bubbling in a tin can with a wire handle that has been hung over an iron tripod above the fire. He is hunkered down in the semi-dark, hugging his rifle, waiting for the food to be ready. There is the SOUND of FEET ECHOING on the stairs coming up. Vic slides the rifle to ready, aims down the stairs below the landing. It is very dark down there and we cannot see what is coming up. CAMERA COMES DOWN CLOSE BEHIND VIC shooting into the darkness.

A VOICE drifts up the stairwell.

POKE
Don't shoot buddy. I'm a minstrel.

Vic lowers the rifle just a bit. He says nothing.

(CONTINUED)

82 CONTINUED:

POKE
Just passing through town and getting some sleep down here. Smelled your food.
(beat)
I've got all kinds of things to tell. Can I come up?

Another beat of silence, then Vic raises rifle again.

VIC
Minstrels wear the armband. You got the armband?

POKE
Sure do. But I ain't got a gun.

VIC
Take off the armband and throw it up here.

There is a beat, then something flips up through the darkness. Vic catches it without the rifle even wavering. He looks at it. An armband of bright yellow with a big red circle in the middle of it.

VIC
Come ahead. Slow.

A shape moves up the stairs. It comes on till we can see POKE, a boy of about twelve or thirteen, with a peculiar instrument slung over his back. He is wearing a battered, chewed-up Stetson. He stops below Vic, waiting to be invited up.

POKE
M'name's Poke. I've got a lot of good stuff to talk about, I can sing; if you feed me.

Vic motions with the rifle at the instrument.

VIC
What's that thing?

POKE
Makes music. Don't know what it's called.

VIC
Yeah? Well, take it off and put it down.

(CONTINUED)

82 CONTINUED (2):

Poke shrugs out of the strap, lays the instrument down. It is a long metal keyboard affair, with two antenna at opposed corners. It is a futuristic version of a theremin, but we will never name it. Vic motions Poke up. Poke opens his jacket to show he's unarmed.

VIC
Food's scarce. What've you got to tell?

POKE
(friendly)
First I eat a little, then I tell a little, then I eat some more an' then I tell some more.

Vic sighs, lays the rifle across his lap, takes his hunting knife with the big mean blade, and spears a piece of something simmering in the tin can. He flips it off the blade to the boy. Poke juggles it for a moment.

POKE (CONT'D)
Ouch, wow... hot!

He sits down on the step below the landing. Vic watches.

83 UP-ANGLE 2-SHOT - FAVORING VIC

FROM BELOW POKE, up the stairs to landing. Poke devours the meat in a few chomps. Vic waits.

VIC
Okay, minstrel, now what's all that good stuff you know?

POKE
(almost mystically)
I seen a far place near here, and it's nothin' but food. Food all over the place. Food in cans and food in jars and food in boxes. Big boxes. Biggest boxes you ever seen. More food than a dozen roverpaks could eat in ten years.

VIC
(ridiculing)
Yeah, sure; and milk runs in the river and the jack rabbits roll over so's you can cut their throats.

(CONTINUED)

83 CONTINUED:

POKE
(defensively)
It's true. I'm a minstrel.
I don't lie about what I tell.
It's a lost land, a magic place,
guarded by hundreds of metal
soldiers and dead cars.

VIC
I don't believe in "lost lands."

POKE
That's what everyone said about
Atlantis, until the missiles
shook everything up during the
Third War... and the lost
continent rose.
(beat)
So, you'd better believe it,
because every roverpak in the
area has started gathering there.

Vic's head comes up sharply.

VIC
You know Fellini and his pack?

POKE
They're there already.

VIC
You actually seen this place?

POKE
(nods)
Lost land, buddy. They even
got a name for it: Eastgate Mall.

Vic contemplates a moment, then spears another piece of meat and hands it across. Poke takes it.

VIC
Can you tell me how to get there?

POKE
I wrote a song about it.
Everybody's been asking.
Wanna hear it?

He reaches for the theremin. Vic puts a hand on the rifle.

VIC
I don't like singin' much. But
go ahead, I suppose.

(CONTINUED)

54.

83 CONTINUED (2):

Poke takes up the instrument, lays it across his lap, throws a toggle switch on it and the theremin's lights flicker then glow dully. He raises the antennae. Then he passes his hands in the air between the antennae and we HEAR the strange, eerie strains of theremin music, as he SINGS.

POKE
Across the dead lands,
Where the highway never goes;
In the misty valley,
Where the starshine never shows;
(etcetera)

As he sings, his voice soothing and mellow, Vic's eyes grow heavy. He shifts position, a man who has had very little sleep. And as the voice drifts upward, CAMERA PULLS DOWN AND AWAY till the scene fades into darkness and we:

FADE TO BLACK

and

FADE OUT

END OF ACT THREE

ACT FOUR

FADE IN:

84 INT. FARMHOUSE - KITCHEN - SPIKE, BLOOD AND PARTRIDGE

as they finish eating. Blood is up on a chair, with an empty bowl in front of him. Spike is drinking a mug of coffee. Partridge is leaning back in his chair, picking his teeth with a gold toothpick hanging from a chain on his coveralls.

PARTRIDGE
Told you m'last name's
Partridge, didn't I?

Spike nods.

PARTRIDGE
(continuing)
Won't tell yuh m'first name.

SPIKE
Have it your way; don't tell me.

PARTRIDGE
You'd only make fun.

SPIKE
So don't tell me.

PARTRIDGE
It's Whistler.

SPIKE
I thought you weren't gonna
tell me?

PARTRIDGE
(as if he never heard)
Whistler Partridge. I'm sixty-eight
or seventy-one years old. And I
remember the war. Yes, I do.
The big war. Before your time,
little girl.

Spike holds out the mug for more coffee. He pours.

PARTRIDGE
(continuing)
I was born in 1954. Right here
in this house.

SPIKE
You lived all that time in this
one place? That's crazy.

(CONTINUED)

84 CONTINUED:

PARTRIDGE
Watch who you're callin' crazy, you young snot. In my day, children had some respect for their elders.
(beat)
Common law goes back a long time afore Blackstone... concept of a man's home is his castle. Still takin' yuh to court.

BLOOD
(filter)
Ask him to tell you about the war.

Spike looks at the dog.

SPIKE
Blood wants to know about the war.

PARTRIDGE
(light dawns)
Ohhh, well I never! That one of them mind-readin' dogs they used in the Third War? Never did believe it.

SPIKE
(to Blood)
He's nuts. He don't know nothin' about the war.

PARTRIDGE
Don't huh?
(beat)
World War III lasted from 25 June 1950 when the Republic of Korea was invaded by 60,000 screaming North Korean troops spearheaded by something in excess of 100 Russian-built tanks... through a long 'cold war' ... and several small 'hot ones' ...to 1 January 1983 when the Vatican _Entente Cordiale_ was signed between the Eastern and Western blocs.

BLOOD
(filter)
He _does_ know. Listen to this, Spike. It's called history.

SPIKE
This's boring.

(CONTINUED)

84 CONTINUED (2):

PARTRIDGE
You got no roots, kid. You got no perspective. First you trespass de bonis asportatis, then you show how bone stick stone dumb y'are.

SPIKE
Watch it, Partridge.

PARTRIDGE
Call me Whistler.

SPIKE
I thought you hated that name?

PARTRIDGE
Where was I? Oh, yup...
(beat)
World War III -- hot and cold -- lasted thirty-three years.
(beat)
World War IV lasted five days, until the few remaining missiles that had jammed in their release phase had left their silos beneath the Painted Desert and the Urals and the Gobi Altay; but by then there wasn't anything much left to fight over. Five days, and 'civilization' as humans knew it was gone. Blotto. Finito. Isn't that sad?

Spike has grown a little interested, despite herself.

SPIKE
Yeah, it's sad.

PARTRIDGE
Not very. Never cared much for the human race. More I saw of danged people, better I liked dogs.

BLOOD
(filter)
Very perceptive gentleman.

Partridge notices the look Spike has given Blood.

PARTRIDGE
What'd he say?

(CONTINUED)

84 CONTINUED (3):

SPIKE
He likes you. Thinks you're smart.

PARTRIDGE
Mark Twain once said, "If you pick up a starving dog and make him prosperous, he will not bite you. This is the principal difference between a dog and a man."

SPIKE
You know about the downunders, too?

PARTRIDGE
You mean those miserable cities the fat middle-class sank down in the Earth, miles down? 'Course I know about 'em. Didn't they try to get me and Miss Vicky Pauline to go with 'em? Like a buncha danged ostriches, strickin' their whole bodies in the sand, not just their heads. Know about 'em? Right proper I know about 'em -- Turned 'em down too. Miss Vicky Pauline and me, we stayed right here.

SPIKE
You're all alone here, aren't you?

PARTRIDGE
No, 'course not! Man'd go crazy bein' here alone all these years.
(beat)
C'mon, I'll introduce you.

He gets up. Spike looks at Blood.

BLOOD
(filter)
Careful. He's a little weird.

SPIKE
Now you agree with me.

She follows Partridge through the kitchen.

85 WITH SPIKE AND BLOOD

as they trail behind Partridge, through the swinging door from the kitchen to the living room and across the living room to a door at the far side.

(CONTINUED)

85 CONTINUED:

PARTRIDGE
Sixty-eight, seventy-one years I lived here. No punk whipper-snappers can drive us outta here.

He opens the door.

PARTRIDGE
(Continuing; calls inside)
Miss Vicky Pauline... want you to meet this nice little girl and her pup... I'm suin' 'em for trespass an' a lotta other tortious behavior...

He waves them inside. They advance to the door. He goes in. CAMERA TIGHT BEHIND THEM shooting into the dim interior.

It is a BEDROOM with the blinds pulled, the ravages of time and the war showing that the room is in patched-up shape. But deep shadows. And there, way at the back of the room is a big four-poster bed with a festooned, ripped, rotting lace canopy.

They edge in slightly. Trying to make out the figure sitting up on the bed.

PARTRIDGE
(Continuing)
Little girl, I'd like you to meet my wife, Miss Vicky Pauline...

86 CLOSE SHOT ON SPIKE

as her eyes bug and her mouth drops open.

87 SAME AS SC. 85

as CAMERA ZOOMS IN on the bed and the preserved, mummified body of an old woman, fully dressed in her Sunday go-to-meeting best. Nothing more than a skeleton, with the leathery skin stretched tight across the face. Miss Vicky Pauline has been dead for thirty years. HOLD that horror for a beat as we:

CUT TO:

88 EXT. EDGE OF CITY - MORNING

Vic and Poke standing overlooking the countryside.

VIC
You sure it's that way?

POKE
That's where it was. Eastgate Mall. The lost land. All the food in the world.

Vic looks uncomfortable. He wants to say something to this young boy, this minstrel, but he's unaccustomed to speaking warmly.

VIC
Listen, uh...
(beat)
You could of taken my stuff, killed me, anything... last night when I fell asleep.

POKE
I don't do that kind of thing. I'm a minstrel. I just go my way and tell what I hear and sing a song for eats.

VIC
Yeah... well... thanks. If I ever run into you again, I owe you one.

POKE
Well, maybe. I might pass back the way you're going. All the roverpaks are out there. It might happen.
(beat)
You're not so sad now... are you?

VIC
You could tell, huh?

POKE
You seemed pretty low. But things're getting better everywhere. Hang on.

VIC
Yeah. Well...

He gives a restrained salute, and turns and goes as Poke watches and we HOLD ON VIC going away as we:

DISSOLVE TO:

89 EMBANKMENT BESIDE RAILROAD TRACKS - DAY

Weed-overgrown railroad spur line. Spike and Blood are down in the bushes, watching as a roverpak of eight or ten mean-looking black kids straggle by, following the tracks. Spike is eating peaches from a can with her fingers.

BLOOD
(filter)
That's the fourth roverpak that's passed us today. All going the same direction.

SPIKE
(whispering)
Something's happening.

BLOOD
(filter)
Gathering of the clans? I wonder.

SPIKE
(whispering)
I'm just glad to be away from that crazy old man. Cheez, that dead wife of his, all propped up and staring...
(beat)
But I got the laser rifle.

BLOOD
(filter)
Hold it...

There is a PINGING sound from Blood. She sets the can down.

BLOOD
(Continuing; filter)
Eastgate Mall.

SPIKE
What's that?

BLOOD
(filter)
I don't know. One of those rovers said it just now. Food.

SPIKE
Yeah? Let's follow them.

BLOOD
(filter)
For a while. But no more commando games like that action back at Partridge's house.

(CONTINUED)

89 CONTINUED:

SPIKE
I got the rifle didn't I?

BLOOD
(filter)
It wasn't worth that kind of risk.
It was anti-survival.

SPIKE
What's that mean?

BLOOD
(filter; testily)
It means that we are adrift in a
world of violence that wants to
kill us, and anything we can do
to avoid violence is pro-survival...
meaning it is good for us... and
anything that looks like trouble
is anti-survival...which means
bad for us.

SPIKE
That makes sense. Any peaches left
in that can?

She picks up the can.

BLOOD
(filter; loud and angry)
Now listen to me! If you want me to
stay with you, you're going to have
to stop playing hotshot..

She has stopped feeding her face. This is a woman who
has grown tough and sharp in a bad situation, and she's
never been talked to like this before.

SPIKE
Listen, dog...

BLOOD
(filter)
And don't call me dog, "little girl!"
(half beat)
If we're together then that means
we work together! No more unilateral
decisions...
(beat)
No more doing what you want to do
without my agreement.

She stares at him. There is a long silence between them.
The dog faces her down. She looks away.

(CONTINUED)

89 CONTINUED (2):

SPIKE
(softly)
Okay... Blood.

CUT TO:

90 FULL SCENE SHOT - PANORAMA - LATE NIGHT

WHAT WE SEE: we are on the ridge of an immense bowl; what might have been a suburban tract community decades before. The ridge is covered with trees and shrubbery, very dense. In the F.G. Spike and Blood are lying out staring down into the bowl.

There is an immense desertlike area at the bottom of the bowl. Here and there are the remains of structures, just poking up out of the ground. But right in the middle, looking as if it's three acres in size, is the top of what must have been a gigantic warehouse. Along its facing wall, right near the roof-line, we can make out the upper-half of block lettering, faded and sand-blasted, but still visible in the full moonlight and the light of campfires that ring the building. The words are barely discernible. (Blood will tell us what they say momentarily.)

The campfires that ring the building are far enough apart and far enough back that there is a large no-man's-land surrounding the building. We SEE people MOVING around near the various fires.

SPIKE
Is this what he called Eastgate Mall?

BLOOD
(filter)
This is it. And I'm simply delighted to see we're not the first ones to arrive at the party.

SPIKE
How many roverpaks are there down there?

BLOOD
(filter)
I make out seventeen, and maybe as many solos. Over there on the right, see the big wagon? That's Fellini and his bunch. About twenty-five of them... he must have hired on five or six more rifles.

(CONTINUED)

90 CONTINUED:

SPIKE
That looks like The Nukes on the left, at about eight o'clock.

BLOOD
(filter)
And The Jolly Stompers, and The Hole in the Wall Gang, and the Cagneys, and that female roverpak, The Flamingos.

SPIKE
What kind of strength have they got?

BLOOD
(filter)
Nukes, eleven; Stompers, sixteen -- as best I can smell them -- they're all rolled up together; Cagneys are running nineteen...

At that moment, a shape breaks from one of the campfires and we can make out the person broken-field running toward the buried warehouse through no-man's-land. It is all dark and distant, but suddenly there is a fussilade of machine gun shots (indicated in the darkness by tracers that light up the area) all coming from other campfires and from around the rim of the bowl, converging on that spot where the man is running. It lasts about ten seconds, all the fire pouring down on that one spot in streamers of light like the spokes of a wheel.

BLOOD
(Continuing; filter)
Make that <u>eighteen</u>.

SPIKE
Wheeew! Ain't <u>no</u>body gonna get in that place for a while. It's a stand-off.
(beat)
No one group is big enough to try and take it with all them roverpaks and solos keeping them away.
(beat)
How do they <u>know</u> there's food in there?

BLOOD
(filter)
Because of what it says on that buried building.

(CONTINUED)

90 CONITNUED (2):

SPIKE
I can't make it out from here. Can't read, anyhow. What's it say?

BLOOD
(filter)
Great Western Produce Market Storage.

At that moment we HEAR footsteps through the brush behind them as Blood leaps up and Spike flops over, holding the deadly laser rifle. She is about to fire, when a young man steps through the brush and looks down at them. It is Vic.

91 CLOSE ON VIC

VIC
Hello, Blood. Who's your friend?

HOLD for beat after beat after beat as we INTERCUT:

BACK & FORTH BETWEEN:

92 thru 95 SERIES OF CLOSEUP INTERCUTS

Blood's face, looking startled.

Spike's face, looking mean and confused.

Vic's face looking bemused and wary.

Blood, as he buries his face in his paws and we:

FADE TO BLACK

and

FADE OUT.

END OF ACT FOUR

ACT FIVE

FADE IN:

96 EXT. RIM OF THE BOWL - MOONLIGHT NIGHT (LATER) - EXTREME CLOSEUP - THE ALMOST BUCK-ROGERS-LIKE MUZZLE OF SPIKE'S LASER RIFLE 96

CAMERA PULLS BACK QUICKLY to show the young woman sighting through the scope atop the mean, futuristic weapon. Her face is even dirtier than we've seen it earlier, and more tense, colder, menacing. CAMERA BACK to WIDER ANGLE so we see Blood still lying there, staring across the fire. BACK FURTHER to show Vic standing there with his rifle aimed at Spile.

SPIKE
Blood! This guy you left behind?

VIC
(filter; bemused)
Oh, so you can hear him, too.

SPIKE
Blood!

VIC
(filter)
Blood... What's that thing she's got there? Tell her to put it down before I blow her away.

SPIKE
Blood! Tell him to stop talking to you!

VIC
Blood! What's goin' on here, buddy?

Blood gets up and slowly walks around in an aimless circle as though he's thinking. CAMERA WITH HIM and IN on his contemplative dog-face. Then he stops and looks at Vic.

BLOOD
(filter)
Put down the rifle, Vic. You were almost out of ammunition a month ago. Chances are good that thing isn't loaded, so put it down.

(CONTINUED)

96 CONTINUED: 96

SPIKE
Thanks Blood.

Blood turns to her.

BLOOD
(filter)
If you fire that laser gun, not only will it wipe out every tree in the vicinity, but it'll draw every solo and rover on the rim. So put it down, Spike.

VIC
Thanks, Blood.
(beat)
Okay, broad, you heard him.

SPIKE
Yeah, I heard him, clown. But he don't know me that well. Put yours down or I burn your head off!

VIC
He's only guessing that I didn't come up fat with ammo... so put yours down!

BLOOD
(filter; to himself)
Why me? Why do I have this endless aggravation?

VIC
(angrily)
Who is this dippy chick?

SPIKE
(furious)
I'm the "dippy chick" that's gonna slaughter you if you don't drop that thing!

Suddenly CAMERA ZOOMS IN on Blood as he bares his fangs and growls deep and menacing. He looks crazed.

CAMERA BACK to include a startled Spike and Vic.

(CONTINUED)

96 CONTINUED (2):

BLOOD
(filter)
Drop them! Both of you! Now!

They are so startled that, watching each other very carefully, they lay down their weapons.

Everything suddely settles down. And as it does, Vic jumps across the fire, spewing ashes in every direction, and goes for Spike. But she hops out of the way very quickly; and as Vic turns, she hauls back and belts him as hard as she can with a roundhouse that lifts him off his feet and sends him sprawling on his back. In a second she's on top of him, fumbling for her sheathed knife.

BLOOD
(continuing;
filter)
Spike! Stop it, let him alone!

She pauses, the command of the dog overriding her fever. Vic lies there, absolutely amazed at what has just gone down, including himself.

BLOOD
(continuing;
filter)
I mean it, Spike. Let him alone!

She slowly pulls back. Then, in a very casual gesture, she slaps him twice across the cheeks, back and forth ... but very gently as an act of superiority; of disdain. To prove he's vanquished.

Then she gets off him.

BLOOD
(continuing;
filter)
Get up, Vic.

He gets up and stands there naked. Spike now has the knife unsheathed.

97 CLOSEUP - VIC

He is so chagrined, and so unseated at what has happened, he looks almost ludicrous. It is a new way for us to see Vic. And makes him more human.

(CONTINUED)

97 CONTINUED:

VIC
(innocently)
That was awful!

SPIKE
You ever touch me again, punk,
I'll kick off your kneecaps.

VIC
But... but you're a chick!
You been handed around... you
must have...

BLOOD
(filter)
She's a virgin. Leave her
alone.

Vic regains some of his previous superior attitude.

VIC
I've had enough of this. Come
on, let's get out of here;
leave this lousy broad by
herself.

SPIKE
You're the one's leaving, pukey.
Blood and me are partners.

VIC
Blood and I...
(then he stops,
horrified)
Blood and you?!?
(beat, to
Blood)
Blood, what is this? I've been
looking for you for a month...

BLOOD
(filter)
I found a new partner, Albert,
old chum.

SPIKE
Albert? I thought his name
was Vic?

VIC
(jumps on it)
See? See? We're still
partners! You called me
"Albert".
(MORE)

(CONTINUED)

97 CONTINUED (2):

VIC (cont'd)
(beat, to Spike)
He calls me Albert, because it's a joke; it's an iron thing from this guy who wrote dog books before the Third War... Tell her, Blood.

BLOOD
(filter, wearily)
An ironic thing, not an iron thing. And his name was Albert Payson Terhune. And it's all done with us, Vic. We lost faith with one another.

VIC
No, Blood, it'll still be a good deal, you'll see...

Blood gets up and starts to trot away. Both of them look at him.

SPIKE
Hey, where you goin'?

VIC
Hey, c'mere! We got to settle this now!

Blood keeps going, doesn't turn around. SHOOT PAST THEM to his shaggy behind, bopping off toward the under-brush.

BLOOD
(filter)
I'm going to look for a fire hydrant. Try not to make me an orphan till I get back.

And he's gone, leaving them alone -- facing each other.

98 thru 100 FULL SCENE WITH INTERCUTS

Darkness but heavily moonlit among the trees on the rim. They stare at each other surlily. Vic tries to be very nonchalant. He turns away from her pointedly. She just stands with arms folded across her breasts, watching him.

SPIKE
(finally, mean)
He's all done with you.

(CONTINUED)

98 thru 100 CONTINUED:

VIC
You know, at first I didn't like you a lot. Now I really want to dance on your face.

SPIKE
Talk big, little fella. The dog's still with me.

VIC
Why don't you go hire on with some roverpack that needs an ugly chick to use for barter. Huh, why don'cha?

SPIKE
No wonder you need the dog so much. Only way you can handle somebody is bigmouth him to death.

Vic takes a step toward her... his only response to anger is frustration and instant mayhem. Spike puts her hand on the sheathed knife. Vic looks around, can't find any exit from his frustration, kicks the ashes of the fire. CAMERA PANS PAST HIM and MOVES IN SLOWLY to show Blood, sitting in the bushes, watching Vic and Spike.

101 SPIKE - VIC IN B.G.

as she goes to her pack and takes out a dirty old chamois cloth. She squats down and reaches for the laser rifle. Vic tenses. She snickers and doesn't even look up.

SPIKE
(continuing)
Take it easy, hero. I won't waste you till Blood says it's okay.
(beat)
That animal's got a stupid soft streak in him.

VIC
(defensive)
Where do you come off talking to me like that? Blood and I, we've been together two years. We're partners.

She doesn't answer him, just keeps polishing the weird futuristic weapon. Vic watches.

(CONTINUED)

101 CONTINUED:

VIC
(continuing; surly, but making conversation)
What is that dumb-lookin' thing?

SPIKE
You talkin' to me?

VIC
No, I'm talking to fat old Fellini down there.
(still no reply)
Well, what is it?

SPIKE
Blood calls it a laser rifle.

Vic is suddenly fascinated, like a child.

VIC
Oh, <u>yeah</u>!!! Wow, I've heard about those. Can I see it?

She looks at him like he's sprung a leak. His enthusiasm vanishes instantly as he realizes what he's asked.

VIC
(continuing)
Mmm. No, I guess not.
(then Sour Grapes)
Don't make any difference. Stupid thing's no good for close work. Too much power, way I hear it.

At that moment, Blood comes out of the bushes where he's been sitting, watching them. Clearly, he has been giving them a chance to get to know each other -- to let their natural antipathy sink to a lower level.

102 BLOOD - UP SHOT TO VIC AND SPIKE

BLOOD
(filter; brightly)
Well, how are Mommy and Daddy getting along?

SPIKE
(without looking up)
Ready to let me burn this creep?

(CONTINUED)

102 CONTINUED:

BLOOD
(filter)
Not just yet, Spike.
(beat)
I want to talk to you two.

VIC
No time to talk. We've got to get some ammo. Let's go.

BLOOD
(filter)
Sit down, Vic. I want to talk to both of you.

Vic stands there defiantly for a moment till Blood looks at him pointedly. Vic squats, then sits cross-legged.

BLOOD
(continuing; filter)
Things are changing. Neither of you has ever had to work with someone else. Just Vic and me, and you all alone, Spike. But it can't go on like that.

VIC
(filter)
Aw, c'mon, Blood; it's worked fine except for a couple of little arguments.

BLOOD
(filter)
No, I mean all over the country, Vic. Things have to change. In a little while there'll be no room for solos or roverpacks.

103 ANGLE - PAST BLOOD TO VIC - SPIKE IN B.G.

VIC
(filter)
You mean Fellini's going to take over everything?

BLOOD
(filter)
No, I mean people are going to start rebuilding.

SPIKE
Rebuilding what?

(CONTINUED)

103 CONTINUED:

BLOOD
(filter)
Rebuilding the world, Spike. Homes and factories and roads and farms and no more guns and no more digging in garbage cans for food.

VIC
(filter; toward Heaven)
Here we go again, folks: "Over the hill" -- where the deer and the antelope play, and everybody grows food in the ground.

SPIKE
Shut up, dummy. Let the dog talk.

VIC
(filter)
"The dog", as you call him, Lady Pinhead, has a name. He's also full of it.

Blood's head snaps around. Vic catches himself.

BLOOD
(filter)
Full of it or not, Vic, the three of us have a far better chance of making it, of surviving -- of perhaps being one of the first units to start living like civilized, rational creatures, if we link up.

Vic cuts him off, a wave of the hand, a dismissing gesture.

VIC
(aloud, amazed)
The <u>three</u> of us? Me, with <u>her</u>?!

SPIKE
No way. Forget it. I'm out of it.

Blood gets up, walks toward the bushes again. He stops, looks back at Vic.

BLOOD
Vic, come on -- I want to talk to you. Spike... just wait.

(CONTINUED)

103 CONTINUED (2):

He goes off into the bushes. Vic looks at Spike. She gives him a dirty look, then cursing beneath his breath, gets up and walks INTO CAMERA.

CUT TO:

104 EXT. CLEARING IN BUSHES - PAST BLOOD IN F.G.

TO Vic brushing his way through the foliage. He comes into the clearing, stands with legs apart, fists on hips, angry.

VIC
Boy, this is some reunion.

BLOOD
(filter)
I'm glad to see you, Vic. I've worried about you.

VIC
Not enough to come looking, though, I guess.

BLOOD
(filter)
You were pretty down the last time we talked. You wanted me to leave, so I left. It wasn't my idea, remember?

VIC
Yeah... well... I was just tired of it all.

BLOOD
(filter)
They call it battle fatigue. Two years without any peace...
(beat)
... Nonetheless... we have to stay alive... that's what it's all about, Vic.

VIC
(reluctantly)
Yeahhh, I know... only...

BLOOD
(filter)
Only nothing, old chum. That woman out there is tough and smart and just what we need.
(MORE)

(CONTINUED)

104 CONTINUED:

BLOOD (Cont'd)
Now you're going to have to get used to the idea. If I had to choose between you, I'd have a tough time.

VIC
After two years, all we been through, it'd be tough to choose?

BLOOD
(filter)
She's very pro-survival, Vic -- And you've been acting a little off-center lately. Don't make me choose. Back off. We'll make a fine team.

VIC
She'll never go for it. She hates me.

BLOOD
(filter)
All I ask is that you try. For my sake. I need both of you.

Vic shakes his head in mild bother, trying to conceal his pleasure at being back with Blood, trying to keep up a Macho pose; but it's clear from his resigned expression that he'll at least try.

VIC
Oh, what the heck... okay. I'll try. But tell her to let up on me. I don't have to take that stuff from no chick.

Blood wags his tail. Vic smiles. He bends down and scratches him behind the ear.

VIC
(continuing)
How's our friend, the flea?

BLOOD
(filter)
You mean Franz Kafka?

VIC
Hey, you named him at last. I was wondering what you'd call him.

(CONTINUED)

104 CONTINUED (2):

BLOOD
(filter)
And if you're a very nice boy
I'll explain who Franz Kafka
was.
(beat)
Now let's go back and try to
sign the Magna Carta.

They start back through the bushes.

105 SAME AS SHOT 96

as they emerge from the bushes. Spike is lying on her stomach, the laser rifle aimed in the other direction. As they emerge, she cranes around and frantically makes a "get down" motion. They drop.

VIC
(filter)
What's the matter with her?
Can't she teep us?

BLOOD
(filter)
Not yet. She doesn't know she
can do it. I'll teach her.

106 FULL SHOT

MOVING IN ON TREES BEYOND the area where Vic, Spike and Blood lie watching. SHOT INCLUDES THEM as it BEGINS AND MOVES PAST VIC AND BLOOD FIRST (as we HEAR V.O. dialogue) THEN UP TO AND PAST SPIKE so we FOCUS ON AREA BEYOND.THEM. We see movement out there... something going past.

VIC (V.O.)
(filter)
What is it, Blood?

BLOOD (V.O.)
(filter)
Half a dozen rovers. Carrying
something... No, carrying
somebody.

CAMERA HOLDS on the group working its way around the side of the bowl, passing very near our three.

VIC (V.O.)
(filter)
Scouting pack? Maybe it's a
deer.

(CONTINUED)

106 CONTINUED:

BLOOD (V.O.)
(filter)
No, it's a human. Dying, I think.

Vic and Blood MOVE INTO SHOT as rovers pass close. They move close enough that we can see them fairly clearly by moonlight. Six mean-looking rovers, each wearing a thick black leather armband from wrist to mid-forearm.

VIC (V.O.)
(filter)
Lookit the wrist bands. That's some of Fellini's people.

Then he sees what they're carrying: A young boy, draped across the shoulders of four rovers like an ancient Aztec offering, his arms hanging down, the body limp. One of the rovers wears a familiar battered, chewed-up Stetson. Another carries a long metal instrument on a cord, its surface of aluminum and glass keys shining in the moonlight. They vanish over the crest of the bowl, heading down. There is a painful MOAN from Vic.

VIC
(continuing;
filter)
Ohhh, God!

He leaps to his feet and rushes toward Spike.

107 SAME AS SCENE 96

He starts to get up as Vic comes straight across the little clearing without hesitation. He kicks the laser rifle away from her and grabs her scope-mounted .22 rifle. He throws down on her.

BLOOD
(filter)
Vic, what are you --

VIC
I know him! He's a minstrel!

SPIKE
You sneaky creep! Gimme my rifle!

Vic moves toward the edge of the rim, keeping low.

VIC
You were right, Blood. I was out of slugs. But this ought to do for now.

(CONTINUED)

107 CONTINUED:

BLOOD
(filter)
What are you going to do?
Don't be crazy.

... But he turns quickly and vanishes over the side, into the darkness. Spike scrambles for the laser rifle and starts to aim after him, into the darkness. Blood dashes across the clearing and bumps her hard enough to throws her off-balance. She spins on the dog, furious.

BLOOD
(continuing;
filter)
We've got to stop him!

SPIKE
Damned right! He's got my rifle.

BLOOD
(filter)
No, not kill him... stop him!
We've got to save him, Spike.

SPIKE
Are you nuts? He stole my rifle!

BLOOD
(filter, frantic)
Spike, we need him! Spike,
please help me save him! He's
my friend.

She looks down at him.

SPIKE
I thought so.

BLOOD
(filter; softly)
Won't you be my friend, too?

They look at each other for a long moment. Then she nods.

SPIKE
Now I understand why he's so
angry you're with me. You're
a helluva dog, Blood.

He wags his tail, pants happily, and starts off over the edge of the rim.

(CONTINUED)

107 CONTINUED (2):

BLOOD
(filter)
Come on. Follow me... I'll track a clear passage down there.

CUT TO:

108 ARRIFLEX - WITH VIC

as he rushes down the hill into the bowl. CAMERA WITH HIM in all its jerky, action-indicating MOVEMENT. He rushes down through the darkness, toward the campfires in the bowl. We GO WITH HIM in a long, FOLLOWING SHOT that shows how large the bowl actually is.

HARD CUT TO:

109 EXT. SLOPE - NIGHT - UP SHOT - THE SLOPE - ROVERS IN F.G.

We see the procession carrying Poke COMING TOWARD US and HOLD it for a beat as <u>suddenly</u> a whirlwind rushes down off the hill and is on top of them before they know what's happening. It is Vic!

110 thru 116 SAME AS 109 WITH INTERCUTS - ARRIFLEX

TILT ANGLES AND SMASH INTERCUTS to indicate wild movement but sufficient to mask the specifics of this encounter.

Vic is on them, whirling the rifle to club one, suddenly spinning to use it as a quarter staff against the rifle of the other rover. Poke is flung down, rolls into darkness.

Three more ROVERS come out of the darkness and jump into the fray. Vic is hurled to the ground, two rovers aim their hand guns at him while two others hold him down.

A BLUR OF FUR leaps out of the darkness. Blood is on them, and... arms, legs, bodies, furry balls, go every which way. A mad tangle, a jumble, nothing distinct, but <u>much</u> action.

Then Spike is there, leveling the laser rifle and we get an even MORE FRAGMENTED VIEW OF THE ACTION as the CAMERA TILTS AND WHIP PANS and GOES OUT OF FOCUS so we do not see her FIRE the weapon at anyone specifically, but see a BURST OF GOLD AND BLUE AND RED LIQUID LIGHT (SPECIAL OPTICAL EFFECT) and we HEAR a scream and then there are rovers running away and Spike and Blood are there with Vic on the ground. Spike grabs up her .22 and slings it.

117 VIC

as he scrambles to his feet, goes sliding and running down the hill to a stand of low bushes where Poke's body has come to rest, tossed unceremoniously into the thicket by his roll down the hill. Vic slides to his knees, drags him out of the bushes. It is dark, but there is sufficient moonlight to see the young boy is broken and dying.

VIC
Poke... hey...

The eyes unglaze and the little minstrel looks up.

POKE
(weakly)
I know... you...

VIC
Why? Why'd they hurt you?
Nobody's s'posed to hurt a minstrel...

POKE
Wh-where's my...
(reaches out)

Vic looks around wildly, sees the theramin lying above them on the hill.

VIC
(filter; frantically)
Blood! The song-thing, the metal thing there... quick!

Blood goes to it, takes the thong in his mouth and drags the theramin to Vic. Vic pulls it to him and lays it on Poke's chest.

POKE
(faintly)
Th-That's swell... now I can make up a s-s --

He dies. HOLD for three beats as Vic holds the dead boy in his arms and then CAMERA PULLS UP AND BACK and we:

DISSOLVE TO:

118 SAME AS SCENE 104 - CLEARING IN BUSHES 118

as Vic shovels the last dirt onto the mound. He drops the shovel and picks up the slim theremin. He jams it into the soft dirt near the head of the grave; a marker.

(CONTINUED)

118 CONTINUED:

Spike and Blood stand watching him for a moment.

BLOOD
(filter)
I can't fault you for trying to help a friend. It's not like you, but maybe after all this time what I've been saying about people acting kinder is taking hold.
(beat)
But that was a stupid move, Vic. You could've gotten us all killed.

VIC
(softly)
I -- I know. It was just seeing him being carried around like ... like meat.

He looks around, sees Spike watching him malevolently.

VIC
(continuing;
to Blood)
Did she... ?

BLOOD
(filter)
Yes. She saved your hide.

VIC
I was wrong. You're tough, and like Blood says -- I owe you. You can join up with me and...

But he doesn't get it finished. Without warning, Spike swings a roundhouse and clips him full on the jaw. Vic goes over backwards and is out unconscious again.

CAMERA PANS TO BLOOD AND ZOOMS INTO CLOSEUP.

BLOOD (V.O.)
(wearily)
Oh, my.

HOLD on Blood for several beats then FADE TO BLACK.

FADE OUT.

END OF ACT FIVE

ACT SIX

FADE IN:

119 EXT. WOODED AREA - NIGHT - MED. SHOT - LEAN-TO

Spike has erected a structure so they can have a fire and it won't be seen. CAMERA COMES IN SLOWLY on the lean-to as we HEAR Blood and Spike in FILTER V.O.

SPIKE (V.O.)
(filter)
So that's how you talk mind-to-mind.

BLOOD (V.O.)
(filter)
You're a quick learner, Spike.

SPIKE (V.O.)
(filter)
You teach good, Blood.

BLOOD (V.O.)
(filter)
I teach well, not good. "Well" is an adverb, "good" is an adjective. An adverb can only be used to modify a verb, or another adjective.

SPIKE (V.O.)
(filter)
What's "modify" mean?

BLOOD (V.O.)
(filter)
That'll be our first lesson in grammar. There are more important things right now.

SPIKE (V.O.)
(filter; reminded)
Yeah, you know, there's something I been wanting to ask you?

BLOOD (V.O.)
(filter)
What's that?

SPIKE (V.O.)
(filter)
That crazy old man, Partridge? You know, all that history stuff he was telling me? Was all that true?

(CONTINUED)

84.

119 CONTINUED:

BLOOD (V.O.)
(filter)
Yes.

SPIKE (V.O.)
(filter)
I been thinking about it. But it gets me all confused. Makes me want to ask more questions.

CAMERA HAS NOW COME IN FULLY on the lean-to and we:

CUT TO:

120 INT. LEAN-TO

Vic lies unconscious.

BLOOD
(filter)
Such as?

SPIKE
(filter)
Well, like this mind-to-mind thing we do. Teeping? And when you get a feel that there's somebody around... you called it pinging?

BLOOD
(filter)
Right... and?

SPIKE
(filter)
Well, how come it is that dogs can do it?

BLOOD
(filter)
It happened during the war. But it's hard to explain. I might use words you won't understand.

SPIKE
(filter)
So I'll ask you what they mean. Tell me.

(CONTINUED)

120 CONTINUED:

BLOOD
(filter)
Well, let's see. Where to begin. Okay -- There was once a science of living things called genetics. And people who studied it found something called DNA.

SPIKE
(filter)
What's that?

BLOOD
(filter)
Well, just think of it as the basic material we're made of. And these geneticists, as they were called, they mixed up the DNA in different ways. Re-combining it.

SPIKE
(filter)
Okay, I think I understand so far.

BLOOD
(filter)
So they recombined the genes and changed them... mutated them. And they injected certain intelligent breeds of dogs with the spinal fluid of dolphins.

SPIKE
(filter)
What's a dolphin?

BLOOD
(filter)
It swims in the ocean. Looks like a fish, but it's like you and Vic, a mammal. Very smart.

SPIKE
(filter)
And dogs got the ability to teep.

BLOOD
(filter)
Correct.
(MORE)

(CONTINUED)

86.

120 CONTINUED (2):

BLOOD (Cont'd)
My great-great-great-grandfather, Ahbhu, he was the first. Then, using X-rays and drugs, the gene change mutation bred true. And here I am.

SPIKE
(filter)
So how come everyone can't do it?

BLOOD
(filter)
It was never universal. There were only a few soldiers whose DNA could adapt for telepathy. Same for dogs. Some dogs can only talk to certain people.

SPIKE
(filter; awed)
You know, you're really smart, Blood.

BLOOD
(filter)
Smart enough to get you to hook up with me and Vic?

SPIKE
(filter)
And what happens when he starts to act like every other guy I've ever seen?

BLOOD
(filter)
He won't.

SPIKE
(filter)
How do I stop it? Chain his hands together? This creep looks to me like no better than any of the others.

BLOOD
(filter)
He is. He's smarter, quicker...

SPIKE
(filter)
I haven't seen any sign of it.

(CONTINUED)

120 CONTINUED (3):

BLOOD
(filter)
He is, Spike. Because I taught him. The way I'm going to teach you.

SPIKE
(filter)
I don't know how you talked me into this. But God help you if it don't work out, Blood.

BLOOD
Doesn't work out, not don't work out. And it'll be okay -- I promise you.

121 ANOTHER ANGLE - PAST SPIKE - FAVORING VIC

He stirs, begins to sit up groggily.

SPIKE
(filter)
Here he comes. It's your game now.

Vic sits up, and then holds his head. He moans.

VIC
Ohhh... water...

Spike fills a canteen cup from a canteen, comes over to him and kneels down. CAMERA IN on them as he looks up at her with something between fear and trepidation. She takes a tiny bit of pity on him when he cannot raise up enough to si from the cup, lifts his head, and tilts the cup so he can drink. Then she lowers him gently, and stares at him for a moment. It might be the moment in which she sees him for the first time as a human being, and not as another potentia killer and rapist. She stays that way another beat, then gets up and retreats to the far side of the lean-to. Blood moves in and sits down.

BLOOD
(filter; method-ically)
She can fight.

VIC
(nods reluctantly)
She can fight.

BLOOD
(filter)
You're not as smart as you think you are.

(CONTINUED)

121 CONTINUED:

VIC
(sighing)
Sometimes I'm stupid.

BLOOD
(filter)
We have a better chance of finding "over the hill" -- not to mention simply staying alive, if we join forces.

Vic is silent.

BLOOD
(continuing; filter)
We have a better chance of --

VIC
Okay, okay. I hate it, but as usual you're right.

BLOOD
(filter)
You will not touch her.

VIC
That's for sure!

BLOOD
(filter)
Have something to eat, and then we'll figure out a way to get into that warehouse.

Vic closes his eyes. Finally, he exhales his breath, indicating he accepts Blood's terms, purses his lips and nods. He gets up and goes to the opened cans of food. He lifts one and looks at it.

VIC
(to Spike)
Were these mine or yours?

BLOOD
(filter; before Spike can answer)
Ours.

VIC
(bitterly)
Right.

He sits down and begins digging out food with his fingers. No one speaks for a few moments. We can HEAR the night beyond the lean-to: Crickets, birds, bullfrogs.

122 BLOOD

BLOOD
(filter)
All right. Pragmatically, the situation is this... correct me if I miss anything --
(beat)
Vic is out of ammunition, and we don't have any 30.06 loads, or .45's. Only .22's and the laser rifle.
(beat)
We have a little food left, putting both our supplies together; but that'll be running out very soon.

VIC
There's plenty of everything down there in that warehouse.

SPIKE
How do you know that for sure?

Vic looks at her with annoyance. He answers reluctantly.

VIC
I've been around here for a week, trying to figure a way in. I, uh, got some data from a solo I met!

SPIKE
(chilly)
Yeah? How do we know he was tellin' the truth?

VIC
I asked him a couple of times.

There is a hidden meaning that escapes no one.

BLOOD
(filter)
What else?

VIC
Well, they started arriving about a month or two ago. Fellini heard about it from some minstrel and got here fast. Found a small roverpack trying to break in through the roof and killed them all. But before he could get in, others started showing up.

BLOOD
(filter)
And it's been a standoff ever since.

(CONTINUED)

122 CONTINUED:

ANGLE HAS WIDENED to include the three of them, but still features Blood, who is running the show now. Vic nods. He finishes eating, going through every can for what leftovers he can find. He turns them upside-down and shakes them -- He's unhappy they had their fill before he came to.

SPIKE
Then that does it. No way in.
So what good does our joining up
together do? We're only three.

BLOOD
(filter)
Hmmm.

VIC
What's that mean -- hmmm?

He falls on his back, legs in the air, and a soft humming SOUND can be heard. Spike looks alarmed.

VIC
(continuing)
Don't worry. He's thinking.

SPIKE
Does he always do that?

VIC
Only when it's a strain, a big
think.
(beat)
Disgusting, ain't it.

SPIKE
Not <u>ain't</u>. <u>Isn't</u> it.

He gives her a class one dirty look.

123 HIGH SHOT - LOOKING DOWN - FEATURING BLOOD

He lies there for several beats, humming, then rights himself and starts toward the exit to the lean-to.

VIC
(filter)
Where you goin'?

BLOOD
(filter)
When was the last time you had
some cow's milk?

(CONTINUED)

123 CONTINUED:

VIC
(filter; perplexed)
Maybe a year ago. What's that got to do with anything?

BLOOD
(filter)
Well, I was going to answer you with an enigmatic quote from Louis Pasteur, but then you'd have only asked me who Louis Pasteur was, and I'd have had to tell you he was the man who discovered that bacteria produced certain diseases -- one of which was in milk, and then I would have said that Pasteur once made the remark -- "Chance favors the prepared mind" -- and -- as I am now doing -- I would have sauntered away into the night, leaving you confused enough that you wouldn't slaughter each other till I got back.

And he saunters out of the lean-to, into the night. HOLD on Vic and Spike -- She looking totally confused; he looking much put-upon.

VIC
Don't worry, it never gets any easier to take.

DISSOLVE TO:

124 EXT. ROVERPAK CAMP - SHOOTING PAST DOBERMAN

A couple of tents, a bunch of feet sticking out of the tents, some SNORING. A fire being tended by a sleeping rover sentry and a wide-awake, extremely mean-looking Doberman... who suddenly perks up his head and stares into the darkness beyond the fire. A VOICE comes out of the darkness.

BLOOD
(filter)
Good evening. Nice night, isn't it?

The Doberman stares into the darkness, and now we can see -- faintly -- a pair of bright little eyes. The Doberman answers in a voice faintly tinged with a Bavarian accent. (NOTE: It is imperative that there be nothing "funny" about this voice. The Bavarian heritage should be there, but as easily accepted as Blood's Americanized voice.)

(CONTINUED)

92.

124 CONTINUED:

WOLF
(filter)
How did you creep up on me?

BLOOD
(filter)
Listen, Bruno --

WOLF
(filter)
My name is Wolf, not Bruno.

BLOOD
(filter)
Short for Wolfgang, perhaps?

WOLF
(filter)
I am of exceeding good stock.

BLOOD
(filter; imatiently)
No doubt. Listen, kiddo, how goes it around here? Enough food? The tempers of your rovers getting short? They kicking you a little too much?

WOLF
(filter; haught-ily)
I serve. I do not ask questions, I do not question decisions.

BLOOD
(filter)
That's terrific. Really a bit of the old terrific. A friend to man.

WOLF
(filter)
Das ist how I vas trained.

BLOOD
(filter)
Yeah, right. But wouldn't you like to get a full belly, and then move out, get back to your turf?

WOLF
(filter)
Who, it is, you are?

Blood creeps in a little closer. The Doberman does not move. Should he jump, he would no doubt give Blood one hell of a fight. It is this restrained power that informs Wolf's attitudes.

(CONTINUED)

124 CONTINUED (2):

BLOOD
(filter)
I'm just a wayfaring stranger, doing his best to be a Force for Good in his Own Time.

WOLF
(filter)
I do not understand vat it is you say. I vill signal my master and raise the alarm.

BLOOD
(filter)
Not too smart.

WOLF
(filter)
Vas is loss???

BLOOD
(filter)
Wouldn't you much rather look like a champ? Bring your master and the rest of the roverpack a way of having all that food in there?

WOLF
(filter)
You know such a ting?

BLOOD
(filter)
What do I look like -- just another pretty face? Of course I know a way.

Wolf sits up and listens attentively.

WOLF
(filter)
I vill attend vat you say.

BLOOD
(filter)
Swell, because I've got a bunch of other mutts to see tonight, and frankly, I could do with some sleep.
(beat)
Okay. First you go to your master and you say...

DISSOLVE TO:

125 INT. LEAN-TO - EARLY MORNING - MOUTH OF LEAN-TO LOOKING IN - SPIKE AND VIC

each wrapped in soggy blanket or sleeping bag, both SNORING loudly. But as Blood comes INTO SHOT in f.g. they both start awake; Spike with the laser rifle in her mitts, and Vic with Spike's .22 leveled. They relax as they see it is the dog.

BLOOD
(filter; wearily, sarcastic)
Oh no, don't arise on my behalf.

He flops down wearily.

SPIKE
Where were you all night?

BLOOD
(filter)
Talking to the League of Nations. Did you ever try carrying on an intelligent conversation with an Akita? Between the Japanese accent and all that "honorable ancestor" nonsense, it's a wonder my brains haven't been puree'd.

VIC
Come on, Blood, what's happening?

BLOOD
(filter)
Softly, Albert, softly. I have a vicious headache right behind my left eye. I'm tired and hungry.

VIC
You're always hungry.

BLOOD
(filter)
That was high on my list of utterly classless remarks.

He settles down and seems to be going to sleep.

SPIKE
Blood... ?!!

BLOOD
(filter; somno-lently)
I will sleep now. If anyone comes around to see me, wake me.

(CONTINUED)

125 CONTINUED:

And he goes to sleep. Vic and Spike stare at each other as IRIS IN ON BLOOD TO BLACK AND IRIS OUT TO:

126 EXT. WOODED AREA SEEN AS NIGHT IN SCENE 119 - DAY

as three rover dogs trot up to a perimeter circle around the lean-to. A huge German Shepherd, an Akita, and Wolfgang the Doberman. They sit and watch the lean-to.

WOLF
(filter; shouts)
Herr Blood! Kommen see aussen!

They wait. After a moment, Blood emerges with Vic and Spike behind him. Speaking, he trots over to them and they form a small group as Spike and Vic watch from the lean-to. CAMERA ANGLE NARROWS to the group.

BLOOD
(filter)
Hi, fellows. What's new?

AKITA
(filter; Oriental accent)
Blessings of the day to you, good messenger.

BLOOD
(filter; wearily)
Please! Will you! Give me a break. Wolf, you speak for the delegation.

WOLF
(filter)
I am honored.
(beat)
Our assembled roverpaks have agreed to your master's suggestion. We meet on the open plain at high noon.
(beat)
One representative and dog -- no weapons.

BLOOD
(filter)
Right. See you down there.

The dogs rise, turn and leave. Blood returns to Vic and Spike.

127 THREE SHOT - FAVORING VIC

as Blood comes up to them and sits. He looks up.

VIC
What was that?

BLOOD
(filter)
Peace party.

SPIKE
Blood, you'd better tell us what's happening.

BLOOD
(filter)
Well, it's not good to let humans think we dogs are smarter than they think we are -- present company exempted, of course -- so I went down last night and suggested a parley.

VIC
A what?

BLOOD
(filter)
Parley. Conference. Communal and group discussion. A sodality meeting.
(beat)
Drop the rifle, get your canteen and a couple of cans of food, and let's go.

SPIKE
Why him? I'm as much a leader of this group as he is.

VIC
No way, broad.

SPIKE
(to Blood)
Tell it to shut it's face, before I bust it in the mouth.

VIC
Listen, woman, I don't have to take any of that --

SPIKE
(to Blood)
Tell it I'm going, and it can just sit here quietly.

(CONTINUED)

127 CONTINUED:

BLOOD
(filter; to Vic)
She says to tell you she's going
and you --

VIC
(screaming)
I hear her, I hear her!

BLOOD
(filter)
Except, he's right this time,
Spike. Think about it.

She stops, reins in her anger, and thinks. After several beats she nods.

SPIKE
They wouldn't respect a woman and
we wouldn't have as strong a
voice.

BLOOD
(filter; warmly)
You know, I like you more and
more every day, kiddo.

Vic snorts. He stamps his foot impatiently.

BLOOD
(continuing; filter)
Okay, Vic, let's go.

He starts off, with Vic beside him. Then stops.

BLOOD
(continuing; filter)
Take off the .45 and leave it.

VIC
It's empty.

BLOOD
(filter)
All the more reason.

Vic drops it, and starts out. Blood stops. He goes back to Spike and she leans over as he speaks to her. Vic is almost over the edge of the rim, a distance from them.

128 PAST VIC - TO BLOOD

as the dog finishes saying whatever it is he's said to Spike. She nods, and the dog trots over to Vic. He keeps going, toward the rim of the bowl, and Vic runs after him as CAMERA TURNS TO GO WITH THEM.

129 VIC AND BLOOD - ARRIFLEX

as they go over the rim and start down. CAMERA CLOSE WITH THEM.

VIC
(filter)
What kept you?

BLOOD
(filter)
Just some last minute instructions on how to protect the area while we're gone.

VIC
(filter)
Why don't I believe that?

BLOOD
(filter)
You're a basically suspicious type.

VIC
(filter)
Y'know, ever since you been with that chick you've gotten really sneaky.

BLOOD
(filter)
To quote Sir Walter Scott, 1771 to 1832 -- "Recollect that the Almighty, who gave the dog to be companion of our pleasures and our toils, hath invested him with a nature noble and incapable of deceit."

VIC
(filter)
And humble to a fault.

BLOOD
(filter)
Humble won't buy it when we're talking to Fellini.

Vic stops. Blood keeps going, realizes Vic has stopped -- and comes back to him.

BLOOD
(continuing; filter)
Now what's the matter?

(CONTINUED)

129 CONTINUED:

VIC
(filter)
You want me to go down there and talk to Fellini?

BLOOD
(filter)
And maybe twenty others.

VIC
(aloud)
Fellini hates me. He's been trying to kill me for years.

BLOOD
(filter)
That's only because he doesn't understand what a wonderful person you are.

VIC
You're tryin' to get me slaughtered!

BLOOD
(filter)
Gird thy loins, stalwart one.

VIC
Knock it off! I ain't going down there.

BLOOD
(filter)
I'm sure Spike will understand.

Vic stares at him a long moment, then snarls and starts walking down the hill again. Blood chuckles in V.O. and follows him. CAMERA HOLDS them as they walk swiftly away down the slope and we FADE TO BLACK and...

FADE OUT.

END OF ACT SIX

ACT SEVEN

FADE IN:

130 NEUTRAL MEETING AREA - ON THE PLAIN - DAY

High noon. The bulk of the buried warehouse rising behind the gathering of solos and rovers sitting in a big circle. CAMERA PANS AROUND so we can see each representative, including two tough-looking women sitting individually at two poles of the compass, the men a little apart from them. The group is perhaps thirty in all. Mean, young, dressed individually. And FELLINI, wearing his Napoleon style admiral's hat with the cockatoo feathers, his cape, his high boots, his ragtag finery. He is far older than anyone there, perhaps forty, perhaps fifty, but looking old and crusty and meaner than spit. Everyone else there is alone or with a dog. Only Fellini has three SIDE-BOYS with him; they are bare-chested, ripplingly muscular, tanned and stupid-looking. But super-spit mean. All of Fellini's people wear that black leather wrist-band. CAMERA COMES TO FELLINI and HOLDS so we can have a good long look at him, just as his face breaks into an evil, gap-toothed smile.

FELLINI
(mock jocular)
Well, well, well. Look who's here! Hello, boy! Good to see you again! Come on in and sit yourself down!

131 REVERSE ANGLE - FELLINI'S P.O.V.

Vic coming in across the no-man's-land to the circle that has been set up. Blood at his side. The other rovers turn to look. One of them, STARKIO, a black rover with a livid scar down his face and all dressed in black, a boy of perhaps seventeen, with a Great Dane beside him, rises and moves out a few steps to greet Vic as he comes in. They shake hands solemnly, indicating they have met before and are friends, if not allies. Starkio comes back to the circle and Vic sits down beside him.

132 PAST VIC - FAVORING FELLINI

as the solo checks out the small traveling litter-chair in which fat old Fellini sits, and the two brass-bound sideboys with him.

(CONTINUED)

132 CONTINUED:

FELLINI
I should've known, boy. It must of been you and that dingo-dog of yourn that got up this meeting.

VIC
I see you're still cheating on the rules, old man.
(beat)
Way I heard it, each roverpak or solo sent one man and a dog.

FELLINI
Wellll... I'm an old, tired man, little fellah, and it's hard for me to get around without I'm helped by these boys. You know how it is.

VIC
I know _just_ how it is, jelly-belly.

BLOOD
(filter)
Vic! Careful!

FELLINI
Missed you, boy! Downright missed you. Did'ja enjoy all that food you stole from me?

VIC
The food _and_ the ammunition.

FELLINI
You know, boy, you cost me two good riflemen.

VIC
Oh? The second one died, too?

FELLINI
You shoulda heard him screamin' all night for a coupla nights till I had Victory here put him out of his misery.

He nods his head toward the taller of the two muscular side-boys. VICTORY is a behemoth. No neck, just a bull head sitting down on his shoulders, muscles oiled and rippling in his shoulders and back.

(CONTINUED)

132 CONTINUED (2):

VIC
Everybody says what a thoughtful guy you are, Fellini.

Another of the emissaries, CRICKET, speaks up.

CRICKET
How long is this gonna go on? I thought we came here to talk? If I didn't know better, I'd think you really like this solo, Fellini!

Another solo, BATTLE, joins in.

BATTLE
My dog told me this was an open parley. We gonna have to sit out here in the sun and listen to you two jerks fight?

BLOOD
(filter)
Okay, Vic. Just repeat what I tell you.

VIC
(filter)
Can any of them tune in on us?

BLOOD
(filter)
Maybe, but I don't think so.
(beat)
Tell them it's a standoff and we have to call a truce and work together.

VIC
I've been doing some heavy thinking about this situation. We've been here a month or two already... a lot of guys have tried to get in and been burned. So it's a standoff, and we got to start using our heads.

133 CIRCLE

SLOW PAN around circle as various solos and rovers speak, and Vic answers them behind Blood's coaching. They should be dressed in individual ways and each have a character trait expressed in their clothing and manner, at director's discretion.

(CONTINUED)

133 CONTINUED:

CHARLIE CHAN
Yeah? Well who pays for Benny Takeda?

BRONCO
You shouldn't'a sent him in and he wouldn't'a got blown away.

SWEET ALICE
I don't trust any of you slobs!

VORKIMER
(simultaneously)
My boys can make it on their own, we don't need no truce!

BIG DANNY
I'm solo. Who's to say I join in and get blown up? Huh, who? C'mon!

Blood's voice can be HEARD over the din as we come in CLOSE on Vic in PAN.

BLOOD'S VOICE
(filter)
Tell them about rebuilding. And do it right. As if you meant it.

VIC
Listen... listen to me... hey, shut up!

They fall silent. Fellini has a bemused expression as if he has the hoodoo sign on all of them, no matter what they say.

VIC
(continuing)
Maybe the time's come to stop all this solo against rover stuff. Maybe we ought to try to get together so we don't all starve to death or kill each other. This's a good place to start. There's enough food and ammo in there for all of us.

FELLINI
Just one thing wrong with that, boy.

VIC
Yeah, and what's that?

FELLINI
I want all of it. And I've got the firepower to take it.

(CONTINUED)

133 CONTINUED (2):

VORKIMER
And there's enough roverpaks here to stop you.

BIG DANNY
And enough solos all together to make sure!

VIC
See? It's nothin' for nobody unless we work out a way to do it. I say we talk it out and work up a system.
(beat)
All you people who want to try, just raise your hand.

Slowly, one by one, the hands go up. All but Sweet Alice and Fellini.

VIC
(continuing)
Okay. That's all but two of you. Now we're gonna talk, and if you don't wanna get left out, you talk too. That's called democracy, or majority rule... or somethin'.

Everybody nods as we:

SLOW DISSOLVE TO:

134 DIFFERENT ANGLE ON CIRCLE - SUNDOWN - FAVORING VIC

as we see that time has passed and they've obviously been working it out.

VIC
Then that settles it. We go in six at a time, two men... or women... to a team, with sacks. As much as you can carry in one trip, then the next shift of six teams goes in.
(beat)
How about you two?
(to Sweet Alice and Fellini)

SWEET ALICE
Okay, I guess. If my team goes in when The Flamingos go in, just to make sure none of you guys decide to supply women instead of food.

135 TWO-SHOT ACROSS CIRCLE - FELLINI AND VIC

as Vic turns to the fat man.

VIC
What've you got to say, Fellini?

FELLINI
Walll, boy, I guess you've all got me boxed in. So I'll go along with it on two conditions... otherwise I set up a crossfire'll do you _all_ in.

BRONCO
What conditions?

FELLINI
First of all, I get all the pudding. Every can of it.

CHARLIE CHAN
You _got_ to be crazy as a doodlebug, old man.

FELLINI
(disingenuous)
But I _love_ pudding.

BLOOD
(filter)
Careful, Vic. Stay out of it; let the others negotiate with him. That's a lot of hate for you there.

FLAMINGO
What's the other condition?

FELLINI
(points to Vic)
I want him.

STARKIO
Forget it! We're all even here!

VORKIMER
Whaddaya mean "you want him"?

FELLINI
This boy's been raiding my larder, shooting up my camp, raising hell with my rovers... I want him.

There is much _sotto voce_ ad lib around the circle. Vic and Blood sit silently. Vic starts to say something and Blood edges closer, indicating he should be silent.

136 THRU 142 SERIES OF RAPID INTERCUTS - ON ROVER & SOLO FACES

as they look at one another and their expressions harden. They have no stake in Vic, no allegiance (except Starkio), and they're not going to screw up their chance to get food without a fire-fight.

FELLINI
Everybody who agrees to my pudding and lettin' me have him, just raise your hand.

INTERCUT as the emissaries raise their hands.

143 FULL SHOT - THE CIRCLE - DYING SUN BEHIND THEM

as all hands in the circle go up but Starkio's.

144 ON BLOOD AND VIC

as Vic watches, starts to object.

BLOOD
(filter)
Don't object. Just go with it.

VIC
(filter)
That old honey-dipper'll stake me out and run bayonets through me!

BLOOD
(filter)
Let it go!

145 ON FELLINI

FELLINI
(joyful)
Well, boy, seems all your parley-people wanna give you up. You <u>mine</u> now, son.

BLOOD
(filter)
Ask for a one-on-one.

VIC
(filter)
Whaaaaaat!?! Are you nuts?!?

BLOOD
(filter)
Do it, Vic! I've got it figured.

(CONTINUED)

145 CONTINUED:

VIC
(filter)
I'll just bet you do, dog. You're gonna get me killed yet.
(aloud)
Okay, Fellini -- I won't fight it, but how about you give me a decent chance?

CAMERA BETWEEN FELLINI AND VIC.

FELLINI
Decent chance? You talkin' some fancy dancin' there, boy.

VIC
I say you're too yellow to give a guy a chance to save himself.

FELLINI
You got it right, son. I don't want you savin' yourself. I want to put some real hot fire to the soles of your feet. I want to hear you shiver and shake.

VIC
I say you're pretty tough and salty when you got all your beef around you. But you haven't got the gut for one on one.

FELLINI
(amazed)
With who?

VIC
With you, fat man.

FELLINI
(mock startled)
With me? That don't be no kind of challenge, boy. I'm just too old and soft. I'm a captain here, son, not some bean-field hand.

VIC
(to crowd)
Hey, wouldn't you people like to see a good fight? Huh, how about it?

He looks straight at Starkio. The black solo picks up on it, trying to aid his friend.

STARKIO
(loud)
Yeahhhh! I been sittin' around here on my tail too long without nothin' been happenin'! Howzabout a little show, everybody? A little entertainment!

(CONTINUED)

145 CONTINUED (2):

Starkio whips them up with enthusiasm. First one rover joins in, calling for the show, then another, then another, and soon the entire ring is clapping and yelling "fight, fight, fight, fight!" Fellini's face goes from angry to annoyed to bemused to thoughtfulness, and then he bursts out laughing with the nastiest laugh ever heard.

FELLINI
I agree! You been doggin' me so long, little fellah, it'll be nice seein' your nose down in the dirt a few times.
(beat)
But not me. I got just the bo to see you into this.
(beat)
You let me pick the man? You got the spunk for that, boy?

VIC
Name him.
(then, in filter to Blood)
I don't like this. A lot.

FELLINI
Victory! Do it to him!

And the huge colossus called Victory lumbers out into the center of the circle as Vic scrambles to his feet. The big bruiser (aged twenty or twenty-one) towers over Vic. Fellini's laugh roars out.

FELLINI
(continuing)
Put 'em up, boy! Put up your dukes!

VIC
(filter; to Blood)
I hope you're satisfied.

BLOOD
(filter)
Great. Just great. Just the way I planned it.

He tosses Blood a strained look as Victory lumbers toward him. And we:

DISSOLVE THROUGH TO:

146 EXT. NO-MAN'S LAND PARLEY CIRCLE - EVENING - EXTREME CLOSEUP - A PAIR OF THE BEADIEST, MOST MALEVOLENT EYES

you've ever seen.

(CONTINUED)

146 CONTINUED:

CAMERA PULLS BACK to show these are the piggy little eyes of Victory, standing there with his mightily-thewed arms swinging like scythes. CAMERA BACK TO FULL SHOT and we see that torches on stakes have been set up to mark the big circle. Vic is on the other side of the circle, shirt off, looking puny in the face of the man-mountain Victory. Fellini is drinking a warm beer and loving every minute of this. Starkio is serving as "second" for Vic, and looking terribly worried. Blood sits near.

STARKIO
He got a terrific reach on him.

VIC
How'd I get into this?

BLOOD
(filter)
Listen...

VIC
(filter)
It's listenin' to you that put me here. That monster's gonna pull my arms off and beat me to death with them.

BLOOD
(filter)
Just listen! Keep it going as long as you can.

VIC
(filter)
If I live that long.

BLOOD
(filter)
Keep away from him, keep it going, just waste a lot of time.

STARKIO
Blood tellin' you somethin'.

VIC
Yeah. He's big on advice.

FELLINI
Gentlemen, why don't we begin?

VIC
(shouts)
Why don't you get your fat gut out here and start, Fellini...?

(CONTINUED)

146 CONTINUED (2):

Victory moves in on him, circling. Vic gulps and moves in the opposite direction, widdershins, trying to keep out of his way. The crowd starts to cheer for blood.

147 ACTION WITH THE DUEL

(NOTE: this segment will, naturally, be handled wholly at director's discretion, entailing input from stuntmen and natural locations. Thus, only specific incident necessary for plot will be indicated here.)

Vic is smaller, but quicker. Victory has trouble getting his hands on the boy. But when Vic goes to punch him, he literally has to leap off the ground to reach Victory's face. Much scuffling in the dirt. Fellini throws the beer can, hitting Vic in the back. Vic turns, and Victory rushes him, grabbing him in a bear-hug, lifting him off the ground. Vic is facing forward and manages to kick backward between Victory's legs, pulling them both off-balance. They go down and Vic squirms loose. He knees the big man in the gut. Both are covered with dirt that sticks to them from their sweat. Vic is good at rolling and coming up feet-first, kicking like a mule. Victory is stunned, Vic moves in, punching him under the heart, in the sternum. But it doesn't seem to hurt the big man very much. He grabs Vic's arm and twists it back up behind him. This looks like the finish. Vic is in bad pain. Shouts from the crowd. Victory has Vic down on one knee, raises his ham-like fist for a punch straight down on Vic's head... a killing blow.

148 WITH BLOOD

as he bares his fangs, snarls and as CAMERA ANGLE WIDENS he LEAPS. High through the air and right onto Victory's shoulders. He starts biting Victory on the ear. The big man screams, drops Vic's arm and starts batting at Blood. But the dog leaps away and rushes across the circle.

149 FROM FELLINI ACROSS CIRCLE - PAST HIM IN F.G.

as Blood gallops toward him, getting big in FRAME. He jumps right onto Fellini's face, knocking him and his litter seat over backward. Fellini howls.

150 thru 155 SERIES OF INTERCUTS

TILT-ANGLE SHOTS and SUBLIMINAL FLASHES of Fellini thrashing in the dirt, his cape over his head...

Solos and rovers alike suddenly rushing into the fray...

Starkio locking his hands together and bashing the slowly recovering Victory...

Vic swinging wildly at anyone near him...

Blood dashing about barking, jumping on people, fleeing, finding a new target, wrecking havoc...

Other dogs fighting with each other...

Fellini's second side-boy grabbing Blood by the scruff of the neck, holding him up and away, Blood thrashing...

156 FULL SHOT - FAVORING FELLINI

as he manages to regain his footing, stands up, screaming mad. Three rovers have hold of the twitching Vic, two others sitting on Starkio.

FELLINI
I'll kill him! I'll kill 'em both!

He fumbles in the cape, and from a sewn-in pocket he pulls a pistol. He waves it around, still too furious to get his act together. Everyone is yelling, the din is tremendous.

Fellini aims the pistol at Vic as CAMERA MOVES IN FAST on the barrel and straight up the muzzle as we GO TO BLACK FRAME and

FADE TO BLACK

and

FADE OUT.

END ACT SEVEN

112.

ACT EIGHT

FADE IN:

157 EXT. PARLEY CIRCLE - LATER - CLOSEUP ON SWEET ALICE

screaming. She is screaming with the VOICE OF THE CROWD:

SWEET ALICE
Blow him away! Blow him away!

CAMERA PULLS BACK to show the entire crowd -- with the exception of Starkio -- all shouting for Fellini, who is still aiming at Vic, to shoot this troublesome solo.

CAMERA PANS ACROSS CROWD and COMES TO BLOOD, CLOSE.

BLOOD
(filter)
Vic! Listen! You've got to do this right...

158 ANOTHER ANGLE ON SCENE - FAVORING VIC

as he listens. The noise of the crowd and the screaming of Fellini is so loud it does not permit us -- or the viewer -- from hearing what Blood is telling Vic. But he is clearly listening to Blood's voice, and the ongoing turmoil permits us to understand something is in the wind. Vic nods slightly, then suddenly shouts:

VIC
(shouting)
Fellini! Fellini! Go ahead, kill us, shoot us right now!

Fellini is startled, hesitates a moment. The crowd falls silent. Starkio stops squirming under the rovers sitting on him. Blood is sanguine.

VIC
(continuing)
I know what you want to do with us! You ain't gonna do it, you pig! You ain't gonna throw us into that warehouse! So shoot us, shoot us now, you stinkin' fat slob! Shoot! Shoot!

Fellini looks perplexed. For all his rapaciousness, this isn't the brightest man in the world. He narrows his eyes and licks his lips. He walks over to Vic and looks at him. CAMERA IN ON THEM. Vic's face is frightened but there isn't the faintest hint of duplicity there.

(CONTINUED)

158 CONTINUED:

FELLINI
Boy... you're dead, mark it.
Either way, you're a dead thing.
But maybe a little later than sooner.

VIC
(tightly)
Get it done.
(beat)
Just put it up and do it!

FELLINI
You're really scared, ain't'cha,
boy?

VIC
Not of you.

FELLINI
And not of being shot, either, I
guess. But there's somethin' in
that warehouse that scares the
juice outta you, ain't there, boy?

VIC
No. Nothing. I never been in
there, how could I know what's
inside?

FELLINI
That's a good question.
(beat)
But I think you do know.
(beat)
What is it, boy?

Vic turns his head away. He won't talk.

FELLINI
(continuing; to crowd)
He knows somethin' we need to know.
There's a trick here. How come that
place's never been broke into? How
come such a big thing's never been
found before?
(beat)
He knows!

VORKIMER
Make him talk!

CHARLIE CHAN
Make him tell us!

(CONTINUED)

158 CONTINUED (2):

BATTLE
I ain't goin' in there till I find out what's inside!

FELLINI
Okay, boy. Start talkin'.

Vic won't speak. He looks terrified. Fellini turns to the battered Victory.

FELLINI
(continuing)
Open him up.

He turns and walks away, putting the gun back inside the cape. Victory passes him, going to Vic, as CAMERA GOES WITH FELLINI. The other side-boy sets up the litter chair and Fellini sits down, looking tense and mean. We HEAR from OFF-CAMERA the SOUND of Victory working Vic over. Fellini watches and it goes on for a few beats, but there is no sound from Vic. Fellini grows impatient, waves his hand. The OFF-CAMERA SOUNDS STOP

FELLINI
(continuing)
He won't talk. He's the meanest little bugger I ever did see. He's been drivin' me crazy for years.
(beat)
But I know what will make him talk.
(beat, to his other side-boy)
Ratch, bring that mutt over here.

RATCH, the other muscular Fellini-servant, still holding Blood by the scruff of the neck, brings him to the old man. Fellini reaches into the cape again and pulls out the pistol. He cocks it, holding it up to Blood's head.

FELLINI
(continuing)
It don't take much, boy.

BLOOD
(filter)
Tell him, Vic.

Vic is pulled INTO SHOT by Victory. He looks terrible.

VIC
(whispers)
Screamers.

The crowd goes dead. Beat. Beat. Then horrified and dismayed whispers through the crowd.

(CONTINUED)

158 CONTINUED (3):

There is ad lib of "I'm not goin' in there" and "You can get burned to a crisp by them things" and "Not me, no way!"

FELLINI
(smiles evilly)
You all seen screamers, ain't you? I have. Radiation poison victims. They glow the prettiest green. Touch one and die slow. Screamin' like they do.

159 TWO-SHOT - FELLINI AND VIC

as Fellini thinks on it for a moment. He hums to himself, then smiles a rotten smile.

FELLINI
Boy, you gonna be our advance scout.

VIC
(horrified)
No! Please, no!

FELLINI
(to crowd)
No wonder he didn't wanna go down there. He set up this whole parley to get _us_ to go down there, hopin' we'd _kill_ 'em off... but _we'd_ of died, too!

160
THRU SERIES OF INTERCUTS
165

FACES of the rovers and solos. Angry, hateful, mean!

CRICKET
You sneaky rotten slime!

SWEET ALICE
Lemme at him! I'll cut his head off!

BIG DANNY
Give him to us!

BRONCO
I never did trust him, he's _solo_!

FLAMINGO
I want a chance at him!

FELLINI
Hold on, hold on, children! I got just the thing for this boy.

166 TWO-SHOT - FELLINI AND VIC

Fellini puts his face very close to Vic's; malevolent, nasty, and happier than ever.

FELLINI
This boy is some swell solo fighter. We gonna put him and his nice little dog down inside there and let them shake up the screamery.

VIC
You been eatin' onions again, Fellini?

FELLINI
Good, boy, real good. You just keep up that sense'a humor. You gone need it.
(beat, authoritative)
Get him a good gun and a coupla racks of loads. Maybe he can stay alive down there long enough to do us some good.

VIC
(scared)
No! No, Fellini, don't do it! Shoot me now!

Fellini laughs in his face, and waves everyone to getting things ready. People move off toward their camps as Vic and Blood are hustled off into the darkness and we:

DISSOLVE TO:

167 ROOF OF THE WAREHOUSE - NIGHT

Lit by torches, with a gang of rovers and solos all dressed in motley, wearing scarves and jackets to keep the cold off their bones. The wind HOWLS. It is eerie, the licking flames of the torches the pale illumination for the entire scene. No moon. And Victory and Ratch, Fellini's side-boys, bashing in the last of the roof-hole with mauls and pickaxes. They have opened a gaping wound in the warehouse. Vic is being held by two rovers, another has Blood in his arms. Both are quiet, waiting. One of the rovers, Vorkimer, has a Thompson submachine gun and two bandoliers of slugs for a 30.06; another has a sack (which, we will discover, holds circular drums of slugs for the submachine gun); and another has the 30.06 -- which we assume will be given to Vic when he has been dropped into the warehouse.

BIG DANNY
Who's got that rope?

(CONTINUED)

167 CONTINUED:

CHARLIE CHAN
Whose idea was that old chopper?

He points to the Thompson held by one of the rovers.

FELLINI
Now, now, young fellahs, don't get all impatient.

FLAMINGO
It was my idea, stupid. It works real good if you gotta take out a lotta meat all at one time.

The remark breaks her up and she laughs raucously. No one else seems to think it's funny.

CHARLIE CHAN
Just don't give it to him till he's down there... and not that rifle, neither.

BLOOD
(filter)
The quality of grammar in this group is truly antediluvian.

VIC
(filter)
I could learn to hate you.

BLOOD
(filter)
It only burns for a little while.

BIG DANNY
(screams)
Who's got that miserable rope, huh? Huh?

VIC
(filter)
I'm not going down there!

BLOOD
(filter)
I don't notice anyone offering you the option to refuse.

VIC
(yelling)
The screamers'll kill me!!!

FELLINI
Not too quickly, I hope.

(CONTINUED)

167 CONTINUED (2):

BIG DANNY
You're makin' me crazy! Who's got the rope?

Cricket comes up with the rope. Big Danny grabs it from him, looking mightily pissed. He comes to Vic, ties it around Vic's waist, signals to the rover holding Blood, who brings the dog to Vic and hands him to the solo.

VIC
I'll get all of you for this!

SWEET ALICE
Tell it to the screamers, solo.

They march Vic to the hole. He fights every step of the way, howling and punching. They drag him to it and Victory lifts him.

FELLINI
So long, boy. You been fun but we got to say bye now.

He nods to Victory, who positions Vic over the hole while half a dozen others hold the rope. He lowers Vic into the hole in the roof and as Vic begins to disappear, they play out the rope.

VIC
(yelling)
I ain't finished yet!

FELLINI
Sure had us fooled, boy!

Everyone laughs as Vic's head, and Blood's, vanish down into the hole.

CUT TO:

168 VERTICAL SHOT - STRAIGHT DOWN ON VIC AND BLOOD

as they disappear down the hole, twisting around and around on the knotted rope. CAMERA PULLS BACK AND UP to include the rovers paying out the rope, then the shape of Fellini on the roof, his cape blowing wildly in the wind, then the full crowd and the entire roof. CAMERA UP AND AWAY to show us the entire warehouse and the no-man's-land and the camps with their eerie fires flickering in the wind.

CUT TO:

169 CLOSE ON FELLINI AND VICTORY

VICTORY
I think you're givin' him a chance to get away, Fellini.

FELLINI
(softly)
Heh. Looks a little like that, don't it. Walll, y'know, life's pretty dull for an old man like me.
(beat)
That boy's about the only thing I got to hate. He dies, I'm gonna spend a lotta years bein' bored.

VICTORY
That don't make sense.

FELLINI
Wouldn't expect it to; not to a dummy like you. Don't worry, I ain't lettin' him get away... just givin' him a possible rat hole to crawl through.
(beat)
That boy dances real fine.
(beat)
Gonna miss seein' him dance.

CUT TO:

170 INT. WAREHOUSE - VERTICAL ANGLE - UPSHOT

with the fitful light from the torches on the roof casting meager illumination, we see Vic and Blood overhead, coming down toward us, twisting on the rope. As they APPROACH CAMERA the ANGLE FLATTENS to a MED. SHOT on them.

FELLINI
(voice from above)
You down, boy?

VIC
Throw me those guns, Fellini!

BIG DANNY
Look out! Get away from under the hole. Here they come.

Vic and Blood (whom he has set down) retreat a short distance. CAMERA TILTS UP SMOOTHLY as a sudden pinwheel of light falls through the hole and crashes down. It is a flaming torch.

(CONTINUED)

170 CONTINUED:

VIC
What the hell'd you do that for? You tryin' to tell them screamers where I am?

FELLINI
You bet we are... ain't that why we put you down there, boy?

BIG DANNY
Shut up, Fellini!
(to Vic)
It's so you can see the guns when I drop 'em. Look out. Here they come.

And down come the Thompson, the 30.06, the sack of drums for the submachine gun, and the two bandoliers of ammo for the 30.06. Vic runs to the pile, rips open the sack, pulls out a circular drum of slugs for the machine gun, slaps it in, and without a moment's hesitation aims up at the hole and FIRES off a long burst, then another. There is silence for a moment, then Fellini's rotten laughter.

171 CLOSE ON VIC

as he stands in the darkness only barely, shadowly lit by the torch on the floor, and he listens to Fellini ridicule him. His face tenses and his lips skin back from his teeth.

FELLINI
(jocular)
Missed us, boy. That's why we didn't give the stuff to you up here. That's why we sent it all down unloaded.
(beat)
Better not waste that ammo, son; you gonna need it when you see that green light comin' for ya.

SWEET ALICE
Have fun, solo. We'll be back tomorrow sometime... see how you did.

172 ANOTHER ANGLE ON VIC - SHOOTING UP PAST HIM

to the hole, as the light dims and vanishes. CAMERA TILTS BACK DOWN to HOLD Vic and Blood.

(CONTINUED)

172 CONTINUED:

VIC
(filter; softly)
I'm scared, Blood.

BLOOD
(filter; softly)
I know, Vic. Take it easy. It's going to work out, I promise you.

VIC
(filter)
We'd better find a good place to hide. They must know where we are by now... damn that Fellini!

BLOOD
(filter)
Follow me, I'll find the perfect spot.

173 WITH THEM - ARRIFLEX

as Vic, with the 30.06 slung over his shoulder along with the bandoliers, the sack hung from his belt, and carrying the Thompson at the ready, follows Blood. The boy carries the torch and as CAMERA ANGLE WIDENS to follow their path we see the huge warehouse around us. It rises up into utter darkness, with beams and catwalks, and enormous stacks of goods piled atop one another. Apart from dust and desert sand that has drifted in, it is untouched by time or the war. It was apparently buried intact. They move down a corridor between huge cartons marked with the names of the items they contain. They GO AWAY FROM US in ARRIFLEX.

174 THRU 180 SERIES OF TRACKING SHOTS - ARRIFLEX

through the warehouse, the boy following the dog and the dog moving as if he knows exactly where he's going.

181 SHOT - DOORWAY

as Vic and Blood come into SHOT IN F.G. LARGE. There is a flickering light through that doorway. Vic stops.

VIC
(filter)
Light. Screamers!

BLOOD
(filter)
Come on.

(CONTINUED)

181 CONTINUED:

VIC
(filter)
But you led us right <u>to</u> them!

Blood goes on ahead, through the doorway. Vic hoists the Thompson into his armpit, pulls back the spring-bar that puts the weapon on automatic fire, and follows slowly. CAMERA TRUCKS IN STEADILY BEHIND VIC as he goes through the doorway. The light inside is from a torch. There is someone in there, moving around. Vic jams the torch into a space between cartons, lifts the submachine gun and is about to fire, when the person in the shadows turns around.

SPIKE
Took you long enough to get here.

Vic is dumbfounded at the sight of Spike. She has a dozen or two cartons opened... food, ammo, bottled water, everything they could possibly want for a six month hike.

VIC
What the...

BLOOD
(filter)
It was necessary to divert their attention while Spike sneaked into the area and burned open the wall of the warehouse, with the laser rifle.

VIC
You almost got me killed by that big freak Victory, and took a chance I'd be shot by Fellini? Just so she'd have it clear?!?

SPIKE
How'd he do in the fight, Blood?

VIC
I damn near got killed, that's how.

BLOOD
(filter)
Spike, how are we set for supplies?

SPIKE
More than enough of everything.

VIC
Where are the screamers?

BLOOD
(filter)
There are no screamers.

(CONTINUED)

181 CONTINUED (2):

VIC
But you let me believe...

BLOOD
(filter)
It was necessary that you think the place was full of them, or you might not have seemed terrified enough to fool Fellini.
(beat)
It's called the 'tar-baby in the briar patch' gambit. Many thanks to Uncle Remus, an early 20th Century battle tactician.

VIC
Why you low, miserable, eggsucking...

BLOOD
(filter)
Are we ready to go, Spike?

SPIKE
I've got everything packed in these sacks. He and I can load up on our backs. One of us can carry you up the rope.

VIC
You two are the most sneaky...

BLOOD
(filter; authoritatively)
Not now. When we're out of this, then you can upbraid me for my duplicity.
(beat)
Right now, we'd better load up and get going.

Vic throws his hand up in exasperation. He'd throw up the other one, but it holds a Thompson. He wanders around a moment, trying to get his temper under control, then goes to Spike and just stands there. She grins at him.

SPIKE
My hero.

VIC
(angry)
Just load me up and shut your face!

Still grinning, she turns him around and starts to fit the sacks with their attached ropes to the back of him. He is nearly bent double with goods, but suffers in silence. Then he does the same for her. Once loaded, Spike picks up the laser rifle and starts toward the doorway with her torch. Vic takes his torch and, with Blood, follows.

124.

182 thru 186 SERIES OF PANS AND TRUCKS - THRU THE WAREHOUSE

WITH THEM as they move down corridors and through rooms to the place where Spike entered the building.

SPIKE
I picked a spot all the way around on the far side, just to be safe.

BLOOD
(filter)
You did very well indeed, Spike. My congratulations.

VIC
(ruefully)
Yeah, just peachy-keen. I'm sorry I was loafing around and couldn't help.

BLOOD
(filter)
We each do what we're best suited to do, Vic. Get used to it.

VIC
I'll <u>never</u> get used to it.

187 EXIT ROOM - ON DOORWAY

as they ENTER. Spike lifts her torch and they SEE a long knotted rope hanging down. It disappears into darkness high above them. We cannot SEE the hole she burned out.

SPIKE
Up there. It's a good long climb.
(beat)
You want me to carry you, Blood?

VIC
I can carry him. You just get your butt up there and stand guard on the outside. They're probably all around, watching for screamers to come out.
(beat, mirthless)
Screamers! Hah!

Spike starts up the rope. Vic unbuttons his jacket and bends down with difficulty because of the sacks on his back. He picks up Blood and awkwardly manages to stuff him inside. Blood's head and forepaws protrude. He holds the wildly swaying rope and CAMERA TILTS UP to show Spike vanishing into darkness above them.

(CONTINUED)

187 CONTINUED:

VIC
You really set me up for this one.

BLOOD
(filter)
We were in a bad place, Vic. I don't have to rehash it with you. It was one of the few ways I could think of to get us fat again.

VIC
I'd like to know what the other ways were.

BLOOD
(filter)
There were four of them... each one more chancey and dangerous than this one.

VIC
You've got too many smarts for _my_ skin.

BLOOD
(filter)
Is it my fault I suffer from aristophrenia?

VIC
That's a new one; I never heard you use that before.

BLOOD
(filter; chuckles)
It's the condition of having a superior intellect.

VIC
I should have known... uh... uh...

BLOOD
(filter)
What's the matter?

VIC
(filter)
I don't want to argue with you, Mr. Superior Intellect, but if you look around back there, do you see what _I_ see?

(CONTINUED)

187 CONTINUED (2):

Blood cranes his head around Vic's chest and CAMERA GOES WITH HIS P.O.V. and we SEE the damnable green glow of three hideous SCREAMERS in the doorway. They are standing, silently, watching the boy and the dog. At that moment, from above, comes Spike's VOICE O.S.

SPIKE (V.O.)
Okay! I'm up! Come ahead!

188 FULL SHOT - FAVORING VIC

as the SCREAMERS stare at him, and he stares at the green radiation victims. A low MOANING comes from them, and one of them starts forward. Vic, almost without thinking, throws the torch. It hits and spatters flame all around the SCREAMER, who falls back, now HOWLING in that characteristic SOUND we have come to know and be chilled by. In a moment, the tinder-dry cartons have caught fire and a sheet of flame leaps up. Vic jumps and gets on the rope. He starts pulling himself up. One of the SCREAMERS breaks through the fire and, FLAMING himself, grabs the rope. The rope catches fire.

189 ARRIFLEX - WITH VIC

as he pulls himself hand-over-hand up the rope, the fire coming up behind him. Up and up as CAMERA GOES WITH and the flames below rise and spread, the SCREAMING of the damned radiation victims rising in a terrifying symphony.

CAMERA STAYS WITH HIM as he goes up. He is sweating, can barely make it with the combined weight of food, ammo, submachine gun and Blood weighing him down. He slips back a few feet, burning his hands which WE SEE IN CLOSEUP.

190 SHOT FROM ABOVE - DOWN ON VIC

with the fire ILLUMINATING everything below, and Vic coming up through it. His face comes UP INTO CLOSEUP and we know he won't be able to make it. His hands in EXTREME CLOSEUP can be seen to be slipping with sweat, and just as he's about to let go, a hand reaches down INTO FRAME and grabs him.

191 FROM BELOW - ON VIC

as Spike's hand grabs him and yanks him up. He manages to fling himself a foot up the rope and grab onto the edge of the hole in the wall. Then his shoulders go in, his upper torso, and his legs squirming through.

192 EXT. WAREHOUSE - NIGHT

As Vic emerges high up on the wall of the warehouse, through a hole with MELTED sides, like a giant running sore. He comes over the lip, hangs there a moment, then slides down the rope on the outside. Just before he reaches the ground, where the rope is being held by Spike, Blood wriggles free and jumps out of his jacket, onto the ground. Vic SLIDES down and FALLS to the ground, exhausted. At which point SHOTS RING OUT and we realize they have been spotted.

VIC
Oh my God... I'm tired...

BLOOD
(filter)
Later you can be tired!

SPIKE
Let's get out of here!

She starts firing the laser rifle off in the direction of the shots. But before Vic can get to his feet, there are half a dozen rovers coming at them out of the darkness. Then Spike's laser rifle gives out, exhausted after all these years, and she's weaponless. Vic is on his feet, knocking her down with a body-block, and from one knee he sprays the darkness with the Thompson. There are HOWLS from the darkness and the SOUND of people running away.

BLOOD
(filter)
Over here, this way! Follow me, it's clear.

And then all three of them are running for their lives as CAMERA HOLDS for several beats and they vanish into the darkness. Then CAMERA SMOOTHLY PANS UP AND LEFT to the roof of the warehouse, where Fellini stands with Victory, watching them disappear.

VICTORY
You <u>did</u> let him get away.

FELLINI
Maybe, son. Maybe.
(beat)
You ever hear that boy talk about "over the hill"? Supposed to be a real fat place. Food grows right in the ground like it did when I was his age.
(MORE)

(CONTINUED)

192 CONTINUED:

FELLINI (CONT'D)
(beat)
That'd be some fine place to go, wouldn't it? Just come in there and take it over, run it my way.
(beat)
I'd bet anybody ever find it, gonna be that Vic and his dog.

He watches them go. Then cups his hands and yells:

FELLINI
(Continuing)
Keep on dancin', boy! You dance real fine! Keep dancin', cause I'm right behind you!

CAMERA HOLDS ON FELLINI on the roof as we:

DISSOLVE THRU TO:

193 SAME AS SHOT 73 - AREA FEATURING FARMHOUSE

Old man Partridge's farmhouse. Vic and Blood and Spike, decked out in full rucksack and weaponry, are approaching across the grassy area. We see the crater made months ago by the laser rifle. Spike carries the useless laser weapon. SHOOT FROM A DISTANCE so we HEAR THEIR VOICES OVER.

SPIKE (V.O.)
Did I say thanks for knocking me down?

VIC (V.O.)
Forget it. We're even.

SPIKE (V.O.)
You still sore about us fooling you?

VIC (V.O.)
How could I be sore about you two getting me into a fight that could've got me crippled, putting me up the barrel of Fellini's gun, burned to death by screamers, blown away by rovers...?

CAMERA CATCHES UP WITH THEM so we need not do V.O.

BLOOD
(filter)
But we made it. With plenty of food and ammunition.

(CONTINUED)

193 CONTINUED:

VIC
And you can forget that "we" stuff. I take back what I said about joining up. I still think you're crazy as a cockroach; you're too mean for me, lady.

SPIKE
(filter; to Blood)
Tell it that I'm not fond of it, either. Tell it that it messes up too often.

BLOOD
(filter)
She says to tell you that she isn't fond of you, either, that you...

Vic stops dead, turns and glares at both of them. At that moment there is a YELL from the farmhouse.

PARTRIDGE (V.O.)
Just hold up there! You're niether guests nor licenses... I can get you in a court'a law for trespass...

SPIKE
(yells back)
Mr. Partridge! Mr. Whistler Partridge!

PARTRIDGE (V.O.)
Who's that? Who's callin' me that hateful name?

SPIKE
(yelling)
It's me, Mr. Partridge. Spike! I came back to say hello, got a friend I want you to meet.

VIC
I'm no friend of yours.

Partridge comes out onto the porch, rifle folded over his arm. He waves at her.

PARTRIDGE
Well, c'mon up, little girl.

They are now very close, and come the rest of the way.

(CONTINUED)

193 CONTINUED (2):

SPIKE
Mr. Partridgë, this is Vic.

PARTRIDGE
Howdy, son.

VIC
(reserved)
Hi.

Spike unslings her rucksack and fishes around in it. She comes up with the theremin from Poke's gravesite.

SPIKE
We were just passing back through this way, and well, we got to thinking how lonely it must be out here, and all, and we wanted to give you this.

She hands it up to him. He takes it, looks at it curiously.

SPIKE
(Continuing)
It's a music maker, Mr. Partridge.
(beat)
We were just thinking you could teach yourself how to play it; it'd be real nice when it's lonely some nights, play something pretty for yourself and Miss Vicky Pauline.

The old man is touched. He tightens up his mouth and his eyes start to water.

PARTRIDGE
Well, ain't that a nice thing. Very thoughtful of you, little girl. You're nice kids, the both of you. Good to see young folks still got a little respect for their elders.

He wipes his nose.

PARTRIDGE
(Continuing)
You gonna stay for supper?

(CONTINUED)

193 CONTINUED (3):

SPIKE
No, we've gotta get goin'. We're going to see if we can find a place Blood knows about.

They start to edge away.

PARTRIDGE
Well, you stop by again some time. Miss Vicky Pauline and me, we'll be lookin' for you.

They wave and move out quickly. CAMERA HOLDS WITH PARTRIDGE and after several beats he yells:

PARTRIDGE
(Continuing)
Did I tell you, that's a nice doggie you got there!

CAMERA MOVES PAST HIM to eliminate him from FRAME, as it HOLDS on the trio cutting across the grassland area, and we HEAR BLOOD'S VOICE OVER, diminishing in volume as they walk away.

BLOOD (V.O.)
(filter)
As long as we're all going in the same direction, why not run through a bit of history?
(beat)
I'll bet niether of you ever heard about a very interesting scandal in American history. Well... once upon a time there was this big building called The Watergate, and there was this strange old man called...

CAMERA HOLDS their retreating forms as we:

FADE TO BLACK

and

FADE OUT.

THE END

CHRONOLOGY OF BOOKS BY HARLAN ELLISON®

1958 – 2019

SHORT STORY COLLECTIONS:

THE DEADLY STREETS [1958]

SEX GANG *(as "Paul Merchant")* [1959]

A TOUCH OF INFINITY [1960]

CHILDREN OF THE STREETS [1961]

GENTLEMAN JUNKIE *and Other Stories of the Hung-Up Generation* [1961]

ELLISON WONDERLAND [1962/2015]

PAINGOD *and Other Delusions* [1965]

I HAVE NO MOUTH & I MUST SCREAM [1967]

FROM THE LAND OF FEAR [1967]

LOVE AIN'T NOTHING BUT SEX MISSPELLED [1968]

THE BEAST THAT SHOUTED LOVE AT THE HEART OF THE WORLD [1969]

OVER THE EDGE [1970]

ALL THE SOUNDS OF FEAR (British publication only) [1973]

DE HELDEN VAN DE HIGHWAY (Dutch publication only) [1973]

APPROACHING OBLIVION [1974]

THE TIME OF THE EYE (British publication only) [1974]

DEATHBIRD STORIES [1975/2011]

NO DOORS, NO WINDOWS [1975]

HOE KAN IK SCHREEUWEN ZONDER MOND (Dutch publication only) [1977]

STRANGE WINE [1978]

SHATTERDAY [1980]

STALKING THE NIGHTMARE [1982]

ANGRY CANDY [1988]

ENSAMVÄRK (Swedish publication only) [1992]

JOKES WITHOUT PUNCHLINES [1995]

ВСЕ ЗВУКИ СТРАХА (ALL FEARFUL SOUNDS) (Unauthorized Russian publication only) [1997]

THE WORLDS OF HARLAN ELLISON (Authorized Russian publication only) [1997]

SLIPPAGE: *Precariously Poised, Previously Uncollected Stories* [1997]

KOLETIS, KES KUULUTAS ARMASTUST MAAILMA SLIDAMES (Estonian publication only) [1999]

LA MACHINE AUX YEUX BLEUS (French publication only) [2001]

TROUBLEMAKERS [2001]

PTAK ŚMIERCI (THE BEST OF HARLAN ELLISON) (Polish publication only) [2003]

PULLING A TRAIN [2012]

GETTING IN THE WIND [2012]

PEBBLES FROM THE MOUNTAIN [2015]

CAN AND CAN'TANKEROUS (edited by Jason Davis) [2015]

COFFIN NAILS [2016]

NOVELS:

WEB OF THE CITY [1958]

THE SOUND OF A SCYTHE [1960]

SPIDER KISS [1961]

BLOOD'S A ROVER (edited by Jason Davis) [2018]

SHORT NOVELS:

DOOMSMAN [1967]

ALL THE LIES THAT ARE MY LIFE [1980]

RUN FOR THE STARS [1991]

MEFISTO IN ONYX [1993]

OMNIBUS VOLUMES:

THE FANTASIES OF HARLAN ELLISON [1979]

DREAMS WITH SHARP TEETH [1991]

THE GLASS TEAT & THE OTHER GLASS TEAT [2011]

COLLABORATIONS:

PARTNERS IN WONDER: *Collaborations with 14 Other Wild Talents* [1971]

THE STARLOST: *Phoenix Without Ashes* (with Edward Bryant) [1975]

MIND FIELDS: *33 Stories Inspired by the Art of Jacek Yerka* [1994]

I HAVE NO MOUTH, AND I MUST SCREAM: *The Interactive CD-Rom* (Co-Designed with David Mullich and David Sears) [1995]

"REPENT, HARLEQUIN!" SAID THE TICKTOCKMAN (rendered with paintings by Rick Berry) [1997]

2000^X (Host and Creative Consultant of National Public Radio episodic series) [2000–2001]

HARLAN ELLISON'S MORTAL DREADS (dramatized by Robert Armin) [2012]

SCREENPLAYS & SUCHLIKE:

THE ILLUSTRATED HARLAN ELLISON (edited by Byron Preiss) [1978]

HARLAN ELLISON'S MOVIE [1990]

I, ROBOT: The Illustrated Screenplay (based on Isaac Asimov's story-cycle) [1994]

THE CITY ON THE EDGE OF FOREVER [1996]

RETROSPECTIVES:

ALONE AGAINST TOMORROW: *A 10-Year Survey* [1971]

THE ESSENTIAL ELLISON: *A 35-Year Retrospective* (edited by Terry Dowling, with Richard Delap & Gil Lamont) [1987]

THE ESSENTIAL ELLISON: *A 50-Year Retrospective* (edited by Terry Dowling) [2001]

UNREPENTANT: *A Celebration of the Writing of Harlan Ellison* (edited by Robert T. Garcia) [2010]

THE TOP OF THE VOLCANO: *The Award-Winning Stories of Harlan Ellison* [2014]

THE HARLAN ELLISON DISCOVERY SERIES:

STORMTRACK by James Sutherland [1975]

AUTUMN ANGELS by Arthur Byron Cover [1975]

THE LIGHT AT THE END OF THE UNIVERSE by Terry Carr [1976]

ISLANDS by Marta Randall [1976]

INVOLUTION OCEAN by Bruce Sterling [1978]

MOTION PICTURE (DOCUMENTARY):

DREAMS WITH SHARP TEETH (A Film About Harlan Ellison produced and directed by Erik Nelson) [2009]

CHRONOLOGY OF BOOKS BY HARLAN ELLISON®

1958 – 2019

GRAPHIC NOVELS:

Demon with a Glass Hand (adaptation with Marshall Rogers) [1986]

Night and the Enemy (adaptation with Ken Steacy) [1987]

Vic and Blood: *The Chronicles/Continuing Adventures of a Boy and His Dog* (adaptation by Richard Corben) [1989/2003]

Harlan Ellison's Dream Corridor, Volumes One & Two [1996 /2007]

Phoenix without Ashes [2010/2011] (art by Alan Robinson and John K. Snyder III)

Harlan Ellison's 7 Against Chaos (art by Paul Chadwick and Ken Steacy) [2013]

The City on the Edge of Forever: *The Original Teleplay* (adaptation by Scott Tipton & David Tipton, art by J.K. Woodward) [2014/2015]

Batman '66: *The Lost Episode* (adaptation by Len Wein, art by Joe Prado and José García-López) [2014]

AUDIOBOOKS:

The Voice from the Edge: I Have No Mouth, and I Must Scream (Vol. One) [1999]

The Voice from the Edge: Midnight in the Sunken Cathedral (Vol. Two) [2001]

Run for the Stars [2005]

The Voice from the Edge: Pretty Maggie Moneyeyes (Vol. Three) [2009]

The Voice from the Edge: The Deathbird & Other Stories (Vol. Four) [2011]

The Voice from the Edge: Shatterday & Other Stories (Vol. Five) [2011]

Ellison Wonderland [2015]

Web and the City [2015]

Spider Kiss [2015]

The City on the Edge of Forever (full-cast dramatization) [2016]

AS EDITOR:

Dangerous Visions [1967/2002]

Nightshade & Damnations: *The Finest Stories of Gerald Kersh* [1968]

Again, Dangerous Visions [1972]

Medea: *Harlan's World* [1985]

Jacques Futrelle's "The Thinking Machine" Stories [2003]

ON THE ROAD WITH HARLAN ELLISON:

On the Road with Harlan Ellison (Vol. One) [1983/2001]

On the Road with Harlan Ellison (Vol. Two) [2004]

On the Road with Harlan Ellison (Vol. Three) [2007]

On the Road with Harlan Ellison (Vol. Four) [2011]

On the Road with Harlan Ellison: *His Last Big Con* (Vol. Five) [2011]

On the Road with Harlan Ellison: *The Grand Master Edition* (Vol. Six) [2012]

On the Road with Harlan Ellison (Vol. Seven) [2018]

THE WHITE WOLF SERIES:

Edgeworks 1: Over the Edge & An Edge in My Voice [1996]

Edgeworks 2: Spider Kiss & Stalking the Nightmare [1996]

Edgeworks 3: The Harlan Ellison Hornbook & Harlan Ellison's Movie [1997]

Edgeworks 4: Love Ain't Nothing But Sex Misspelled & The Beast That Shouted Love at the Heart of the World [1997]

NON-FICTION & ESSAYS:

Memos from Purgatory [1961]

The Glass Teat: *Essays of Opinion on Television* [1970]

The Other Glass Teat: *Further Essays of Opinion on Television* [1975]

The Book of Ellison (edited by Andrew Porter) [1978]

Sleepless Nights in the Procrustean Bed (edited by Marty Clark) [1984]

An Edge in My Voice [1985]

Harlan Ellison's Watching [1989]

The Harlan Ellison Hornbook [1990]

Bugf#ck! *The Useless Wit & Wisdom of Harlan Ellison* (edited by Arnie Fenner) [2011]

HARLAN ELLISON BOOKS PRESERVATION PROJECT

The Dimensions of Harlan Ellison [2019]

The Ephemeral Ellison [2019]

The Ellison Treatment [2019]

This Book Needs No Introduction By Harlan Ellison [2019]

EDGEWORKS ABBEY OFFERINGS (Edited by Jason Davis):

Brain Movies: *The Original Teleplays of Harlan Ellison* (Vol. One) [2011]

Brain Movies: *The Original Teleplays of Harlan Ellison* (Vol. Two) [2011]

Harlan 101: *Encountering Ellison* [2011]

The Sound of a Scythe *and 3 Brilliant Novellas* [2011]

Rough Beasts: *Seventeen Stories Written Before I Got Up To Speed* [2012]

None of the Above [2012]

Brain Movies: *The Original Teleplays of Harlan Ellison* (Vol. Three) [2013]

Brain Movies: *The Original Teleplays of Harlan Ellison* (Vol. Four) [2013]

Brain Movies: *The Original Teleplays of Harlan Ellison* (Vol. Five) [2013]

Honorable Whoredom at a Penny a Word [2013]

Again, Honorable Whoredom at a Penny a Word [2014]

Brain Movies: *The Original Teleplays of Harlan Ellison* (Vol. Six) [2014]

Harlan Ellison's Endlessly Watching [2014]

8 in 80 by Ellison (guest edited by Susan Ellison) [2014]

The Last Person to Marry a Duck Lived 300 Years Ago [2016]

Brain Movies: *The Original Teleplays of Harlan Ellison* (Vol. Seven) [2016]

Brain Movies: *The Original Teleplays of Harlan Ellison* (Vol. Eight) [2019]

Brain Movies *Presents* Blood's a Rover [2019]

FOE: *Friends of Ellison* [2019]

Why Do You Call Me Ishmael When You Know My Name Is Bernie? [2019]

HARLAN ELLSON has been characterized by *The New York Times Book Review* as having "the spellbinding quality of a great nonstop talker, with a cultural warehouse for a mind."

The Los Angeles Times suggested, "It's long past time for Harlan Ellison to be awarded the title: 20th century Lewis Carroll." And the *Washington Post Book World* said simply, "One of the great living American short story writers."

He has written or edited 118 books; more than 1700 stories, essays, articles, and newspaper columns; two dozen teleplays, for which he received the Writers Guild of America most outstanding teleplay award for solo work an unprecedented four times; and a dozen movies. *Publishers Weekly* called him "Highly Intellectual." (Ellison's response: "Who, Me?"). He won the Mystery Writers of America Edgar Allan Poe award twice, the Horror Writers Association Bram Stoker award six times (including The Lifetime Achievement Award in 1996), the Nebula award of the Science Fiction Writers of America five times (including the Grand Master Award), the Hugo Award 8 ½ times, and received the Silver Pen for Journalism from P.E.N. Not to mention the World Fantasy Award; the British Fantasy Award; the American Mystery Award; plus two Audie Awards and two Grammy nominations for Spoken Word recordings.

He created great fantasies for the 1985 CBS revival of *The Twilight Zone* (including Danny Kaye's final performance) and *The Outer Limits*, traveled with The Rolling Stones; marched with Martin Luther King from Selma to Montgomery; created roles for Buster Keaton, Wally Cox, Gloria Swanson, and nearly 100 other stars on *Burke's Law*; ran with a kid gang in Brooklyn's Red Hook to get background for his first novel; covered race riots in Chicago's "back of the yards" with the late James Baldwin; sang with, and dined with, Maurice Chevalier; once stood off the son of the Detroit Mafia kingpin with a Remington XP-100 pistol-rifle, while wearing nothing but a bath towel; sued Paramount and ABC-TV for plagiarism and won $337,000. His most recent legal victory, in protection of copyright against global Internet piracy of writers' work, in May of 2004—a four-year-long litigation against AOL et al.—has resulted in revolutionizing protection of creative properties on the web. (As promised, he has repaid hundreds of contributions [totaling $50,000] from the KICK Internet Piracy support fund.) But the bottom line, as voiced by *Booklist*, is this: "One thing for sure: the man can write."

He lived with his wife, Susan, inside The Lost Aztec Temple of Mars, in Los Angeles.

The Harlan Ellison® Books Preservation Project was made possible by

---

Gary Wallen
Andrew Hackard
Jay Kemp
John Farmer
Stanley L. Korwin
Sven-Hendrik Magotsch
Dan Melin
Jay Corsetti
Eliot R. Weinstein
James Bocchinfuso
David Loftus
Stanford Maxwell Brown
William M Feero
William Dennehy
Mark L Cohen
Curt M Snyder
Rod Searcey
John Palagyi
Suzzii Barrafato, P. Stashio Nutz & Tortoni Spumoni & Co.
Dan McCormick
Andy Bustamante
Samantha A. Vitagliano
Mike Jacka
Alice Tatarian
David Jessup & family
Paul Guay & Susan S. Knight
J. Michael Straczynski
Raymond McCauley
David M. Barsky
Gordon H. Schnaper
Joel T. & Carole Hampton Cotter
Gerald R. Parham
Michael J. Dymond, MD
and 725 other Friends of Ellison.

50726751R00161

Made in the USA
Columbia, SC
10 February 2019